ON COMMUNICATION. AN INTERDISCIPLINARY AND MATHEMATICAL APPROACH

THEORY AND DECISION LIBRARY

General Editor: Julian Nida-Rümelin (*Munich*)

Series A: Philosophy and Methodology of the Social Sciences

Series B: Mathematical and Statistical Methods

Series C: Game Theory, Mathematical Programming and Operations Research

SERIES A: PHILOSOPHY AND METHODOLOGY
OF THE SOCIAL SCIENCES

VOLUME 40

Assistant Editor: Thomas Schmidt (*Göttingen*)

Scope: This series deals with the foundations, the general methodology and the criteria, goals and purpose of the social sciences. The emphasis in the Series A will be on well-argued, thoroughly analytical rather than advanced mathematical treatments. In this context, particular attention will be paid to game and decision theory and general philosophical topics from mathematics, psychology and economics, such as game theory, voting and welfare theory, with applications to political science, sociology, law and ethics.

The titles published in this series are listed at the end of this volume.

ON COMMUNICATION. AN INTERDISCIPLINARY AND MATHEMATICAL APPROACH

by

JURGEN KLÜVER
University of Duisburg-Essen

and

CHRISTINA KLÜVER
University of Duisburg-Essen

Springer

A C.I.P. Catalogue record for this book is available from the Library of Congress.

ISBN-10 1-4020-5463-7 (HB)
ISBN-10 1-4020-5464-5 (e-book)
ISBN-13 978-1-4020-5463-1 (HB)
ISBN-13 978-1-4020-5464-8 (e-book)

Published by Springer,
P.O. Box 17, 3300 AA Dordrecht, The Netherlands.

www.springer.com

Printed on acid-free paper

TABLE OF CONTENTS

PREFACE

This book originated in the last four years when we were lecturing both in communication and computer science at the University of Duisburg-Essen, Germany. Therefore, it was rather obvious for us to integrate these two scientific disciplines and to analyze the problem of the general logic of communicative processes by the use of suited computer models and mathematical concepts. The result of these efforts is this book and it is up to the readers if our attempts are successful.

We could never have finished this study without the enthusiastic interest of many students in both sciences. Several of them are named in the book who implemented specific computer programs as part of their respective MA-thesis. We have also to thank several colleagues in communication and computer science, who supported our work in many ways. We frequently experienced that the old and venerable paradigm of especially the German University "the unity of research and teaching" (Humboldt) is far from dead and can be updated any time, provided a suited research project.

Our special thanks go to Jörn Schmidt from the former Center for Interdisciplinary Research in Higher Education at our University, whose constant help was invaluable to us.

Each new scientific approach is only possible because it stands, to quote Newton, “on the shoulders of giants”. Therefore, we dedicate this book *in memoriam* to two great pioneers in communication science, namely Claude E. Shannon and Gerold Ungeheuer.

Essen, Summer 2006

Jürgen Klüver Christina Klüver

CHAPTER 1

INTRODUCTION: COMMUNICATION – PROBLEMS OF A CONCEPT AND A NEW METHODICAL APPROACH

If any researcher wants to write about the social and/or cognitive conditions of human life then it is nearly impossible not to mention communication in one or another sense. Therefore, one can take any social and cognitive discipline like sociology, economics, psychology or anthropology and one will find communication at its core or at least at its periphery. The number of books that have been written on communication from one point of view or the other has for a long time transcended the receptive capabilities of single researchers. Thus being the case it seems quite hopeless to write about this subject without repeating considerations and insights that others have found out long ago.

To make matters even worse, communication is also a concept that is frequently used in the natural and computer sciences. Biological cells are "communicating" in order to generate and to preserve the organism; computer programs are "communicating" and sharing "information" and of course humans and computers are also "communicating". Apparently the whole universe can be looked at as one gigantic communicative system; therefore, writing on communication is to write about everything.

Yet despite the fact that communication is probably one of the most used concepts in scientific – and non-scientific – discourses there is no general theory of communication scientific users of this concept will agree upon. On the contrary, it may be that the nearly universal use of the term of communication is only possible *because* there is no general theory of communication, and not even a general definition that is obligatory for scientific users. Communication seems to be fruitful for rather different applications because no particular discipline may claim it as its rightful domain and define it in a way all scientific users have to acknowledge.

To be sure, there are numerous definitions of communication and many theoretical attempts to analyze it. But none of these, as important as they are for specific disciplines, are obligatory for other scientists and in particular for scientists from other disciplines. The sociologically grounded definitions by Luhmann (1984) for example are not relevant for cognitive scientists; the considerations of Bateson (1970 and 1972) are not interesting for most of social scientists, and reflections on communication by psychologists will be ignored by computer scientists, natural scientists, and social scientists likewise.

In our opinion it is not by chance that communication is one of the most used concepts in scientific and everyday discourses. In a rather abstract sense communication is indeed the key concept for many different phenomena and, therefore, scientists from different disciplines are bound to use it in their own fashion, although the term is often not precisely defined. The general definition of communication that we shall introduce and use for the purpose of this book is in contrast to the different definitions used in specific disciplines applicable to rather diverse realms of research, i.e., physical, biological, and social-cognitive fields as well as to computer science. Of course, definitions on such general levels often tend to be empty, that is they are not fruitful for particular empirical investigations. Yet we hope that the definition we give and that is formulated in terms of complex systems theory will be not only general but also useful to specific empirical research.

As there is no general definition of communication there is also no general precise theory of it that earns the name. There is of course the "mathematical theory of communication" by Shannon and Weaver (1949) that is frequently used in the natural and computer sciences. But this theory deals "only" with the concept of information, as Shannon and Weaver explicitly pointed out, and it does not analyze the concept of meaning. In particular, nothing is said by this theory about the aspects of human communication. Therefore, the theoretical schema of Shannon and Weaver may be still useful for technical purposes and in the natural sciences, but a lot of social and cognitive scientists has often and rightly stressed the point that human communication cannot be reduced to the information processing models in the tradition of Shannon and Weaver (e.g. Krallmann and Ziemann, 2001). Although we believe that the Shannon-Weaver approach is still useful and hence use the basic idea of their definition of information for our theoretical goals, we also believe that this approach must be enlarged in several ways. In chapter 3 we shall reformulate their famous definition of the degree of information and show that it is possible to give a similar definition that is compatible with an according definition of meaning.

Although the approach of Shannon and Weaver is much too restricted for the use of social and cognitive investigations it is one of the few attempts to deal with the problem of communication in a precise, i.e. mathematical manner. Therefore, it is, e.g., no accident that often the term "theory of communication" is identified with their theoretical frame, i.e., as "the study of the principles and the methods by which information is conveyed" (Oxford Dictionary 9th edition). In this sense their approach still must be looked at as paradigmatic and other approaches like, e.g., the "situational theory" of Barwise and Perry (1987) did not reach the level of that classical theory (cf. also Devlin, 1991). On the other hand, the numerous attempts of philosophers, cognitive and social scientists to catch the complexity of communication and to take into account the fact that communication has something to do with the transfer of "meaning", never succeeded to give precise, i.e., formal foundations for a theory of communication in a strict scientific sense. On the contrary, many researchers on communication from the social and cognitive sciences and the humanities seem to believe that a formally precise theory of communication is not possible at all. As a result, nearly each theorist gives his own definitions and uses the concepts accordingly.

It is not the purpose of this book to enumerate and discuss all the important approaches with respect to the theoretical foundations of communication (cf. e.g. Anderson, 1996; Favre-Bulle, 2001). We rather try to develop some new ways to deal with this problem and to show the possibility of a precise theory of communication. Because the methodical way we use in this study is still comparatively new for most researchers in the social and even cognitive sciences we first have to explain our own theoretical framework and give some introduction into the key concepts and formal methods that we shall use. To put it into a nutshell, we shall define communicative processes as complex dynamical systems that depend on their social context on the one hand and the particular cognitive dynamics on the other hand that is generated by the communicative processes. Therefore, communication has to be understood as the interdependency of two kinds of dynamics, i.e., a social interactional one and a cognitive one. Because we are able to demonstrate that both social and cognitive dynamics can be defined in a precise mathematical way, it seems possible to reach the goal of a mathematical theory of communication that is not restricted in the way the classical approach of Shannon and Weaver and their followers was and still is.

By aspiring such an ambitious goal we have to prove, of course, that our theoretical frame is capable to define not only the concept of information but at least also that of meaning. Although the terms of information and meaning are often used as equivalent in everyday language – and not only there – it is quite clear that these concepts are by no means synonymous. On hindsight it seems a bit unfortunate that Shannon and Weaver on the one hand explicitly stated that they did not deal with "meaning" but that on the other hand they named their theory as a mathematical theory of *communication*. In this way they suggested that communicative processes are just the transfer of information and because they defined "information" in the famous way burrowed from thermodynamics they seemed to imply that communicative processes are something akin to thermo dynamical ones. In other words, they seemed to postulate a particular form of epistemological reductionism, i.e., the reduction of communication to physical processes. We do not know if this was indeed their intention, but it is a fact that their theory was not seldom understood that way. It is no wonder that social and cognitive scientists often believed that such a theory is rather useless for their own problems.

The basic assumption of our approach is at the core a truism: communication is understood as a basically social process that is regulated by certain social rules of interaction on the one hand and determined by cognitive processes of the communicators on the other hand. Therefore, communication is indeed at the core of society and cognition likewise: social actors communicatively interact via the regulation of social rules and thus generate social reality, but social actions are also determined by the cognitive world views of the actors in a specific situation (Berger and Luckmann, 1966). In this sense all social interactions are communicative processes because they depend on the respective social rules *and* the beliefs, knowledge etc. of the communicators, i.e., their cognitive processes. Being a social actor is being a communicator – even Robinson had to construct his own communicative community first with himself and later with Friday in order to remain a social being.

To be sure, human actions are not to be reduced to communication alone. The well-known distinction of Habermas (e.g. Habermas, 1968) between labor as action in regard to material reality on the one hand and social interaction on the other demonstrates that societies are not only communicative systems as, e.g., Luhmann and his followers believe. The "material basis" (Marx) of society is not to be neglected if one thinks about society as a whole. Societies are not isolated monads but are systems within a material environment and the according development of the *Produktivkräfte* (forces of production) determine the evolution of societies as much as the development of social structures. Therefore, it is necessary to place communication in the context of Max Weber's famous definition of *social* action distinguished from the non social form of labor. By taking this *caveat* into account one can say that society is generated and reproduced by social actions and the *social* organization of labor; in this sense communication is indeed at the core of society and hence it is no accident that all social sciences have to deal with this concept.

The social process of communication is also crucial for cognitive processes, in particular cognitive development, as has often been pointed out. It is also no accident that even neurobiologists recently admit that the human brain can only completely be understood as the result of communicative processes, i.e., social interactions (cf. Singer, 2000). Of course, cognition cannot be reduced to communication either. There are a lot of cognitive processes that can only be understood as "autopoietic" (Maturana, 1982) self-organizing processes of the brain (or the mind, respectively). But cognitive development as well as every advanced cognitive achievement depends on social environments and that is on communication. Therefore communication is a key concept not only in the social sciences but in the cognitive sciences too. We shall more thoroughly deal with these problem in the following chapters.

In contrast to the definition of the Oxford Dictionary we understand communication not only as the transfer or exchange of information but also and probably even more important as an exchange of *meaning*. We are quite aware of the fact that "meaning" is even more ambiguous than "communication"; that is why we have to give a precise definition of meaning in the terms of our theoretical frame. But no theory of communication can claim conceptual completeness that does not capture the concept of meaning; in particular it must be shown that "information" and "meaning" are on the one hand different concepts but that on the other hand they must be understood as two aspects of the same process.

The methodical approach we develop in this book consists of a) the theoretical frame of complex dynamical systems theory and b) the use of computer simulations, i.e., the construction of formal models and their experimental investigations by the runs of the according computer programs. In addition we shall show that and how particular computer based models of communicative processes can be empirically validated. Because we use specific models and computer programs of a kind that is called "Soft Computing" – a term created by Zadeh, the inventor of fuzzy set theory – we shall introduce not only the theoretical frame but the formal models of Soft Computing too. To put it into a nutshell, we "translate" the concept of communicative processes into the particular theoretical and mathematical concepts of complex systems theory, develop according computer programs based on the techniques of Soft Computing, perform computer experiments in order to gain some general insights into the regularities of communicative processes, and last but not least undertake to validate some of the programs by comparisons with empirical social experiments. In order to do this we have, of course, to define – and discriminate – the different aspects or "dimensions" respectively of the complex process of communication. In particular, we shall demonstrate how the modeling of the social and cognitive dimensions of communication can be done.

To be sure, we do not claim to give a *complete* theory of communication in this book, which is for several reasons at present not possible. But we hope to demonstrate that a "mathematical theory of communication", to quote Shannon and Weaver again, can now be considered as a concrete goal, namely a theory that is not reductionist in the sense that it reduces the general phenomenon of communication to the too narrow frames of physical concepts.

According to these theoretical and methodical considerations we can now present a general definition of communicative processes; if it is not explicitly said otherwise communication is understood here as communication between human communicators: Communication is a (dynamical) process that consists of at least two *communicators* A and B who perform *communicative* acts. Each communicator must be considered as a *complex cognitive system*; the communicative acts generate a *cognitive dynamics* in each of the respective communicators. The communicative acts are to be understood as the transfer and exchange of *meaning and information*; the acts are regulated by *social rules and rules of the production of signs*; the signs are often coded as symbols. Therefore a communicative situation – or a communicative system respectively – consists of different communicators, certain social rules that regulate the *interactional dynamics* between the communicators, *semiotic production rules* that regulate the combination of the signs or symbols respectively, which are used in the communicative situation, and *cognitive rules* that regulate the cognitive dynamics of the communicators. The communicative process understood this way is started with the introduction of a communicative theme that generates certain initial cognitive states of the communicators.

The communicative process then must be considered as a two-dimensional dynamical process: on the one hand the social rules and social "topology" (see below next chapter) generate a particular interactional dynamics between the communicators; on the other hand cognitive rules and cognitive topologies generate a certain cognitive dynamics, i.e., the cognitive processing of the messages; finally the whole communicative process and its particular dynamics is regulated by a mutual interdependency of the interactional and the cognitive dynamics. We may therefore characterize the dynamics of communication as the result of two interplaying kinds of dynamics, which is determined by three types of rules. Yet in many cases it is sufficient to consider only the social and cognitive levels of communication.

Readers who are acquainted with the general semiotic theory of signs will immediately perceive the proximity of this general definition to the three-dimensional model of signs by Morris (1970). "Meaning" and "information", of course, refer to the semantic dimension of signs; social rules and topologies refer to the pragmatic dimension and the concept of semiotic production rules refers to the syntactical dimension. In a rather abstract sense our general definition may be understood as the transformation of the classical model of Morris into the framework of complex dynamical systems. By the way, this definition of communicative processes demonstrates the advantages of our particular approach. It allows to model communication, cognition and social interaction quite naturally within one and the same theoretical framework.

To be sure, such a general and abstract definition tells us nothing about the particular kinds of dynamics and the kind of interdependency between them. In particular nothing is said about the definitions of meaning and information in terms of complex systems theory. Because these two concepts are the decisive concepts for each communicative theory we have to clarify them. But as the according definitions are based on the conceptual framework of complex systems theory we have to start with an excursion into this field. Readers who are already acquainted with the general concepts of complex systems theory may, of course, pass over this chapter and go directly on to the definition of meaning and information.

CHAPTER 2

EXCURSION INTO COMPLEX SYSTEMS THEORY

2.1. GENERAL CONCEPTS

Although or perhaps because the concept of "complex systems" is nowadays used in rather different contexts the meaning of this concept is by no means always clear; in particular the combination of "complex systems" with the methodical and theoretical terms of "systems dynamics" is still not very frequent in the cognitive and social sciences. Therefore we give a brief introduction into the main concepts of these fields; for more details we refer to the respective literature (cf. Kauffman, 1995; Mainzer, 1997; Gell-Mann, 1994; Holland, 1998; Klüver, 2000). Nevertheless we shall see that it is necessary for our purposes to enlarge the well-known definitions.

According to the classical definition of von Bertalanffy (1956) a system is defined as a set of elements, which interact via local rules of interaction. The elements of the system are characterized by a particular state at a certain time t; the interactions of the elements determine the changing of the element's states. The whole system is at time t in a systems state S_t ; this state is usually defined by a mathematical aggregation of the element's states at the same time. Because the local rules of interaction determine the changing of the element's states, the rules also determine the changing of the system's state. Therefore, we may consider the ensemble of the local rules of interaction as a system function f that recursively generates new systems states from the preceding ones. In a more formal sense we obtain

(1) $$f(S_t) = S_{t+1},$$

if we designate S_{t+1} as the system's state at time $t+1$. In general, if we call S_0 the initial state of the system, e.g., at time $t = 0$ when our observations of the system start, we obtain

(2) $$f^{n+1}(S_0) = S_n,$$

if we designate by f^n the nth iteration of f and by S_n the nth state that is generated by the recursive applications of the ensemble f of the rules of interaction. In a mathematical sense we may consider f as a mapping from state S_k to the state S_{k+1}.

This general definition, of course, says nothing about the particular rules and the order of recursively generated states. The system function f may be a deterministic one, if all the local rules are deterministic, and it may be a stochastic function. In the later chapters of this book we shall introduce rather different kinds of rules and according systems functions.

The dynamics of a system is now defined as the particular succession of states that is generated by the local rules, i.e., the system function. It is important to note that the dynamics of systems defined in this way is always an emergent phenomenon produced by the local interactions. Often the dynamics of a system is considered as a path in the state space of the system: each specific state is defined as a point in a multi-dimensional space that consists of all possible states the system can *principally* realize. The particular path a system generates by applying the system function is called the trajectory of the system. Note that a specific trajectory is dependent not only on the rules, i.e. the systems function f, but also on the particular initial state(s) S_0.

Often the trajectories of systems are visualized in a two-dimensional state space or in a plane that is defined by two dimensions of the states of the elements and hence of the system. As an example we give two visualizations of the model of a predator-prey system that was constructed by us and Jörn Schmidt on the basis of a cellular automaton (see below). The figure 1 shows the trajectory of the system, the figure 2 shows the variation of the number of preys and predators respectively with a time curve for each population.

Often the dynamics of a complex system is characterized by particular states S_A that have the property

(3) $$f^n(S_A) = S_A,$$

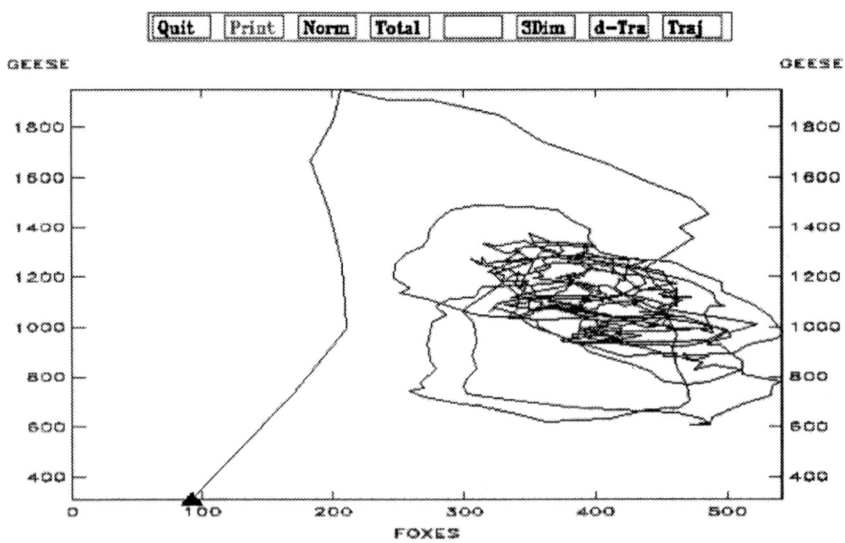

Figure 1. The trajectory of a predator-prey system in a two dimensional state space; the dimensions are defined by the numbers of prey and predator respectively

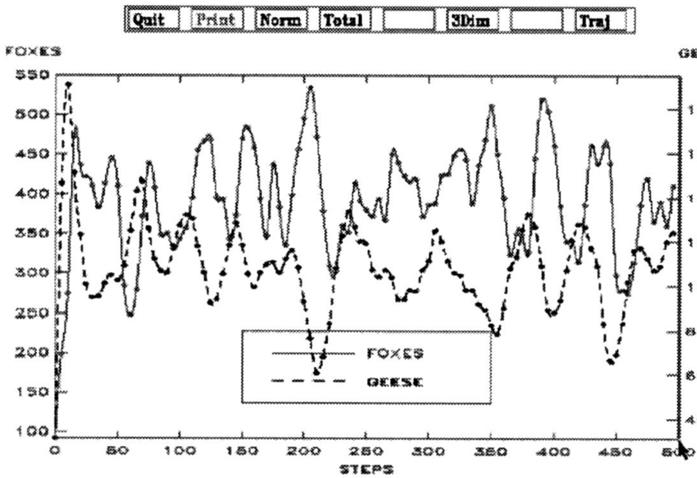

Figure 2. The interdependent variations of the numbers of prey and predator; the connected curve illustrates the variation of the number of prey, the other that of the predator

for all n. In this case S_A is called a point attractor of the trajectory of the system or briefly a point attractor of the system. If we get

$$(4) \qquad f^k(S_A) \text{ and}$$
$$f^i(S_A) = S_A \text{ for } i = n * k$$

we speak of a (simple) attractor of period k; in this case the attractor contains all the states the system generates between the first and the second time of the generation of S_A. In other words, an attractor "attracts" the trajectory of the system and keeps it at this state (point attractor) or in the successive k states that define an attractor of period k. Mathematically speaking, an attractor is characterized as a point or a segment in the state space that draws the trajectory to the point or segment respectively. Readers who are acquainted with the mathematics of function theory will perceive that the attractor concept is basically nothing else than the well known "eigenvalues" of a function introduced by Hilbert. The definition given above is a generalization of it in the sense that it is also applicable to discrete system functions. In chaos theory often so called "strange attractors" are investigated too. Strange attractors are also defined by a segment of the state space that the trajectory does not leave any more; in that segment the trajectory may reach any point of the segment and is only difficult to predict. Such systems are called chaotic or quasi chaotic.

Because the specific trajectories of a system are, as we said, dependent on the system functions and the respective initial states, a system may generate rather different attractors according to the respective initial states. In particular a system may generate several different states after the initial state before it reaches an attractor. The succession of these states is called the preperiod of the respective attractor.

The trajectories of a system which start at different initial states may finally reach the same attractor. The set of all initial states that are characterized by the same attractor S_A as the final point or segment in the state space of their trajectories is called the basin of attraction of the attractor S_A. With a picture from Kauffman (1995) one canvisualize the basin of attraction as a set of different creeks all flowing from different mountains into the same lake. The set of all basins of attractions of a system is the basin of attraction field, i.e., the set of all equivalence classes of initial states defined by their generation of the respective same attractors. In other words, an element of the basin of attraction field is a class of trajectories that all end in the same attractor.

Wolfram (2002) has classified the dynamics of complex systems by introducing four different complexity classes, the so called Wolfram classes. Class 1 is the simplest and is characterized by the fact that all different initial states lead to one and the same attractor, usually a point attractor. Class 2 generates different attractors but only point attractors or those with rather short periods. Class 3 is the class of chaotic or quasi chaotic systems: their trajectories are characterized by attractors with very long periods and even strange attractors. Class 4 is a mixture between class 2 and class 3: it generates all types of attractors with the exception of strange attractors; the different attractors do not influence the whole system but can remain locally fixed. In contrast to class 4, systems of class 3 literally never get any rest, i.e., never reach point attractors because all parts of the system influence the other ones. Systems belonging to class 3 and 4 are very sensitive in regard to initial states: they generate nearly always different attractors when starting with different initial states. Systems of class 1 and 2 on the other hand always or often are not susceptible to the changing of initial states; that fact explains in a very general mathematical way why many complex systems, e.g., physical ones, come back to rest after having been disturbed by external causes.

Kauffman (1993, 1995), Langton (1992) and others have shown that it is possible to predict the *principal* kind of dynamics a system may obtain by so called ordering

Figure 3. Visualization of a basin of attraction (drawn by Magdalena Stoica)

parameters (Klüver, 2000, 2002). Ordering parameters are a property of the specific rule ensembles of a system: for example, if the number of possible states that the elements of a system may obtain is two, e.g., 1 and 0, and if the rules are such that the state 1 is reached in proportion ¾ to state 0, then the so called P-parameter of the system's rules is $P = 0.75$; if both states can equally frequent be obtained, then $P = 0.5$ and if only one state can be reached for all elements then $P = 1$. The interesting point is now that only rules with $0.5 \leq P \leq ca.0.65$ can generate trajectories that belong to Wolfram class 3 or 4. Rule ensembles with all other P-values generate only trajectories belonging to class 1 or 2. The other known ordering parameters have similar characteristics, namely that only small ranges of their values generate trajectories with complex dynamics, i.e., dynamics belonging to Wolfram classes 3 or 4. It seems a safe conclusion that the "origins of order" (Kauffman, 1993), i.e., complex systems whose trajectories reach simple attractors with only very small periods is just a question of mathematical probability: order must necessarily evolve because it is much more probable than systems with no simple attractors or those with long periods.[1]

When speaking of the rule ensembles of complex systems another important distinction must be made: complex systems are not only defined by their local rules of interaction that determine the changing of the element's states but also by "topological" rules that determine which elements can interact with which others (Klüver, 2000; Klüver and Schmidt, 1999a). Rules of interaction are executed if the respective local conditions are fulfilled, but the rules do not tell us which elements of the system will interact at all. This is determined by the topology of the system, i.e., rules that define the possibility of local interaction. The frequently only metaphorically used concept of the "structure" of a system means in a precise sense just that. In many cases the topology of a system can be characterized by a binary adjacency matrix that tells if certain elements interact or if they interact only via other elements (cf. Freeman, 1989 for the case of social networks).

It is interesting to note that the topology of a system also determines its dynamics: Klüver and Schmidt (1999b) discovered another ordering parameter v that exhibits a characteristic of the adjacency matrix of Boolean networks (see below). Roughly speaking this ordering parameter defines the mean value of the influences certain elements have on other ones. If all elements have equal influence on the other ones, the parameter value is $v = 0$; if the influences are such that they are extremely unequally distributed, then $v = 1$. As an ordering parameter v has the effect that a topology with $0 \leq v \leq 0.25$ generates complex dynamics, i.e., trajectories belonging to Wolfram classes 3 and 4; $0.25 < v \leq 1$ generates only simple trajectories. In other words, the more equal the elements are in regard to the possibilities of influencing other elements, the more complex the system's behavior will be and vice versa.

[1] It must be noted that these results with respect to ordering parameters are "only" statistical ones: there are always exceptions, i.e. systems whose parameter values do not follow these regularities. Therefore, the probability of the emergence of order is still valid but only as a statistical regularity. But these are questions for specialists (cf. Klüver et al. forthcoming).

Because the other ordering parameters also measure certain degrees of inequality, although in other dimensions, it seems plausible to postulate a conjecture of equality:

The more equal a system is in different dimensions, the more complex its behavior – its dynamics – will be and vice versa. Because only rather high degrees of equality will generate complex dynamics the origins of order is a consequence from the fact that most systems will necessarily exhibit more degrees of inequality than of equality (Klüver, 2002).

These considerations demonstrate that a lot can be learned about the regularities that determine the behavior of dynamical systems by applying the concepts of complex systems theory. Yet these concepts do not take into account the important cases when systems evolve, i.e., when they do not keep their rules of interaction and/or their respective topology constant. After all, a lot of very important processes of complex systems can only be understood by taking into consideration that rules of interaction and topologies can and will be changed. Among those processes are biological evolution, individual learning and sociocultural evolution (Klüver, 2002). Therefore the definitions given so far must be extended.

We call a system *adaptive* if it is capable to change its rules of interaction and/or its topology according to certain demands of its environment. In particular an adaptive system must be able to evaluate its own states with respect to the environmental criteria and change its rules and topology accordingly. In order to do this an adaptive system must have some *meta rules* that regulate the changing of the local rules and topology; the evaluation of its own states must be done by the equivalent of some *evaluation or fitness function* respectively. Therefore, an adaptive system is characterized a) by its rules of interaction and its topology, b) by the meta rules that determine the variation of the interaction rules and the topology and c) by an evaluation function that determines if and when the rules of interaction have to be changed. For example, the concept of "environment" may include emotional states of communicative actors. The according evaluation function refers in this case to the emotion of well being of the actors. Another example is the respective scientific community of a certain research group. The according evaluation function measures the research success of the group with respect to the state of the art of the respective scientific discipline.

Well known examples of adaptive systems in this precise sense are biological species (not individual organisms) that change the genomes of the individuals by the well known "genetic operators" of mutation and recombination with respect to certain physical environments (biological fitness). It is important to note that these adaptive systems have no goal, i.e., they do not orientate themselves explicitly to the environment. They rather try different possibilities, that is different individuals, and keep the most suited ones. The meta rules in this case are the genetic operators and their operations on the individual genotypes; the evaluation function is the natural selection that determines the individual fitness of the members of the species. Although the meta rules operate on the individual genotypes only the species as a whole is adaptive in a strict sense.

Another example that will be studied in the next chapters is the learning process of single systems. We shall see that in a strict sense individual learning consists mainly of the variation of local cognitive topologies; the meta rules in this case are different learning rules that operate on the topology. The evaluation function is mainly an immediate feed back from the environment of the learning system that consists in the measuring of the respective learning errors the system has made during its learning process.

A final example of adaptive systems are sociocultural systems that evolve by the variation of their social structure, i.e., their rules of interaction and their social topology, and by the enlargement and variation of their culture, i.e., their knowledge about the world (Klüver, 2002). The meta rules in this case can be very different, for instance the "rules" of social revolutions, democratic reforms, cultural exchange and so forth. The same holds for evaluation functions that have to take into account the material wealth of the citizens, cultural traditions, national identities etc.

In the case of adaptive systems the concept of attractor has to be extended too. Whether a trajectory reaches an attractor depends, as we saw, on the rules of interaction, the topology and the initial states. Adaptive dynamics on the other hand are characterized by the variation of rules and topology likewise and therefore adaptive systems can become independent from the constraints of their initial states. In particular, because the adaptive processes are characterized by certain criteria – learning goals, biological fitness, the welfare of a country –, they may be mathematically considered as special kinds of optimization processes: they are judged according to the criterion if they have reached certain optima in their whole space of possible goals; evolutionary biologists speak in this respect of a fitness landscape. The respective goal or optimum is the point in the state space where the adaptive process will stop, i.e., the meta rules will not change any more the rules of interaction including the topology. This aspect must be a bit more thoroughly analyzed.

The variation of the rules and topology by meta rules is itself a process that must be understood as the iterative application of certain rules – in this case meta rules. In the case of non adaptive systems we saw that usually the iteration of the rules leads to attractors, in particular point attractors and attractors with only small periods. The question now is whether the iterative application of meta rules to interaction rules and topologies also leads to attractors, i.e., to rule ensembles and specific topologies that the application of the meta rules does not change any more, although the meta rules are still applied. This is one of the most important questions, e.g., in the field of machine learning and of the adaptation of complex systems in general.

Holland (1975) has constructed a mathematical model of biological evolution, the so called genetic algorithm (GA). It is basically nothing else than an optimization algorithm that uses the operators of biological evolution, namely mutation and recombination (crossover). In this case Michalewicz (1994) has given a proof that a certain form of GAs indeed has attractors in the sense just described: by iteratively applying the genetic operators on an artificial "genotype", i.e., different vectors consisting of symbols for specific rules, the vectors converge and do not change any more.[2] This convergent characteristic of the GA gives a mathematically expressed explanation for the fact that most biological species do not change any more after some time of evolution although their environment may change. For the same general problem it was demonstrated that artificial neural networks, formal models for the simulation of individual learning processes, converge under specific conditions, in particular if the networks are "recurrent" (cf. McLeod et al., 1998). In a literal sense we may speak here of "meta attractors" that can be defined just the way attractors are defined:

Let F be the ensemble of meta rules that regulate the rule and topology variations of a system at a certain time t and let f_t be the ensemble of rules of interaction and topology at this time.[3] Then a meta point attractor f_A is obviously defined as

$$(5) \qquad F^n(f_A) = f_A,$$

for all n. An attractor with larger periods is accordingly defined; we leave it to the imagination of the readers if there is anything like strange meta attractors in the domain of rule changing.

It is rather unfortunate that the concept of attractor is often used for both cases, namely the "one-dimensional dynamics" considered above and the adaptive dynamics, which is some kind of optimization process. In the first case the states of the system reach an attractor by the iterative application of the rules of interaction, in the second case the rules and topology of the system reach an attractor by the iterative application of the meta rules. The concept of "meta attractor" is more precise, but this term is not frequently used. To avoid confusion we shall speak of attractors only in the first case, i.e., an attractor of the system's states; in the second case we shall use the terms "meta attractor", "local optimum", "point of convergence" or in the case of individual learning processes "learning goal".

It is also possible to analyze the adaptive processes in regard to the efficiency of their optimization as a formal parallel to the ordering parameters described above. One can introduce so called "meta parameters" (Klüver, 2000) that measure different degrees of rule variations. Apparently the meta parameters regulate the adaptive optimization processes in a formal similar way as do the ordering parameters in regard to non-adaptive dynamics.

For the sake of brevity we designate non-adaptive dynamics as *first order dynamics* and adaptive dynamics as *second order dynamics*. The evolution of complex systems is in some special cases determined by still another type of dynamics that we call *third order dynamics*. (Klüver, 2002). Third order dynamics is characterized by its ability to change its own initial structural conditions, in

---

[2] The proof of Michalewicz uses a famous theorem from the theory of metrical spaces, i.e. the Banach fix point theorem, and is valid only for so called elitistic GAs.

[3] Over a longer period of time the meta rules may vary also, as is the case for example with social systems where the change of social rules can be obtained in different ways-civil wars versus democratic legitimatized reforms etc.

particular its topology, without the selective force of an environment. In this sense third order dynamics has the capability of structural change like second order dynamics, but it is in important aspects independent from the environment of the system – like first order dynamics. Processes of third order dynamics seem to occur only in cases of sociocultural evolution and ontogenetic learning (Klüver, 2002); because we shall later deal with these processes in some detail these remarks are enough for the moment.

To be sure, a lot more could and should be said about the dynamics of complex systems. However, our purpose is not a treatise on the research on complex systems but the unfolding of that theoretical framework that we shall use for a theoretical analysis of communicative processes. Therefore we now shall sketch some methodical consequences.

2.2. UNIVERSAL MODELING SCHEMAS AND MODELS OF SOFT COMPUTING

In the introduction we remarked that we shall use computer simulations as a methodical tool for our research. Unfortunately neither in the natural nor in the social and cognitive sciences the concept of computer simulation is unambiguously used. In particular in the natural sciences the tradition of constructing formal models and computer programs by the use of the classical differential equations of physics is still dominant; the same can be said about many computer simulations in biology where for example variants of the Lotka-Volterra equations are applied when simulating eco-systems (e.g. Pimm, 1991).

Because we use the theoretical frame of complex systems dynamics it seems appropriate to look for modeling schemas and formal tools, i.e., classes of formal models, that are immediately applicable to the task of the modeling of communicative complex systems. In consequence of our theoretical considerations of the last subchapter we therefore use a modeling schema that is a direct methodical transfer from our theoretical frame and that is, for reasons given below, universally applicable (cf. Klüver et al., 2003):

Consider any empirical domain, for instance social groups, whose members communicate according to certain rules, or a learning system with certain elements that interact – neurons in the case of the brain, concepts in the case of the mind. Then the construction of a formal model of this domain is its representation as a formal complex system just defined in subchapter 2.1. We saw already that such systems are characterized by rules of local interactions and a certain topology, i.e., a structure that defines which elements are interacting with which others. It is now an empirical question which kind of dynamics the model of our system should have. Social groups for example do not change their rules and/or topology over short times of observation; in this case first order dynamics is enough for the construction of an adequate model. In the case of learning systems obviously second order dynamics has to be introduced into the model, and sometimes even third order dynamics is necessary.

A little example may illustrate this procedure. It is well known in the analysis of social groups that their "structure" may be characterized by a so called sociomatrix or Moreno matrix (cf. Freeman, 1989). In many cases the sociomatrix describes the mutual feelings of the group members towards the others, i.e., the matrix contains different values v, say 1, 0 and -1. $v(a,b) = 1$ means that a has positive emotions towards b; 0 means neutrality, -1 means negative feelings. Apparently these values can be defined as the topology of this social group. As each member has particular feelings towards all other members the topological relations of one group member must be modeled as a (n–1)-dimensional vector if the group has n members. Now we have to introduce specific rules of interaction which are in this case simply that a group member interacts frequently with those members he likes, that he interacts only sometimes with members neutral for him and that he avoids to interact with members he does not like. In addition we have to determine if all members can interact with all others or if only with certain members; then we have a formal model of that particular group and its probable dynamics.

Before we sketch the formal tools that are especially suited for this kind of modeling we have to make a methodical *caveat:* it is a *methodical decision* which "level" one wants to take as the system level and accordingly it is a methodical decision whether the elements of the respective system are just represented by their states – scalars, vectors or other symbols. For instance, in many social cases it is sociologically sufficient to represent the elements of social systems, i.e., the social actors, by simple states and to concentrate just on the social level. In this case, of course, one neglects the obvious fact that social actors are not simple finite state automata but are themselves complex systems that should be modeled the same way as the systems on the social level. This is a methodical reduction every sociologist is aware of (cf. Luhmann, 1984). The theoretical and methodical reason for this often justified abstraction is the knowledge that in many cases the differences between the individual elements, in this case social actors, dissolve in the statistical average. In the case of social systems there is the additional theoretical reason that via the process of socialization individuals tend to act rather uniformly according to the specific social rules that are valid in particular situations of action. However, in certain cases this reduction is not valid, and the analysis of communication is such a case where the participants of communicative processes must be represented as complex systems themselves. The reason for this is the mentioned fact that communicative processes in general are determined by both social rules of interaction and the cognitive processes of the communicators. Therefore, we have to model communication as a complex system whose elements are complex systems themselves.

In this sense communication as the core of social reality mirrors the dual character of society: on the one hand a society can be characterized by its social *structure*, i.e. the social rules of interaction and the respective topology; on the other hand a society is defined by a certain *culture*, i.e., the sum of the knowledge that is hold to be valid in that society (cf. Habermas, 1981; Geertz, 1973). That is why communication as the basic generating principle of societies has to be analyzed in just that dual manner (see below).

Because we shall deal with this problem in the next chapter we may for the moment return to the modeling schema in its simple version, i.e., single elements are just represented by the value of the finite states they have obtained at certain times.

Why is this schema universal? The answer is grounded in a mathematical characteristic of the formal models we use when we transfer the models of empirical domains into formal systems and according computer programs. Take for example the formal model of cellular automata (CA) that has been mentioned above and which is frequently used in the social and some natural sciences (cf. Wolfram, 2002; Klüver, 2000).

A CA is an algorithm that generates a grid of cells, usually visualized as squares. The cells are in particular states – scalars or vectors. In the logically simplest case the cells just have two possible states: 1 or 0, on or off, dead or alive. Each cell has eight adjacent cells, i.e. on its sides and at its edges. The topology of this formal system is usually that a cell interacts with these eight cells in its neighborhood – the so called Moore neighborhood – or only with the four adjacent cells at its sides – the so called von Neumann neighborhood. The rules of interaction, in the terminology of CAs the rules of transition, are simply that the next state of a cell depends on the states of the four or eight adjacent cells in the respective neighborhood and on its own previous state. A classical rule of a famous CA, the Game of Life by Conway, is that the state s of a cell becomes or stays $s = 1$ if exactly three adjacent cells in its Moore neighborhood are in the state 1.

CAs and their generalization in form of Boolean networks (BN) are obviously rather simple systems, at least with respect to their basic logic. Therefore, on a first view it is quite astonishing that they are logically equivalent to universal Turing machines (Rasmussen et al., 1992), which means that it is possible to model literally all complex systems by using these formal models.[4] There is little doubt that this assumption is valid for all empirical systems. The modeling schema we present in this subchapter is universal because it is always possible to construct a model according to this schema and to map the model onto a suited formal system like a CA or a BN. To be sure, this general proof of the universality of our schema says nothing about the task how to capture the peculiarities of a specific empirical domain in such a model; that is up to the creativity of the constructors. But the decisive point is that the application of the modeling schema will always yield a model that is suited to capture *in principle* each characteristic of the empirical domain one wishes.

---

[4] To be more exact, universal Turing machines are able to compute any computable function and by this it is possible to model every system by such a formal system that is computable in the abstract sense of mathematical logic. No scientist seriously believes that there are physically real systems that cannot be modeled by a suited universal Turing machine or some logical equivalent (the so called physical Church-Turing hypothesis).

The logical universality of formal systems like BN or CA opens an additional methodical way: the analysis of these "pure" systems by itself obtains results *that are valid for all empirically real systems.* This is a direct consequence of the characteristic of universal Turing machines. Given one general property of such universal systems, i.e. a property that all such systems will show then each empirical system must *a priori* also have this property. Indeed, for every empirical system there exists at least one CA or BN as a suited model of the empirical system; in particular the respective CA or BN is able to exhibit all the characteristics of the empirical system that is to be modeled. Therefore the specific CA or BN is the result of an isomorphic mapping of the empirical system. Because all CA or BN have this specific general property our empirical system must also have it – q.e.d. That is why the results about the ordering parameters with respect to CA and BN are also valid with respect to, for example, social or cognitive systems (cf. Wolfram, 2002; Kauffman, 1992; Klüver, 2000; Rasmussen et al., 1992).

Our universal modeling schema has two other advantages that makes it extremely suited for the analysis of complex systems. On the one hand it allows to model the empirical domains in a rather direct and immediate way. Take for example the model of group dynamics we sketched above. One only has to investigate the specific group in the well known way of empirical social research, i.e., one has just to construct a sociomatrix by interviewing the group members and has to observe the interactions or communications respectively between the different members. The results of the interviews, i.e., the values of the sociomatrix can be given to the computer programs that are themselves nothing else than the *direct* formal representation of the observable group. Then the predictions of the programs can be immediately compared with the empirical observation; examples of this procedure will be given in the fourth chapter. In this sense the modeling schema allows to make a very natural transfer from the methods and results of empirical social research to the construction and analysis of formal methods. In contrast to the classical mathematical methods of physics or the statistical methods of survey research it is not necessary to abstract from the individual interactions and/or individual beliefs in order to aggregate the data on a general level, i.e. that of the system as a whole. One may remain at the level of the observed individual cases, so to speak, and can transfer them directly into the model and therefore into the computer program.

In this sense the modeling schema directly allows to transfer social reality, as we observe and experience it, into the mathematics of formal systems and according computer programs. This great advantage of the modeling schema and the according formal tools like CA, BN or artificial neural nets (NN) is not only important for social research; we shall see that it is equally important for research in the cognitive sciences.

On the other hand the modeling schema quite naturally allows the enlargement of initial models that served as a beginning in particular research processes. It is always possible to start with a rather simple model that captures only very general properties of the empirical system. The more detailed the model should be the more additional aspects can be inserted into the model: for example, the state of the elements may not just be represented as a scalar but as a vector; the possibility of interactions may not only be represented by a binary adjacency matrix – interaction or no interaction –, but the interactions can be modeled according to a degree of interaction, that is by a matrix coded in real numbers; the adaptive behavior of the system is represented by the addition of meta rules and so forth. Therefore, it is not necessary to construct always new models if one wants to go from simple cases to complex ones, but one has only to start with a simple model and to enlarge it step by step.

The modeling of individual learning processes may serve as an example, which will become important later. Although CA and BN are in principle universal Turing machines it is only with certain difficulties possible to model learning processes in a direct way by them.[5] But one can easily extend, e.g., a BN into a learning neural net (NN):[6]

A logical or Boolean net is *in nuce* a generalization of CA in the sense that a) the size of the neighborhood and b) also the rules of interaction may locally vary. If one takes as the size of the neighborhood $K = 1$ or $K = 2$, then one gets as rules of interaction just the classical logical functions of propositional calculus. In particular it is possible to characterize elements that influence others but are not influenced by them (see above the remarks about the v-parameter). In this sense BNs are CAs with locally different topologies and locally different rules of interaction. The topology of a BN is represented in a binary adjacency matrix that consists only of values 1 or 0.

The first step to extend this formal model into a learning system is to code the adjacency matrix in real numbers to represent, as we said above, the *degree* of interactions. Then for the sake of lucidity in the second step we omit the different rules of transition (interaction) and replace them by a single function that regulates the state values of the elements in dependency of the states of the other elements that interact with a specific element. If there is no interaction, i.e., if the extended adjacency matrix contains a value $w_{a,b} = 0$ for two elements a and b then no influence of a will occur in b. Because we have substituted the binary values of the simple adjacency matrix by real numbers, i.e. by the degree of interaction we have to take into account also the respective degree. This is usually done by multiplying the state value of an element a that influences an element b with the value of the degree w_{ab}. Then we get as the general function of interaction for two elements i and j

(6) $$A_j = A_i * w_{i,j},$$

if A_j designates the state value (the "activation value") of an element j.

---

[5] This is not a contradiction to the postulated universality: every *single* learning process that has been observed can be modeled with a suited BN or CA (cf. Wolfram, 2002). But a usual BN or CA does not have the *general* property of learning.

[6] We discussed the transformation of a BN into an arbitrary NN in detail in Stoica-Klüver et al., 2006.

Any element j may be influenced by more than one other element; the influence of these on j is computed accordingly. The influence of all elements i that interact with j is simply summed up; then we obtain

$$(7) \qquad A_j = \sum A_i * w_{i,j},$$

which is the most used activation formula for artificial neural nets.

To give this formal system the capability of learning in a third step one has to introduce a specific meta rule, in this case called a learning rule that has to change the topology of our artificial system (the activation rule is usually not changed although this is possible too). A frequently used learning rule is for example the "delta rule":

$$(8) \qquad w_{ij}(t+1) = w_{ij}(t) \pm \eta(t_i - a_j)o_i = \eta o_i \delta_j$$

where $w(t+1)$ and w(t) are the values at time $t+1$ and t respectively, η is a so called learning rate and n is the number of elements ("neurons") that influence j, δ is the size of the error the system has made in regard to j, that is the difference of the state value of j with respect to some predefined goal value and o is the factual activation – the factual state value – of j. To put it into a nutshell, our formal system learns by varying its topology, i.e., the single values of degrees of interaction, in dependency of the errors it has made in the respective previous learning steps. In the terminology of neural networks the degrees of interaction are usually called "weight values" or simply "weights" – hence w_{ab} for two elements a and b. We shall also use this term in the following chapters.

Apparently it is rather easily possible to extend a Boolean net into a learning neural net; the extension was done in this case by the generalization of the binary adjacency matrix to a "weight" matrix coded in real numbers and by adding a particular learning rule. However, the formal system also became simpler because we substituted the different logical rules of the BN by one general rule or function of activation. To be sure, it is possible to construct neural nets with locally different activation functions too but for the most known learning problems such a simplification of an original BN will do.

It is certainly possible to insert a general learning capability into BN by other means than by transforming a BN into a learning neural net (NN) in the manner just described. For example, one can vary the locally different rules of interaction and the topology of a BN by using certain "evolutionary algorithms" as meta rules, like, e.g., GAs or evolutionary strategies (cf. Wuensche, 1994; Stoica, 2000). For reasons that will become clear in the next chapters we shall use mainly neural nets to model individual learning processes although this second possibility will also be used.

The modeling schema that we introduced at the beginning of this subchapter apparently is universal not only in a logical sense but also in a methodical manner: literally all complex processes or dynamics of complex systems can be modeled by applying the schema and extending the initial model as far as necessary. In particular it is apparently rather easily possible to introduce different kinds of dynamics into an initial model that started only with rather simple forms of dynamics. Because we shall use the theoretical framework as well as the modeling schema in the course of the following chapters we discussed both in some length. We shall see that it is possible to capture any feature of communicative processes within this theoretical and methodical frame and to obtain this way the foundations of a general mathematical theory of communication.

2.3. COMPLEX SYSTEMS APPROACH AND SYSTEMS DYNAMICS

Before we start with the conceptual foundations of our communication theory it is necessary to briefly characterize our approach with respect to the also well known tradition of systems dynamics.

Port and van Gelder (1995) emphasize the point that in cognitive science systems dynamical approaches at least go back to the classical study "Design for a Brain" by Ashby (1952) and that these attempts are more suited for the theoretical and methodical characterizing of cognitive processes than "computational-representational" approaches (e.g. Thagard, 1996). This claim has often been criticized (cf. e.g. Grush, 1997; Thagard, 1996) and if our approach would be nothing else than a variation of an old theme in cognitive science we had first to deal with the arguments against systems dynamics in cognitive and social sciences as well.

But what is this classical approach? To be sure, our approach uses several concepts that have been developed in systems dynamics like trajectories, attractors and state spaces. Already Ashby demonstrated how these concepts can be used for the modeling of cognitive processes. To put it into a nutshell, systems dynamics describes dynamical systems by introducing (a) a (small) set of state variables, (b) mostly non-linear differential equations that determine the values of the variables, and (c) the trajectory of the system in its state space as the consequence of the application of the equations. The Lotka-Volterra equations mentioned above are a typical example of such a methodical procedure: state variables represent the numbers of predator and prey respectively; the equations describe the mathematical relations between the variables, and the trajectory is a consequence of the equations (together with initial values of the state variables, of course). In physics and biology this approach is quite successfully used because a lot of systems can be described with a small set of state variables. On the other hand there are serious doubts if cognitive processes can be adequately modeled with a small set of variables (Thagard ibd.).

Port and van Gelder additionally postulate that only models with "real" time, i.e. continuous time variables are meaningful and that discrete time concepts are only "ersatz time" (ibd.). This argument is hardly convincing because who says that "real" time is continuous? Physics says otherwise since the discovery of the Planck time. In addition, it is possible to demonstrate that discrete models are able to capture any real process (Wolfram, 2002). Therefore there is no real argument against the use of discrete models for the analysis of cognitive processes (cf. e.g. the models of Elman (1995) and Pollack (1995) in the volume of Port and van Gelder).

We suppose that the often stressed importance of continuous time variables is simply due to the fact that the classical systems dynamics approach is characterized by differential equations and that means continuous systems functions. In the social sciences, by the way, Forrester (1973) and his school of systems dynamics quite successfully demonstrated the possibilities of using difference equations instead of differential equations (cf. also Hannemann (1988).

Although our own approach is without doubt related to systems dynamics, there are obviously important differences. Systems dynamical approaches in the manner described above are "top down" approaches, i.e., they model the dynamical behavior of the system as a whole via the fundamental equations. The approach that we develop in this book is in contrast to systems dynamics a "bottom up" approach, i.e., we start from the local interactions of the elements of the systems, determine the rules that govern these interactions and obtain the whole systems dynamical behavior *as an emergent consequence of local interactions*. (cf. e.g. Langton, 1988). For example, the trajectory of the predator-prey system we showed above is *not* the effect of the application of the Lotka-Volterra (differential) equations on particular initial values of the predator and prey variables, as is often the case with simulations of predator-prey-systems. In contrast to these systems dynamical approaches we obtain certain trajectories by defining particular rules of local interactions like "*if* a prey is in the neighborhood of a predator, *then* the predator will eat it", "*if* two prey are in the same neighborhood, *then* they will produce an offspring with a certain probability", or "*if* a predator did not get a prey for a certain number of time steps, *then* the predator will die from starvation" and so on.[7] In this sense the shown trajectory is an emergent effect of the local rules (and of course the initial states of the system). Therefore the key concept of our approach is not that of state variables and general systems equation but that of *local rules* of interaction in combination with the element's states as "local" variables. By using such a methodical way it is not necessary to restrict the description of the system to a small set of state variables but the number of variables can be as large as the problem demands. In the same sense Thagard (loc. cit.) refers to connectionist models like artificial neural nets as having many variables: each unit can and must be represented by a particular set of variables that designates the states of activation of the unit. It is quite the same with cellular automata or Boolean nets.

In classical systems dynamics the behavior of the system is often described as dependent on the environment and additional equations are used to describe this dependency. For example, in our predator-prey-system one species may be looked at as the environment of the other and both co- evolve together according to the Lotka-Volterra-equations. Such an assumption is certainly often very useful for the description of physical or biological systems. But in the realms of the social and cognitive sciences a *general* assumption of this sort overlooks the undeniable fact that there are a lot of social and cognitive processes that cannot be understood as

[7] "Neighborhood" means the so-called Moore neighborhood on a cellular automaton (CA).

a *direct* interaction of a – social or cognitive – system with its environment. Many such processes must be interpreted as autonomous ones that follow their own logic. Social and cognitive systems in many aspects are regulated by their own laws that cannot be determined by the environment (cf. Grush loc.cit.; Klüver, 2002). The famous concept of *autopoiesis* (Luhmann, 1984; Maturana, 1982) means exactly that, although it tends to neglect the fact that complex systems are also adaptive in the sense defined in subchapter 2.1. The classical systems dynamics approach cannot capture this phenomenon if it makes the assumption just mentioned.

The approach of complex systems analysis on the other hand can quite easily characterize the autopoietic character of complex systems by distinguishing between rules of interaction that generate the dynamics of the system on the one hand and the changing of these rules via meta rules according to certain environmental demands on the other hand. One may say that our approach combines the advantages of systems dynamics by using certain concepts for describing the behavior of the whole system with the advantages of computational approaches by modeling the dynamics of social and cognitive systems in a bottom up way: the state of each element of the system is computed by using local rules of interaction and neither a restriction of state variables nor implausible assumptions about system- environment relations are necessary.

We already mentioned the fact that social interactions can only be understood two-fold: on the one hand social interactions are determined by social rules that are the precise definition of "social structure" (Giddens, 1984; Habermas, 1981). On the other hand human actions are regulated by the "world-view" of the actors, i.e., their knowledge, beliefs, moral norms etc. This duality of objective rules and subjective world-views is essential for any analysis of social action and that means communication. It would be difficult and rather implausible to model this dialectical duality in terms of traditional systems dynamics. The approach we develop in this study is on the contrary very suited for this task and probably the best way to capture the complexity of (social and cognitive) communicative reality in terms of mathematical models, although the concept of "mathematical models" has to be enlarged in comparison to the traditional approaches borrowed from mathematical physics.

CHAPTER 3

MEANING AND INFORMATION: THE SEMANTIC DIMENSION OF COMMUNICATION

3.1. THE MEANING OF MEANING

Presumably the discourses about the "meaning of meaning", to quote the title of Ryle's famous book, are as ancient as in all the reflections on thinking and communication. There can be no doubt that no theory of communication can claim *principal* completeness in a categorical sense if it does not give a definition of meaning. That is why the theory of Shannon is strictly speaking no theory of communication at all. Therefore, our task is to define this ambiguous concept in terms of complex systems theory.

In a very abstract manner one can say that all the different theories of meaning could be categorized as representatives of three basic types or as combinations of them.[1] The first basic type has its origins in Platon's *Kratylos* and may be called the *referential theory of meaning*. The meaning of a sign – or symbol – is defined here as the relation between the sign and the object that the sign refers to. The famous scholastic definition "*aliquid stat pro aliquo*" – something stands for another thing – quite aptly describes that definition of meaning.[2] Frege and Carnap elaborated the classical referential theory by introducing the well known distinctions between *Sinn* (sense) and *Bedeutung* (meaning) or, as Carnap formulated in a more precise terminology, between intensional and extensional meaning. Yet the problem with all referential theories of meaning was and is that they cannot be formulated in a precise manner. In particular, what is the precise meaning of "reference"? For this reason Carnap restricted his definition of intensional and extensional meaning to formal languages and made, therefore, the definition quite useless for the analysis of human communicative processes. The same objection is valid with respect to the linguistic distinction between connotation and denotation that roughly is equivalent to that between intensional and extensional meaning. In addition, reference understood as a kind of relation between a sign and the object it refers to, is always dependent on the subject, which uses the sign. This fact cannot be expressed in a precise way as Frege and Carnap intended.

The second basic type may be called a *theory of usage* with its most prominent partisans Peirce and Wittgenstein. This theory is expressed most explicitly in

---

[1] To be sure, other kinds of systematization are possible and exist. For our purposes the categorization given above is best suited.

[2] Platon himself identified the meaning of a symbol with the symbolized object but that position of course is untenable.

the famous "pragmatic maxim" of Peirce: "to develop its meaning, we have, therefore, simply to determine what habit it produces, for what a thing means is what habit it involves" (Peirce 1878). In other words, the meaning of a sign – or of any perceived object – is the way in which the perceiving system uses the sign. Wittgenstein expresses the same idea when he remarks "*Die Bedeutung eines Wortes ist sein Gebrauch in der Sprache*" (Philosophical Investigations).[3] In contrast to referential theories of meaning usage theories explicitly take into account that meaning must always be defined with respect to a subject, which uses a sign, and that meaning is always meaning for someone. Yet usage theories usually neglect the undeniable fact that meaning also is always a meaning of something – the *aliquo* in the scholastic definition. Meaning defined by the use of signs is a definition without semantic content and by this reason only partially applicable to the analysis of communicative processes. In particular, neither Peirce, Wittgenstein or other partisans of usage theories were able to define their concepts of meaning within the framework of a precise, that is a mathematical theory.

The third theory type we may call *representational theories* and they are often associated with psychological constructivism (e.g. Piaget). These theories are based on the assumption that meaning is the result of a constructive process in the brain (cf. e.g. Roth 1997) or the mind respectively: Perceived objects, e.g. certain symbols, are not mirrored in the perceiving cognitive system but the system constructs some internal states that give meaning to the perception. In other words, the meaning of a sign is not some undefined relation between the sign and something it designates but the constructive reaction of the perceiving system to the perception. The main argument for this theory type is the often observed neurobiological fact that the brain is able to construct meaningful internal states even when there are no such meaningful signs in the environment of the brain (Roth loc.cit.). The problem with these theories is that they do not explain why the meaning of signs is very often the same for different perceiving systems and why the attachment of meaning to signs is not done in an arbitrary manner. Yet despite this problem we shall introduce a rather similar definition of meaning; to be sure, we try to avoid this particular trap.

All three types have their advantages and their shortcomings. A satisfactory definition of meaning, therefore, has to take all three types into regard and has to combine the respective advantages by avoiding the shortcomings.

By quoting Platon, Peirce or Wittgenstein we may generate the impression that the question of meaning is just an abstract philosophical one without relevance for science proper. But a very actual importance of a clarification of "meaning" is well illustrated by a famous argument of Searle (1990) against the possibility of an "Artificial Intelligence" founded on rule based systems or computer programs respectively. He introduced the so called "Chinese Room", i.e., a man sitting in

[3] "The meaning of a word is its use in language" (our translation).

a room and "translating" texts written in Chinese into French language. The man, a native speaker of English, does not have any knowledge about the Chinese and French languages; he just has a lot of formal rules that tell him how to refer certain Chinese symbols to particular French words. Despite the fact that the result of the combination of the Chinese with the French symbols is a text that speakers of Chinese and French alike would call a correct translation from the Chinese original into French, nobody, so the argument of Searle, would say that the man in the room understands Chinese. Although he performs a correct translation he does not understand Chinese because the Chinese symbols *have no meaning* for him – they are for him just meaningless signs scrabbled on paper and without the combination rules they could be as well the drawings of a little infant.[4]

Searle does not give a definition of meaning in this context, but his argument is clear: the purely formal, i.e., syntactical manipulation of signs, even if they produce correct results, has nothing to do with "understanding" them, because "understanding" refers to meaning and that belongs to the semantic dimension of signs. Therefore, Searle's argument is clearly based on a referential theory of meaning. Because computer programs operate only according to syntactical rules and know nothing about the semantic dimension, they do not understand what they are doing and therefore they will never be "intelligent".

As we do not want to participate in the discussion about "real" Artificial Intelligence, which seems rather fruitless, we can accept for the time being the argument of Searle, although it has been severely criticized (cf. e.g. Churchland and Churchland 1990). By the way, we shall see that Searle's man in the room gives indeed some meaning to the Chinese signs, although it is certainly not the meaning a speaker of Chinese would give to them. Nevertheless, the argument of Searle indicates the undeniable fact that a definition of meaning must be given if one wants to speak about "understanding" (cf. the next chapters) and in particular about communication. A pure syntactical theory of signs will never be sufficient for our task. After all, communicative processes are evaluated by the criterion if and how far the participants do "understand" each other; we may safely assume that understanding has something to do with the sharing of common meaning.

In order to introduce an own definition of meaning that only uses the general concepts of complex systems theory we refer to a non human learning system, that is the famous dog of Pavlov. This dog Vladimir was trained, as is well known, to respond to the ringing of a bell that synchronously occurred with the offering of food. Vladimir learned to identify the ringing of the bell with the opportunity to get some food; the indicator for this learning was the production of saliva at

[4] The original version of Searle's "Chinese room" is a bit more complex. We omit some details because we just want to outline the general argument.

the ringing of the bell alone.[5] In other words, Vladimir learned to give the signal "ringing of the bell" a certain meaning, i.e., the same meaning as the signal "offering of food".

We shall use the example of Vladimir in quite another context later, namely the acquisition of logical concepts. If we now have to define the learning of a certain meaning by Vladimir we may immediately refer to the concepts of complex dynamical systems:

Consider Vladimir as a special type of cognitive systems that consists of particular elements, rules and topology. For the time being we can abstract from the question what kind of elements the system consists of, for example neurons as in the case of Vladimir's brain. Then we can visualize the cognitive system of Vladimir before the training as a dynamical system that reacts to the signal of food and only to that signal by producing saliva. The signal "food", therefore, has a specific meaning for our dog:

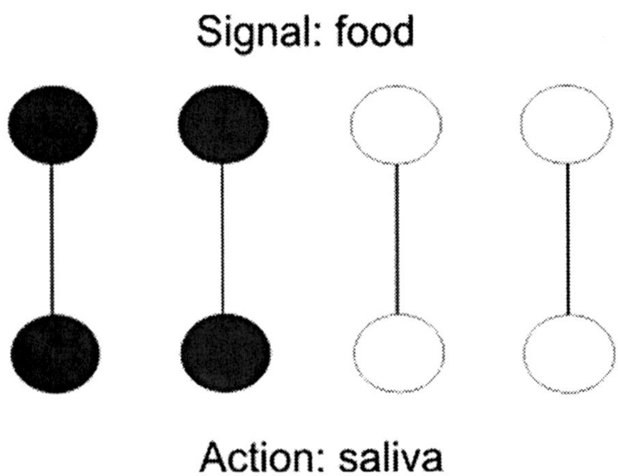

In terms of artificial neural nets we may call the first level of elements the input level, i.e., a level where incoming signals (e.g. by the sensory organs) activate the elements of this level. The second level is the so called output level, i.e. the level by which the system is connected with its environment, in this case in particular the saliva producing parts of the brain and the stomach. The dark color of the elements in the input level mean that the signal "food" is received by them and only by them; the light colored elements in this level mean that nothing is activated. The lines between the elements in the input level and the elements in the output level represent the fact that only these specific elements are connected. According to

[5] The name of the dog was noted by Zoozmann (1917).

the rules of interaction – e.g. the linear activation rule that we explained in 2.2. – the activation values of the first level elements will "spread" to the elements of the second level (the topology of this exemplary system is, of course, only constructed for visualization purposes).

Now a certain problem has to be solved by the cognitive system: the topology of the system has to guarantee that the activation values of the different elements do not generate a dynamics with no attractors or only attractors with rather long periods. One certain signal must generate one definite final state of the system and must not generate a dynamics where the system "oscillates" between different states. If that would be the case then the cognitive system is not able to react adequately to signals like "food".[6] Therefore the signal processing dynamics of the cognitive system has to generate a particular point attractor in order to generate the "right" response. In the case of Vladimir of course phylogenetic evolution has cared for an adequate topology. In our little example the network contains "sinks", i.e., elements that do not interact with other elements anymore once they have obtained their specific activation values. The sinks are in our figure the elements of the output level. The attractor is designated in our little example system by the dark colored elements of the output level; light colored elements mean that these not activated elements are not important for the attractor.

We emphasize this aspect because the generation of a point attractor is the *conditio sine qua non* for solving two problems: On the one hand only a point attractor generates an unambiguous meaning; already an attractor of period 2 would give two different "meanings", i.e. the cognitive system would not be able to identify the input signal in a unique manner. That may often be the case if an unknown signal has to be examined. Yet on the other hand only a point attractor enables the system to act, that is to respond to the signal in a certain way. If, e.g., the cognitive system would generate an attractor of period 2 then the system would be in the position of the famous donkey of Buridan: placed between two identical stacks of hay the donkey could not decide which stack it should eat at first and in the end the donkey starved to death. Action is only possible for a receiving system if it is able to attach unambiguous meaning to a signal and that means the generation of a point attractor. The famous remark of Luhmann (1984) that a certain action closes communication processes must here be understood in the same way: only if a cognitive system reaches a point attractor an according action becomes possible. We shall come back to the question of generating actions from cognitive processing in subsequent subchapters.

Now we can define the concept of meaning of the signal "food": *it is nothing else than the attractor generated by the cognitive system if it receives the according signal*. To be sure, as the particular attractor is generated by a general activation rule and by the specific topology of the cognitive system we might also say that the meaning of the signal "food" is contained in the topology, but that would not

---

[6] In Vladimir's case the production of saliva is the adequate reaction because it causes the stomach to produce the acid necessary for digestion.

be sufficiently exact.[7] In chapter 2 we referred to the fact that many complex systems are rather "sensitive" with respect to different initial states: they generate often different attractors when receiving different initial states, although rules of interaction and in particular the topology remain constant. Therefore we have to define the meaning of a signal by the topology *and* the according attractor, and not only by the topology alone.

Obviously this definition fulfills the criterion that meaning must be a semantic concept, i.e., the meaning of a sign must refer to its *designatum*. A certain topology of the cognitive system generates the according attractor via the activation of the input level by the *external* signal of food. "External" means that the signal is external to the specific cognitive system that processes the signal of food; signals that have their origin not outside the brain of, e.g. Vladimir but in other parts of the brain are of course in this sense external too.[8] In other words, the generated attractor "refers" to the perceived sign and makes it meaningful for the perceiving cognitive system. Therefore, our definition fulfills the criterion of referential theories of meaning that meaning must be defined in terms of semantics. In particular, it is now possible to define the somewhat only metaphorically used terms "reference" or "relation" respectively in a more precise manner: The relation between a sign and its meaning is just the specific topology of the perceiving cognitive network and the activation rule(s) that determine the spread of activation between the units of the networks. We shall see in later chapters how this definition can be expressed in specific mathematical concepts.

In a formal sense we also have with this definition of meaning a parallel to the famous pragmatic maxim of C.S. Peirce "for what a thing means is what habit it involves". To be sure, Peirce did not have in mind neurobiological or systems theoretical definitions of meaning but an operational definition in terms of *logical* interpretants. But we may well argue that the topology that generates the attractor is rather akin to the "habit" of Peirce: the meaning of a signal is not just a *particular* action or behavior caused by the signal but the interplay of a signal, an according initial state of the cognitive system, the topology and activation rule of it, and finally the generated attractor. Because the topology, if it is not changed, will always generate the same attractor if receiving the same signal we have the logical specification of Peirce's habit concept. Therefore, the advantages of usage theories of meaning can also be captured with our definition.

Consider now the situation of Vladimir before the famous training or conditioning process respectively. When his cognitive system receives a signal "bell" then his system reacts like this:

---

[7] Such an inexact definition can be found, e.g., in Favre-Bulle 2000.

[8] The mentioned fact that it is possible to generate practically all reactions to perceptions in the brain by artificially stimulating certain parts of it demonstrates the adequacy of our definition: the brain generates a certain meaning although there is nothing outside of it by generating an according attractor via the stimulations.

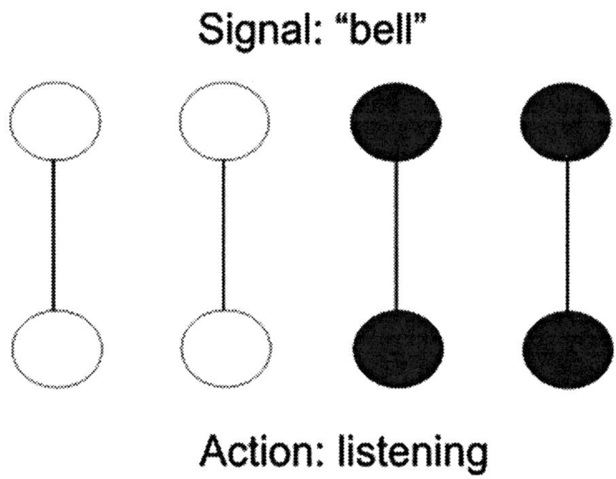

The signal "bell" is only received by the dark elements in the input level. According to the topology of the system only the respective elements in the output level are activated and generate an action like, e.g. "listening".

Now Vladimir is trained and receives the synchronous signals "food" and "bell". We omit in this chapter the logical structure of this training situation and simply assume that Vladimir uses a learning rule like the Delta-rule from chapter 2.2. to change the topology in order to combine the two signals. In particular, the cognitive system must generate the same attractor in three different cases, i.e., three different initial states: a) the offering of food without the bell, b) the offering of food together with the bell, and c) the ringing of the bell alone. The attractor must be the same or nearly the same in all cases because the reaction – production of saliva – must be and is in all cases the same. If the training is finished, the topology of Vladimir's cognitive system is the following

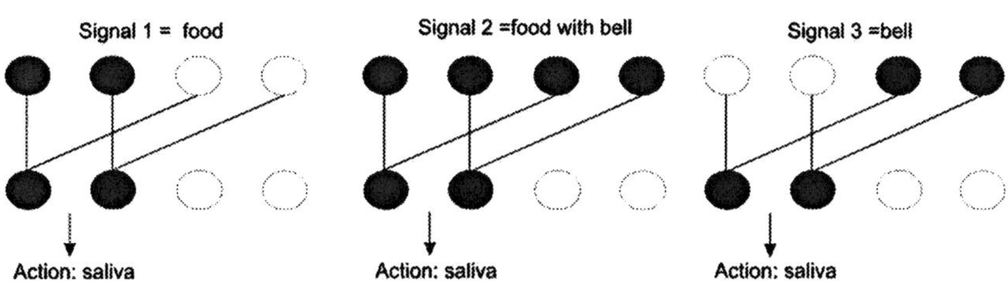

In other words, all three different initial states, caused by different signals, generate the same attractor. It is now clear what "learning" means: learning is the change of a cognitive topology, in this case the construction of new connections between elements of the input level and elements of the output level on the one hand and the vanishing of other connections between the input level and the output level. In terms of complexity classes or Wolfram classes (see above chapter 2.) in the end we apparently have a system belonging to class 1 or 2. It may well be that the result of such fundamental learning or training processes that are very important for the correct functioning of the whole organism is always or often a cognitive system of class 1 or 2. Obviously the training has the result that all three signals now belong to the basin of attraction of the original attractor that was the meaning of "food".

It is important to note that we do not necessarily mean "brain and neurons" when we speak of a cognitive system and its elements. On the one hand we sometimes explicitly refer to artificial systems if we mention cognitive systems; on the other hand we shall often give examples of cognitive systems where the elements are not neurons but concepts. In that case the cognitive system is not the brain in a neurobiological sense of the term but the mind, although of course the mind must be considered as a certain part of the brain. In the case of Vladimir, to be sure, the cognitive system is certainly a part of the brain with its neurons that generates the according attractors. In the case of human beings we often mean the mind with its concepts. However, the relation between mind and brain will be more thoroughly discussed in chapter 5.

The example of Vladimir can be finished with another aspect, namely the advantage of forgetting and the non arbitrary generation of attractors. It is well known that Vladimir forgot the meaning of the signal "bell" when it received some times only the bell signal with no food. To be sure, Vladimir did certainly not understand that he had been conditioned and in that way "tricked". The stomach of Vladimir, as was mentioned, produced the acid necessary for digestion when the attractor "food" was generated in the brain as reaction to the bell. When the brain got reactions from the stomach that acid but no food was there the brain received a negative input, that is, it realized potential danger for the digestive system. Therefore, the brain had again to learn in reaction to the negative stimuli from a certain part of its environment, i.e. the stomach. As a consequence it changed its topology again, namely to the initial structure where the signal "bell" did not generate the attractor "food" in the brain:

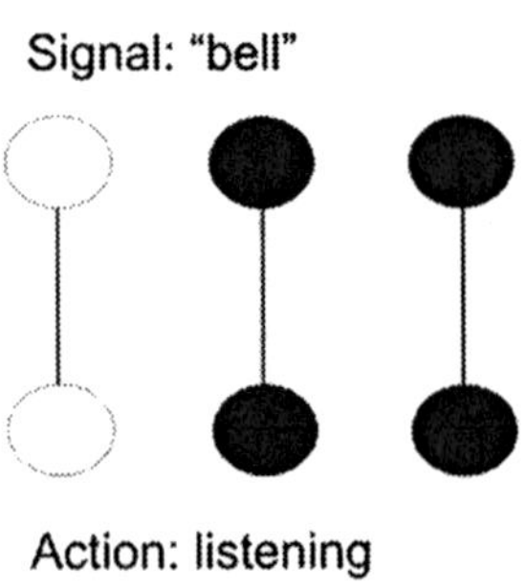

This example demonstrates why the generation of attractors of meaning is not arbitrarily done by a cognitive system. The generation of meaning via an attractor is not a process each cognitive system performs in its own way. The feed backs from the respective environments force each cognitive system to generate very specific attractors and in particular very similar ones to the same signals. In the case of dogs conditioned by some experimental psychologists it is simply a question of survival that all dogs generate after some time an attractor that means "no production of saliva and that is no production of acid" if only a bell signal is received. Otherwise the dogs would die rather quickly because their digestive systems would collapse.

Our proposed definition has of course similarities to the representational definition of meaning, as we said in advance. But it avoids the difficulty of seemingly arbitrary constructions of meaning because our definition explicitly takes into account the feed back from the environment of cognitive systems. As a first result we may, therefore, summarize that the attractor definition of meaning combines the main advantages of the three basic theories of meaning. Yet it is important to remember that the generation of attractors is done by cognitive systems that are self-organizing *and* adaptive in the sense we defined in chapter 2. Only by taking that fact into account it is possible to take over the advantages of the representational theories of meaning too.

The example of Vladimir may be seen as a too simple one and valid only for non human brains without a consciousness. How about human beings? For a more human example we may imagine the visual perception of an old aunt whom we have not seen for some years. The perception of the aunt – the signal – causes again dynamical interactions between particular neurons – or concepts – that generate an attractor state in a certain part of the brain. Only after reaching this attractor we are able to act, e.g., by greeting the aunt. If our brain would not have reached a point attractor or an attractor with a very short period we would not have recognized the aunt, that is, the signal would have no *definite* meaning for us. Therefore the signal "aunt" has a meaning for us if and only if her perception generates a simple attractor – the meaning is the attractor.

The "aunt attractor" also is the memory of her: we remember her only if her perception generates a point attractor. If we have forgotten her then no attractor – at least no simple attractor – will be generated; forgetting is losing the according attractor. That happens in particular if the rules of interactions and the local topology have changed for this part of the cognitive system. *Therefore forgetting may also be described as losing the particular rules of interaction and the specific topology necessary for generating the respective attractor.* We suppose that (the neurobiologist) Edelman (1992) meant something like that when he remarked that memory is a system's achievement, although he did not precisely describe what he meant with this concept. However, as there is no store in the brain in the usual sense of the word or in the sense computers have stores, the memory of a perception or of everything else must be contained in the mathematical structure of the cognitive system and that is in its topology.

Now suppose that the aunt has changed in the last years – for example by another hairdressing. We remember her well, but only with the old hair-style, i.e., the original aunt attractor is generated by the initial state "old hairdressing". In spite of that we immediately recognize her again with the new hair-style. The explanation for this ability is obvious: the new initial state is element of the same basin of attraction as the old one and generates roughly the same attractor with the meaning "aunt". Because complex systems often have rather large basins of attraction for particular attractors at their disposal this recognizing ability is obviously a characteristic of complex systems in general. The same general explanation, by the way, is valid for the often stated though seldom explained capability of artificial neural nets to recognize disturbed patterns that they once have learned in the original version. In all these cases we have to assume that the learning processes, in this case the learning to recognize an aunt, lead to systems of Wolfram classes 1 or 2, because only these systems have real large basins of attraction.

This definition of meaning and memory by the attractor concept is basically not totally new (e.g. Hopfield 1982; Stadler and Kruse 1992; Wuensche 1994; McLeod et al. 1998) although it has scarcely been systematically examined. In particular, it has been empirically confirmed in neurobiological research (Freeman 1992): The analysis of EEG-waves in the brain of rabbits demonstrated that new smell sensor inputs generated disturbances in the brain that soon stabilized, i.e. a new local attractor was generated.

But a short consideration shows that this definition must be enlarged a bit. When we perceive our aunt with the new hairdressing we do not only recognize her *as* our aunt but also as the aunt who has changed her hair-style. In other words, we remember her *and* perceive her changing, in particular the kind of changing. We do this by remembering the aunt with the old hairdressing, i.e., we generate an attractor state of the *original* aunt although we do not see her with the old appearance before us.

Accordingly we have to assume that the part of the cognitive system that deals with the processing of the meaning of "aunt" is not only able to generate the old attractor when perceiving the aunt but is also able to generate another attractor that is the meaning of "aunt with new hairdressing". In other words, our cognitive system generates different local attractors at the same time, i.e., the attractor with the memory of the aunt with the old hair-style and the attractor that is the meaning of the present perception of the aunt. The cognitive topology of the cognitive system that is responsible for these different attractors keeps the attractors that have been generated before in a "latent" manner, that is they become generated again only if the responsible part of the cognitive system receives an according signal – by the environment or other parts of the system. Therefore, the memory of the aunt with the new hair-style will be kept by the topology too.

This aspect must be more thoroughly examined. We may assume that there is a particular whole network that performs the meaning processing in regard to aunts; this network is sensitive to different initial states and, therefore, belongs to complexity class 4. That is why the signal of her *new* hairdressing is transformed into a *new* attractor that is rather similar to the old one. The whole network contains a sub-network of class 1 or 2 that is not influenced by the generation of the new attractor and was trained some time ago to the signal of "aunt as I have perceived her in particular with the old hairdressing". Therefore *it also reacts* to the signal of the new hairdressing and, belonging to class 1 or 2, it generates the old attractor with the old hair-style (and perhaps other characteristics that I remember).

This generation causes the "mental image" of the former aunt. By generating both attractors at nearly the same time we are able not only to recognize the aunt but also to perceive the exact differences between the two images – the one we see and the other we see only "in our mind". In this sense memory can be understood as the construction of a sub-network of class 1 or 2 that generates always the same attractor, regardless if the signal has changed in the meantime; but note that the perception of the aunt with the new hair-style generates also the new attractor belonging to the new signal.

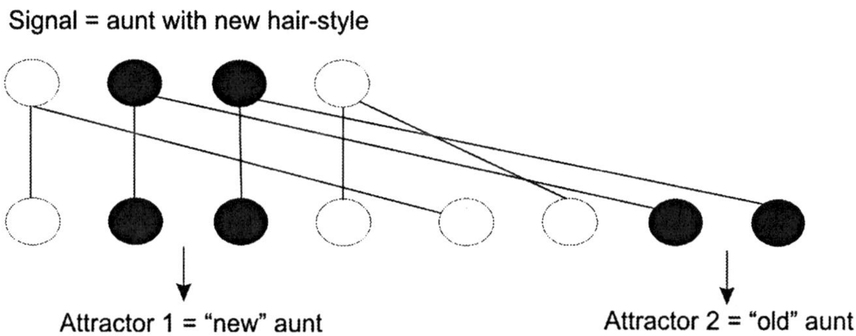

Note that the two networks consist of the same input level and two different output "sublevels".

This process can be iterated: the attractor 2 will be kept by the *whole* network again in a latent manner, i.e., attractor 2 becomes "stored" in another sub-network of class 1 or 2 (that is the exact meaning of the term "local attractor" that was used above). If we meet the aunt again some times later and she has changed her hair-style the second time then we will remember both old hair-styles and so on. Of course, if the aunt keeps changing her hairdressings then after the fourth or fifth time we shall forget the first styles because we cannot or will not keep sub-networks only with respect to new hair-styles. But that is another question.

Now we can enlarge the definition of meaning. The different signals the aunt causes during different times all generate different initial states that may lead to the same attractor or in addition generate a new one. In the second case we nevertheless identify the aunt as the same person. *The meaning of "aunt" is now the set of different attractors that are generated by the signals "aunt at time t and with characteristic$_{ct}$"*. The identifying of the "different" aunts is possible because the according initial states form a subset of the basin of attraction field; the boundaries of this subset are defined by the measures of similarity of the different "aunt attractors".

So far we have spoken only about attractors that are generated at the reception of a certain signal and that are the meaning of the signal. But of course the reception of a particular signal must not be restricted to the generation of just one attractor (or two attractors as in the case of the aunt). It frequently occurs that with the generation of one attractor other attractors are also generated via the activation of other nets and subnets in the cognitive system (see above). This is nothing else than the well known process of *association*, i.e., the formation of other meanings by the reception of a particular signal. When receiving the signal "aunt", we do not only remember her old hair-style and form a mental figure of it in the way just described, but we also think of her husband and other uncles, her dog, other aunts and so on. In other words, we construct an *association field* of different "concepts" that are related to the meaning of aunt in some way or other. Note that this is a constructive performance of the cognitive system without obtaining external signals, a parallel to the formation of the mental figure "old hair-style". Because the attractors that are independently of external signals generated by the cognitive system also belong to the meaning of "aunt", we have to extend our definition of meaning for a second time:

We call the attractors that are generated in regard to the aunt, when receiving the signal "aunt", the *immediate meaning* of aunt. The additional attractors that will be generated by the cognitive system and that form the association field of "aunt" we call the *mediate meaning* of "aunt". In the case of symbolically coded signals, i.e., in the case where signals are transferred and processed as symbols we shall also speak of the semantic field of aunt instead of association field. We shall see in the next chapters that the formation of an association field or semantic field respectively depends not only on the particular cognitive topology of a cognitive system but also on the social situation of communication.

The generation and formation of an associative field is – in terms of complex systems theory – possible in different ways. The logically simplest case is of course the existence of different nets or subnets for each newly generated attractor – uncle, dog, cousins etc. But it is also possible to use, so to speak, one particular network more than once: if a certain network has generated, say, the attractor of "uncle 1", then this state can be "fed forward" to the network again as a new initial state or the generation of a new initial state respectively with the result of generating the attractor of "uncle 2". Feed forward networks are rather common in the technique of artificial neural networks; as far as we know the brain may often (although not necessarily always) operate just the same way. It is obvious that such a solution to the formation of association fields is more economically than the using of different networks for each new attractor of the association field. Probably the brain uses both methods, i.e., constructing new networks for new concepts and using old networks more than once via the feed forward method. It is probably a question of the similarity of signals whether a new sub-network is activated (or constructed) or whether an existing sub-network is used more than once by feed forward activation.

Such a feed forward network has to be at least of Wolfram class 2 in order to generate different although similar attractors by receiving one attractor as the initial state for the generation of a new attractor. A little figure can illustrate the feed forward method:

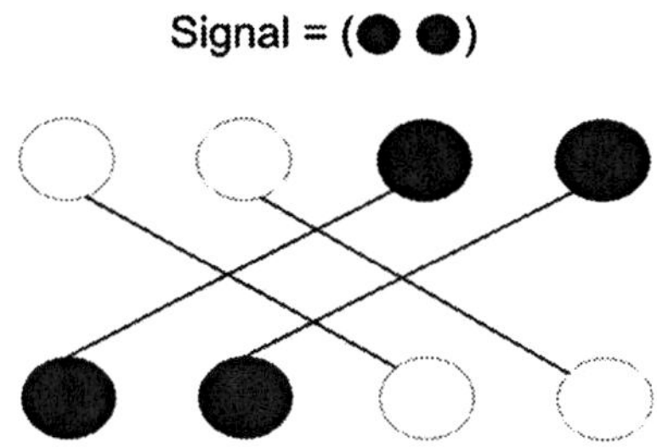

network after the generation of a first attractor

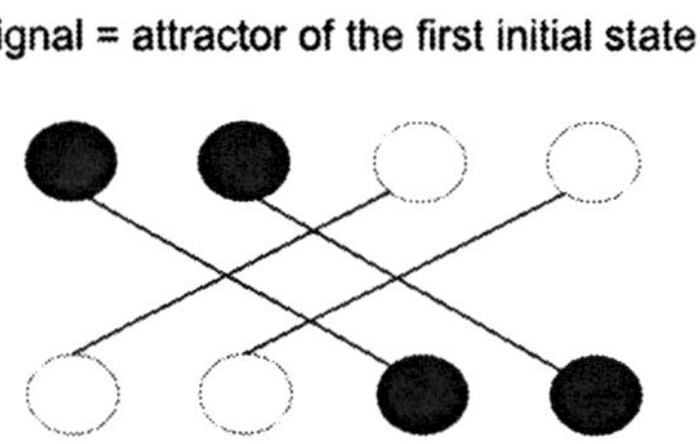

the same network, i.e. the network with the same topology after the input of the first attractor

By the way, the term "first attractor as input" is not quite correct. The attractor state consists, of course, of the states of *all* neurons, in particular also of the neurons of the input level. For the sake of brevity we shall use, as before, the term "attractor" for the final states of the neurons of the output level.

Obviously the definitions of immediate and mediate meaning take into account the fact that the meaning of a signal or a concept as the symbolical code for the signal depends on the individual learning biography of the respective cognitive systems – dogs, humans or, as we shall demonstrate, artificial cognitive systems. Indeed, the meaning of "aunt" is not only different for different people who have one aunt, several aunts or none, but it also depends on the cultural context in which people grow up. In Western societies "aunt" usually signifies just the sisters of the parents or in addition the wives of the parents brothers. In other societies "aunt" may mean any adult female person who cares for the respective children. Because the networks in the cognitive systems that generate the respective attractors are themselves the result of the biography, i.e., the learning process by which the networks have been trained via the adjusting of their topology, it is obvious that these networks will be different for cognitive systems that have learned under the influence of different cultural contexts. We shall more thoroughly examine these aspects in chapters four and seven.

Now we can also define the concept of *the same meaning* of a signal for two receiving systems. A signal means the same for two cognitive systems if a) the same kind of attractor is generated by receiving the signal (usually a point attractor) and b) if the signal generates via its immediate meaning the same association field or semantic field respectively in both systems. Because this happens rather seldom in the case of at least human systems we may assume that in most cases of communication the communicators attach different meaning to the same signal. Of course, insofar meaning also depends on the cultural context people are embedded in, the identity of a cultural context and in particular the similarity of the respective socialization processes in these contexts usually guarantee that the meaning of signals is not very different for any two individuals. If, e.g., in tribe societies socialization is nearly the same for all individuals and if everybody knows all other people of the tribe, then the meaning of signals is very similar to all persons. But even in this society differences of age or of sex will generate at least not identical meanings for any two individuals.

In many cases the meaning of a message or a single concept has a very specific aspect that must also be taken into regard. Consider for example a detective who learns that a certain suspect was at the time of a murder *not* at the place of the crime. Then the detective will generate a specific meaning to this message, i.e., that the suspected person has an "alibi", which means that the person could not be the murderer. In this case the meaning of the message is on the one hand the original attractor for "not being at place A at time B" and on the other hand a second attractor "alibi". In other words, the meaning of this message is for the detective that message X "means" Y – a simple form of "abduction", to quote Peirce again.[9] The attachment of meaning to message X apparently is in such cases the generation of another attractor after receiving the message and after the generation of a first attractor. To be sure, this is just a special case of the generation of mediate meanings, but a very important one. Many learning processes consist of how to construct new attractors that attach the "real" meaning to certain messages.

Before we close this subchapter on the concept of meaning we have to make several final remarks. Readers who are acquainted with concepts of meaning in epistemology and/or cognitive psychology may find it more than a bit strange to define meaning in terms of attractors, i.e., in terms of complex systems theory. After all, meaning is mainly supposed to denote the reference between a sign or symbol respectively and the *designatum* it refers to. In other words, to most people "meaning" refers to the referential theory of meaning that was discussed above. But

---

[9] "Abduction" is according to Peirce a cognitive process by which something "A" is identified as "B". If a child learns that the dolphin Flipper is not a fish but a mammal the child has learned a simple form of abduction.

it is important to stress again the point that meaning is nothing that exists independently of people or cognitive systems who combine a sign with its *designatum*. To be sure, sign systems like particular languages have well defined relations between the single signs and the combinations of signs on the one hand and their respective *designata* on the other hand. In this sense the meaning of a sign is independent of a *single particular* user of it. The languages of the mathematical sciences are such examples where – at least in principle – each sign has an unambiguously defined designatum.

But nevertheless this intersubjective meaning of signs must be realized by the community of users and that means by single users who follow the rules of sign production; elsewhere the meaning would not be existent at all. Therefore meaning is always dependent on those cognitive systems that attach meaning to certain signs. In an abstract orientation to Peirce and other theorists of operative and constructive concepts of meaning our definition just clarifies the *process and the result* of the construction of meaning, i.e. the generation of attractors. The undeniable fact that the meaning of certain signs cannot be arbitrarily constructed by single cognitive systems just refers to the equally well known fact that neither humans nor animals are the isolated monads of Leibniz. They are social beings that construct together and finally share the meanings of the common signs. Socialization, so to speak, cares for the possibility of communication by putting constraints on the arbitrary freedom of constructing cognitive topologies and the according attractors. We shall come back to this subject in the following chapters.

To be sure, it still makes sense to attach the meaning of "Aunt Lucy" to the particular person we "mean" when we produce the sign "Aunt Lucy". That, as we mentioned, was the basic idea of Platon's *Kratylos* and without doubt that is the "meaning of meaning" for most persons in everyday language. But the meaning of this sign is *not* the same for people who have this particular person as an aunt and for people (like us) who have not. The person to whom the sign "Aunt Lucy" refers is the same for all speakers but, to speak in Kantian terms, the individual biography differently constitutes the meaning of the signal for people with and without such an aunt. Factual communicative processes, insofar as they are determined by the exchange of meaning, are dependent on the meaning the communicating systems attach to the signals or messages respectively and by the designatum of the signals.

It is also possible to reformulate the famous distinction of Frege and Carnap between intensional and extensional meaning in our terms. Consider the famous example of Frege of "evening star", "morning star" and "planet Venus". According to Frege, when we use the terms of Carnap, all these concepts have the same extensional meaning, namely a celestial body, i.e., the second planet from the sun. Yet their intensional meaning is different for all three concepts because their use makes sense only in different contexts: Two lovers sitting on a park bank at a summer evening will probably admire just the evening star and neither the morning star nor the planet Venus (if the lovers are not both students of astronomy). Respectively a poet will try to make a poem about the brightness of the morning star if he is an early riser and in a creative mood. A conference of astrophysicists will certainly not speak about evening or morning star but only of the planet Venus. In this sense the referential theories of meaning by Frege and Carnap apparently introduce some aspects of the usage theory because the intensional meaning refers to the use of the signs in dependency of the respective contexts.

Frege and Carnap, as was mentioned above, were only able to define the concepts of intensional and extensional meaning in a precise manner with respect to formal languages. The main problem, of course, is the definition of "context": whether one and the same physical object is designated by "evening star", "morning star" or "the second planet from the sun" apparently depends only on the respective context in which the object is perceived or mentioned. In terms of our definition, however, it is quite easy to preserve that distinction and to apply it to all human communicative processes. Consider again the two lovers on the summer evening. When the girl says "look, how lovely is the evening star" we can understand her message to her boy friend as the reaction to an attractor "evening star". This particular attractor was generated by an input vector, consisting of the different components of the situation – evening sky, boy friend, park with flowers and trees and so on. In other words, the "context" that causes the girl to use the term "evening star" can be represented as a particular vector that generates a particular attractor – in this case the attractor of "evening star". The meaning of the signal "star" in this context is just that.[10]

Now consider the same girl sitting in a course of astrophysics on planet formation. A figure of the same star will of course generate the attractor "planet Venus" because the components of the input vector are rather different – dull elderly professor instead of young interesting boy friend, Kepler's equations on a black board, the announcement of the next examination on planet formation by the professor and so on. The particular cognitive net of the girl that processes the inputs of the situation with respect to planets is sensitive enough with respect to different input vectors to generate the different attractors "evening star" and "planet Venus" according to the different inputs.

To put it into a nutshell, in terms of our definition of meaning there is no difference between intensional and extensional meaning of the signal "star" but there are different attractors as generative reactions to the context in which the signal is received. To be sure, the star is always the same regardless which attractor is generated by the observation of it. But its meaning is always dependent on the context of observation and accordingly different attractors and that means different meanings are attached to it. The physical object that is always the same is just one component of the perception vector which is the representation of the whole context. If with the exception of the component "planet" all other components differ according to different contexts then by necessity the generated attractors will be different too. Therefore, no distinction is necessary between extensional and intensional meaning. The definition for example that the concept

[10] The input vector, of course, constitutes an initial state for the cognitive system of the girl.

"evening star" is attached to the celestial body of the second planet from the sun – Carnap's extensional meaning – is also "meaningful" just in a particular context, namely that of astronomy. Neither the two lovers nor the early risen poet attach their meaning of "evening star" and "morning star" to that astronomical definition.

Therefore, the intensional meaning of two signals is the same if and only if the signals generate the same attractor or, in the terms introduced above, if they belong to the same basin of attraction. But the same holds for the extensional meaning and that is why this venerable distinction is not necessary any more in a precise theory of meaning. To be sure, for pragmatical reasons it may sometimes be worthwhile to use it still.[11]

Finally, a critical objection against our definition of meaning in particular and the theoretical framework of complex systems in general may be that the speaking of cognitive topologies, cognitive systems and "meaningful" attractors is just a metaphor because neither neurobiology nor any other empirical science is still able to look directly into the brain or the mind. Therefore, these methodical and theoretical concepts are rather arbitrary in the sense that one may take them or leave them.

To be sure, we cannot claim to formulate a theory that is *directly* observable and confirmable and nobody else can at present do it. The quoted empirical evidence about the formation of attractors in the brain of rabbits is just an indicator for the empirical validity of our definition and not an exact proof. Yet the numerous "theories of the mind" that have been constructed by cognitive scientists in the last decades share this fate with our theoretical and methodical proposal. For example, nobody has been able to confirm the existence of a "language acquisition device" in the tradition of Chomsky's famous hypothesis. But our proposal has the great advantage that it is possible to construct mathematical models of the dynamical processes that occur when cognitive systems perform certain operations, to analyze these models in computer simulations, and to compare the according results with the empirical facts known about cognitive processes. In a certain sense our models allow us to formulate hypothetical suppositions about cognitive processes that are mathematically precise and light a bit the black boxes of our minds and brains.

From a theory of science point of view our procedure is of course well known and is at least since Popper's great "*Logik der Forschung*" (logic of scientific discovery) characterized as the procedure of many theoretical enterprises, in particular that of theoretical physics. Theoretical models can often not be directly observed but must be confirmed – or refuted – by their observable consequences. Insofar our

[11] In a very general sense these considerations have some formal similarity with the so-called situation theory insofar as the situation theory also takes the situation of perception, i.e. the context as the basis of the constitution of meaning and information (cf. Barwise and Perry, 1987). But in all other aspects this theory tries a totally different approach, which we cannot discuss here.

methodical and theoretical procedure stands on rather firm ground, namely that of modern theoretical science in general.

3.2. INFORMATION AND THE VECTOR OF EXPECTATION

One of the great achievements of Shannon's and Weaver's "mathematical theory of communication" was and is the exact definition of the degree of information. The basic idea, as is well known, is the characterization of the degree of information of a signal by its negative probability; in other words, a signal contains the more information the less probable, i.e., the less expected, it is. By perceiving the proximity of this definition to the concept of entropy Shannon and Weaver were able to define information as "negentropy" or negative entropy respectively.[12] As a reminder we quote the famous formula once again:

If H denotes the mean information degree of a certain message and if p_i denotes the probability, by which a component i of the whole message can be expected, then the degree of information of the message is given by

$$(3.2.1) \quad H = -\sum_i p_i ld p_i$$

Although the foundation of information on thermodynamics is rather unusual for scholars who are not trained in physics, the basic idea is still convincing, even in a common sense of information. If one distinguishes between information and meaning which has to be done at least since the achievements of Shannon and Weaver, then it is very plausible to identify the degree of information of a message by the degree to which the message is unexpected. The more unexpected a message is, the more it contains *new* contents for the recipient and therefore the more information it includes. To be sure, in empirical research it is often rather difficult or even impossible to measure the degree of information, but the basic definition has been frequently used with success in the mathematical sciences and in particular in complex systems theory (e.g. Langton 1992).

Yet despite this great merit of Shannon's and Weaver's approach several problems still remain. We already mentioned that the theory of Shannon and Weaver is not a theory of communication, although they named their approach thus themselves, because no definition of meaning was given (which they themselves already emphasized). Yet they also did not take into account the fact that communication is a dynamical process between receiving systems whose reactions to the messages determine the process at least as much as do the initial messages. Last but not least their definition of the degree of information is not applicable to communicating systems with a certain history for a quite simple reason.

---

[12] Shannon based his famous definitions on the preceding work of Hartley (1928) who used in his early definition of the degree of information only equal probabilities.

Consider the message "country A has declared war on country B". The degree of information of this message, measured by its negative entropy, may be quite small for the head of the intelligence service of country C, because he expected it: the message is telling a probable story *for him*. On the other hand a normal citizen of country C may be very surprised because he believed the announcements of peace of the leaders of country A. Therefore the message is very improbable *for him* and contains a high degree of information. Obviously from a communicative point of view it makes not much sense to ask which degree of information is the "right' one. Each recipient of this message had another knowledge of the political situation between the unfriendly countries A and B. Therefore, no "objective" measurement of the degree of information is possible, i.e. a measurement independent of the different receivers – at least not one that can be applied to factual communicative processes between people.

Of course, a defender of the Shannon-Weaver definition might argue that the objective probability of the declaration of war could be measured, given all information about the situation in regard to both countries. But even if that is granted, then this objective probability does *not* determine factual communicative processes between people with different degrees of political knowledge: the process of communication, insofar the degree of information regulates its dynamics, is dependent on the knowledge the communicators have about the content of the messages when they receive them. In the preceding subchapter we argued the same way for a "subjective" definition of meaning, i.e., a definition that takes into regard the learning biography of the communicators and the particular contextual situation.

This everyday example demonstrates another reason why the theory of Shannon and Weaver is *not* a theory of communication, at least not in the sense that communication is a dynamical process between generally *different* receiving systems. The Shannon/Weaver definition of the degree of information presupposes that it is possible to define and measure the *objective* degree of information. Indeed, if one defines information by the concept of negative entropy such a presupposition makes sense. No physicist doubts that such an objective measurement is in principle possible and that any system is either in this or in that state of entropy or negentropy.

Our example in contrast demonstrated that the degree of information is obviously not the same for sending and receiving systems, at least not in general. Any process of communication between human communicators, however, is not only but also determined by the probability or improbability the message has for the communicating systems. A communicative process between two experts on the foreign affairs between countries A and B will take other directions and will generate other dynamics than the communication between a political layman and an expert about the same subject. Therefore a theory of communication that preserves the general insight of Shannon and Weaver has to take into account the fact that information must be defined with respect to the sending and receiving systems as the bearers of the communicative process.

For an according variation of the Shannon-Weaver definition let us consider a hypothetical case, borrowed from the famous novels about Heidi by Johanna Spyri. Heidi, as is well known, spent some time in the city of Frankfurt where she had to learn how to live in a big town. Now imagine that one day Heidi heard the noise of an approaching vehicle of which she believed that it was a coach. She could not see the vehicle yet but she expected the sight of a coach in the next minute. Accordingly Heidi constructed a "mental image" of a coach that contained its different characteristics like wheels, horses, coachman and passengers (or cargo). This mental image can be represented as a vector $V_E = (1, 1, 1, 1)$ which means that Heidi expected a visual perception with the four mentioned characteristics of a coach. We call V_E the *vector of expectation* or *expectation vector* respectively.[13]

Now imagine that *Frau* Benz, the wife of the famous constructor of the first motor-car Karl Benz, made together with her son a trip from Mannheim to Frankfurt and Heidi saw one of the first automobiles in history.[14] Heidi obviously saw a carriage with wheels, coachman (respectively coachwoman) and passengers, but she saw no horses. Her *vector of perception* V_P then can be represented as

(3.2.2) $V_P = (1, 0, 1, 1)$.

and the difference between VE and VP, measured by the Hamming distance is

(3.2.3) $V_E - V_P = 1$.

The Hamming distance is for two vectors nothing else than the number of different components and in the case of binary coded vectors it is just the difference between the respective components. For any two binary vectors $V = (v_i)$ and $W = (w_i)$ their distance can accordingly be written as

(3.2.4) $V - W = \sum_i |(v_i - w_i)|$.

Following the basic idea of Shannon and Weaver, we define the amount of information of a message as a measure of *the difference between the factual message and the message expected by the receiver*. When we imagine both messages coded as vectors and their components codes as real numbers between 1 and 0, then the amount of information can be measured as a vector distance. The factual message then may be expressed as

$$X = (x_1, x_2, \ldots, x_n),$$

[13] Remember that we defined the perception of some signals with respect to intensional and extensional meaning the same way.

[14] Readers who are not acquainted with either the story of Heidi or the history of the first automobiles may be assured that this fictitious story is historically well grounded: the story of Heidi has to be placed at approximately the time when Karl Benz made his invention; it is also a historical fact that the wife of Benz made some of the first trips with the motor-car.

whereas the expected message is given by

$$Y = (y_1, y_2, \ldots, y_n).$$

To be sure, the more a message is unexpected, i.e., improbable for the receiving system, the greater is the difference between the x- and y-components and the greater the degree of information of the message. Therefore we may define

$$(3.2.5) \quad p_i = 1 - |(x_i - y_i)|$$

to be the *expectation probability* of the component x_i; i.e., the deviation from the expected component y_i. Note that this is a "subjective" probability; i.e., it need not be the same for both communicators, in contrast to the Shannon-Weaver probability.

By summing over all components of the respective vectors and by using the Shannon-Weaver assumption that the degree of information of a message is the *negative* probability of the message we obtain

$$(3.2.6) \quad I = -\sum p_i$$

and by including the logarithm dualis for normalization purposes we obtain precisely the Shannon-Weaver definition

$$(3.2.7) \quad I = -\sum p_i * \mathrm{ld}\ p_i$$ [15]

Despite the formal identity of our formula and the classical definition of Shannon and Weaver we have again to emphasize that the probability concept in both definitions is *not* the same. The Shannon/Weaver equation is based, as we mentioned, on an *objective* concept of probability, following the tradition of thermodynamics. Our definition is based on a *subjective* concept of probability, i.e., the probability the message has for the receiving system and that we call the *expectation probability*. To be sure, "subjective" does not mean an arbitrary probability concept. We demonstrated that the expectation probability is mathematically defined and can in principle be measured with the same degree of exactness as the objective probability of Shannon and Weaver. But the expectation probability is in general *not* the same for sending and receiving systems; it depends on the biography of the according communicating systems insofar as it depends on the degree of knowledge the communicating systems have obtained at the time of the communicative process. The expectation probability measures the difference between the expected and the perceived and in this sense, but only in this sense, it is "subjective".

---

[15] One of the mathematical reasons for Shannon and Weaver to introduce the logarithm as an additional factor was, of course, that by this factor the informational degree as the negative probability becomes a positive numerical value. By taking the logarithm with basis 2 the important definitions of bits and bytes became possible.

By changing the concept of probability we obviously obtain several advantages: On the one hand it is possible to maintain the achievements of the classical definition of Shannon and Weaver. Our definition also postulates that the degree of information is the higher the less expected a message was and vice versa. Because we measure the informational degree by the difference between the expected and the perceived, the basic content of the "objective" definition is preserved, but without the unsuitable reference to physical concepts. On the other hand we are obviously able to apply the new definition to factual communicators by considering their differences with respect to their previous knowledge. In particular we can take into account the changing of informational degrees by the communicative processes themselves: for example, the message of the war between countries A and B has of course a different degree of information for a certain communicator *after* the communicators have spoken about it than it had before the communication. We mentioned above that the informational degree of a message in part determines the communicative process. The converse, of course, is also true: the communicative process changes the informational degree; therefore in regard to real processes only such a subjective concept of information in terms of expectation probability makes sense.

Apparently this definition of (the degree of) information is closely related to the concept of meaning given in the last subchapter. The meaning of a message (or a signal) was defined as the set of attractors that are generated by the receiving system when it gets the message. In our little fictitious example of Heidi and Ms Benz Heidi, when seeing the first motor-car, generated an attractor consisting of the vector of perception $V_P = (1, 0, 1, 1)$. In an informal sense the meaning of this perception was therefore a coach without horses.[16] Heidi expected to see a coach *with* horses, i.e., she generated an expectation vector $V_E = (1, 1, 1, 1)$ which can be understood as *her expected meaning* of the signal. Therefore we can combine the definitions of meaning and information by saying that *the degree of information of a message is the difference between the expected meaning and the meaning obtained by the perceived message*. In this sense meaning and information are, as we mentioned in the beginning, obviously two aspects of the same thing, although by no means identical.

It is not very difficult to construct examples of messages with roughly the same meaning for two communicators A and B and different degrees of information for both of them and of messages with roughly the same degree of information for A and B but different meanings for them. But before we can do this we have to examine the concept of information a bit more in detail.

So far the definition of the informational degree of a message is "only" a cognitive and not a communicative definition because we spoke only of Heidi as a receiving and information processing system. With respect to communicative processes this definition can be enlarged the following way:

[16] We assume here, of course, that Heidi had learned to form symbolic concepts like "coach", "horses" and so on at the time when she was at Frankfurt. The relation between sub-symbolic attractors and the construction of symbols will be dealt with in chapter 5.

A sending communicator A who sends a message performs this on the basis of an immediate meaning of this message, i.e., he/she has generated an attractor. When sending the message or immediately before the sending this attractor activates other attractors as was described in the last subchapter. In other words, the sending communicator activates a certain subset of the association field of the attractor that is the meaning of the message. The size of this subset depends mainly on the communicative situation and of course on the knowledge of the sender. This subset now forms the expectation vector V_E of A, i.e., it defines something like an expectation horizon of A in the sense that A expects an answer inside this horizon. When B receives the message, "computes" the degree of information of this message, and sends an answer to A, then B generates himself an expectation vector in regard to the answer of A. A computes the information degree of B's answer, forms another expectation vector and so on. Insofar as the communicative process is regulated by the information degrees of the messages, i.e. the initial message and the respective answers, the information degrees operate as parameters for the dynamics of the whole process (as do the different meanings of the messages, of course). We shall describe this process in more detail below.

When analyzing the computation of the information degree of the respective answers we have to consider another important aspect. When A generates an expectation vector, then B frequently will give an answer that contains components which are not components of the expectation vector of A. The simple computation of the informational degree that we discussed so far does not take into account an important difference: In some cases new and unexpected components in the answer of B may belong – for A! – to the subject that the two communicators are discussing and in other cases the new components may not. To illustrate this difference we refer to another literary example, taken from a detective novel by Agatha Christie.

In her famous novel "Lord Edgeware dies" the detective Hercule Poirot learns about a conversation at a party. One of the suspected persons, namely Lady Edgeware, hears another person say "the judgment of Paris". She joins the conversation by saying that Paris does not count any more because in questions of fashion New York and London are much more important. Lady Edgeware did not understand that the conversation was about the subject of the Trojan war and that "Paris" was the Trojan Prince. She simply did not know that such a person existed, at least in one of the great epics of world literature.[17]

Now consider conversations about the subject "Paris". Communicators who belong to the Western culture probably have some knowledge about Paris as the capital of France; accordingly they have at their disposal semantic sub - networks which contain concepts like "Tours d'Eiffel", "Champs d'Elyseé", "Seine", "Moulin Rouge", and "Haute Couture". To be sure, these semantic networks differ according to the

[17] For readers who do not know this detective novel we may add that at another party Lady Edgeware was able to speak with great knowledge about Greek and Roman literature. Therefore, Poirot concluded that there must have been two different persons acting as Lady Edgeware and thus Poirot was able to prove that Lady Edgeware had no alibi for the time of the murder.

individual knowledge of the communicators, for instance, if one of the communicators had been at Paris or not. But we can say that all these concepts belong to a network that is "clustered" around Paris as a particular city. On the other hand, "Paris" as a Trojan prince belongs to quite another semantic network that contains concepts like "Troy", "Hector", "Achilles", "Helena" and so on. By the way, experiments that we did in some seminars with students with this example taught us that even in the Western culture and at Western universities one can not presuppose the existence of such networks on classical literature in many communicators.

Both networks are not arbitrarily structured but in dependency of the cultural importance of the different concepts. "Paris" as the capital of France can be imagined as the center of the according network or cluster respectively. In more dynamical terms that means that there is a strong relation, i.e., a connection from e.g., "Moulin Rouge" to Paris but not conversely: if one speaks about Moulin Rouge, then most people will have the association "Paris", but if someone mentions Paris as the capital of France, then associations like "Eiffel Tower" or "Champs d'Elyseé" are at least as probable as the association of "Moulin Rouge".

On the other hand "Paris" as a prince of Troy is certainly not *the* center of the according network. Other figures are at least as prominent in the story, e.g., Hector, Achilles, Helena and Ulysses. The concept "Trojan War" is probably the best candidate for the center of this network because the mentioned concepts all immediately lead to "Trojan War" but not conversely: "Trojan War" may lead to Agamemnon or Patrokles etc.. In a mathematical manner we can represent these different networks as graphs with certain concepts as central nodes and other concepts connected with the central nodes with different strengths. If two concepts A and B have connecting "weights" w(A,B) and w(B,A) that represent the strength of the connection, then $w(A, B) > w(B, A)$ means that A is stronger connected with B than conversely and that an association process leads more often from A to B than from B to A. In this sense "Paris" in the first network has a connection w(P,E) with "Eiffel Tower" and conversely there exists a connection w(E,P) with $w(E, P) > w(P, E)$. We shall use this graph theoretical representation of semantic networks in a computer model shown in the next subchapter. Accordingly "Paris" in the second network can be represented with respect to Trojan War (TW) with $w(P, TW) > w(TW, P)$.

In nuce, the strength of connections between different concepts can be interpreted as the order of associations: If "Paris" is stronger connected with "Eiffel Tower" than with "Moulin Rouge", i.e. $w(P, E) > w(P, M)$, then a communicator will first associate "Paris" with "Eiffel Tower" and then with "Moulin Rouge". Accordingly, this communicator will first send messages about "Paris" and Eiffel Tower" and only after that he will generate messages with "Paris" and Moulin Rouge".

For the sake of mathematical simplicity let us define $0 \leqslant w(X, Y) \leqslant 1$ for all concepts X and Y in a semantic network. Then it is possible to define the degree of information in a more differentiated manner.

Suppose communicator A utters a sentence containing among other concepts "Paris" and "Hector". A expects an answer, i.e. A generates an expectation vector V_E

containing "Patrokles" (the friend of Achilles who was slain by Hector). B generates instead another vector, containing "Ajax" (who had a duel with Hector). Although A did not expect this answer, it makes "sense" to him, because "Ajax" belongs to the same network as "Paris" and "Hector". Therefore the degree of information of B's answer is not high. To compute it we have to measure the "distance" in the network of A between "Patrokles" and "Ajax". Let us assume that B as well as A knows a lot about the Homeric epos and that "Ajax" and "Patrokles" are directly connected in A's semantic network. Then we define the " distance" d(Patr.,Aj.) as

$$(3.2.8) \quad d(\text{Patr.}, \text{Aj.}) = 1 - w(\text{Patr.}, \text{Aj.}).$$

This definition means that two concepts X and Y, which are strongly connected, are rather "near", i.e. if one of them is uttered in a conversation then there is a high probability that the other will be associated. Conversely, if there are only weak connections between two concepts then the probability is low that the second concept will be associated if the first appears in the conversation or, to speak in terms of order of association, the second concept will appear in a message only after several others. Because a concept X is trivially always associated with itself, i.e. $w(X, X) = 1$, we define $d(X.X) = 1 - 1 = 0$.

Now let us assume that B expects an answer containing "Achilles" from A. But A answers with "Laertes" (the father of Aeneas, the mythical founder of Rome). Although B knows about Laertes he did not expect it because Laertes is rather "far away" from Achilles in B's semantic network, i.e., there are no direct connections between the two concepts. B first has to generate a connection from the expected "Achilles" to "Laertes": Both concepts are not directly connected in his network but only with two intermediating nodes, say "Hektor" and "Aeneas". Then the "semantic distance" between "Achilles" and "Laertes" is

$$\begin{aligned}(3.2.9) \quad d(\text{Ach.}, \text{La}) &= d(\text{Ach}, \text{He})^* d(\text{He}, \text{Aen})^* d(\text{Aen}, \text{La}) \\ &= (1 - w(\text{Ach}, \text{He})^* (1 - w(\text{He}, \text{Aen}))^* (1 - w(\text{Aen}, \text{La})).\end{aligned}$$

In other words, we define the semantical distance between two concepts that are not directly connected as the product of the semantical distances of the intermediating pairs of concepts.

Generally speaking a "semantic distance" d(x,y) of two concepts in a semantic network is

$$(3.2.10) \quad d(X, Y) = d(X, U_1) \text{o} \prod_i d(U_i, U_{i+1}) \text{ o } d(U_k, Y)$$

if U_1 is the concept "next" to X in the chain of concepts that lead from X to Y, U_i are the other intermediating concepts between X and Y, and if U_k is the concept "next" to Y, i.e. the concept that directly leads to Y. Note that the association chain from X to Y is defined as the "shortest" way between them, i.e. one has to select the according chain with the smallest number of intermediating concepts U_i.

A small semantic network may illustrate these considerations:

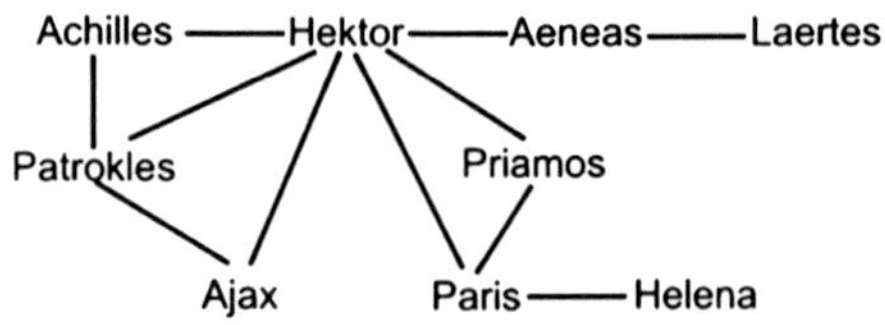

In this network obviously "Hector" is something like a central concept because the node "Hector" is directly connected with nearly all other concepts – with the exception of "Laertes" and "Helena". Despite her important role at beginning of the Trojan War "Helena" is only at the periphery of the network, which can be justified because she played no important role any longer during the ten years of the war.

Now let us return to Lady Edgeware and the unfortunate exposure of her lack of education in the Greek classics. She obviously could not connect the concepts about the Trojan War with her concepts about Paris as the capital of High Fashion. Therefore in a strict sense the semantic distance of "Hector" to any of her concepts is infinite. In this case there is no degree of information, because it would be literally senseless to extend the definition to this case. No communication of course is possible if the other communicators do not change by courtesy their networks and talk about the capital of France. Therefore again in contrast to Shannon and Weaver we restrict the definition of information degree to the cases where communicators are able to connect new concepts, i.e., messages that contain concepts new for them with those they have already in their respective semantic networks. From an abstract point of view this restriction may be a pity. But because we are interested in the analysis of real communicative processes we have to exclude cases like that of Lady Edgeware where neither information can be given nor communication can take place.

A connection of a new concept is possible if and only if the receiver B gets the message in form of "concept X is Y (perhaps of Z)" and both Y and Z respectively are known to B. Then B integrates X into his semantic network with $w(Y, X) = w(X, Y) = 0.5$ and perhaps $w(Z, X) = w(X, Z) = 0.5$. In other words, B adjusts his semantic network to the new message but keeps the connection "neutral", i.e., he waits for new communication acts to make the connections more precise.[18]

By the way, it is a truism in all theories of learning that the learning of new concepts is only possible if the learners are able to connect the new ones with

[18] In a computer model shown in chapter 7 the new connections are weighted according to the social status of sender and receiver respectively.

concepts the learners are already acquainted with. Therefore our restriction can also be justified by this remembrance to the basics of learning theories. This leads to the following definition:

Let V_{ei} be an expected concept and let V_{pi} designate the factually perceived concept, that is the concept the receiver gets in the message instead of the expected one. Let V_{pi} be a new concept for the receiver and let V_{pr} be the concept in the network of the receiver that integrates V_{pi} into his network in the form "V_{pi} is something like V_{pr}". Then

$$(3.2.11)\quad d(V_{ei}, V_{pi}) = d(V_{ei}, V_{pr}) * d(V_{pr}, V_{pi}).$$

Now we can easily generalize our definition of the information degree of a message. We take again the expectation vector $V_e = (v_{ei})$ and the perceived vector $V_p = (v_{pi})$ and measure the difference, but now in terms of semantic distance. Then we get for two components v_{ei} and v_{pi} the expectation probability

$$(3.2.12)\quad p_i = 1 - d\left(v_{ei}, v_{pi}\right) = 1 - \left(d\left(v_{ei}, x_1\right) * \prod d\left(x_i, x_{i+1}\right) * d\left(x_k, v_{pi}\right)\right)$$

if x_j are the intermediating nodes or concepts respectively between the expected component v_{ei} and the perceived component v_{pi} .

The information degree I of the whole message, i.e. the perceived vector V_p is again obtained by summing the probability of the components and by taking again into account that the information degree is the higher the lower is the probability of the message (measured again as a subjective probability). Because the expectation probability of a received vector component v_{pi} is simply measured as the inverse distance, it seems quite natural to define the informational degree I as the distance between the expected components and the factually perceived ones. That gives us the definition

$$(3.2.13)\quad I = \sum d\left(x_{ei}, x_{pi}\right)/n,$$

if n is the dimension of the two vectors. In the case that, e.g., the dimension of the expectation vector is greater than that of the perceived vector, we simply complete the perceived vector with zeroes as in the following example:

$V_e = (a, b, c, d, e, f)$.

$V_p = (r, s, t)$.

Completed vector $V_p = (r, s, t, 0, 0, 0)$.

When we define $d(X, 0) = 1$ for all concepts X obviously the completion of V_p, which we may call a trivial completion, does not change the information degree of the message.

Apparently we obtain a definition that is very similar to the basic equation of Shannon and Weaver, although this time the information degree must be computed in the special way just described. The reason for this is of course that we again have to introduce a "subjective" factor, namely the fact that in different semantic networks the "distance" between the same two concepts is not equal but usually different. In other words, the probability to receive a certain concept is dependent on the connections between the two concepts; the information degree for the receiver when hearing a certain concept is accordingly dependent on the connections between the expected concept and the factually received concept in *the semantic network of the receiver*. Therefore, our definition must be understood as the information degree of a message being a product of the topological relations of the receiver's semantic network. In addition, we do not use the logarithm dualis as did Shannon and Weaver but simply the arithmetical mean. This is done for the sake of mathematical simplicity; the important point, however, is that the basic idea of our definition is nearly the same as that of Shannon and Weaver.

By the way, when we speak of "semantic distance" between two concepts X and Y we have to mention the fact that this is not a "distance" in a strict mathematical sense, i.e., there is no complete metric defined by it. A metric is characterized by the symmetry axiom, i.e., a metrical relation d(X,Y) is defined by $d(X, Y) = d(Y, X)$. This is generally not the case with our semantic distance. Because the other two axioms of a metrical relation are fulfilled by our semantic distance we may speak in our case of a "pseudo - metric" or an "asymmetrical metric". As far as we know, asymmetrical metrics have never been systematically analyzed by mathematicians who always concentrated on the analysis of metrical spaces with symmetrical distance relations. But short considerations demonstrate that the experience of asymmetrical distance relations are quite common in everyday life and not peculiar to cognitive spaces. We often speak of a "social distance" between two persons and mean the fact that A is not allowed to interact directly with B if B is socially superior – e.g., the chairman of the board and a worker in a big firm. The worker has to communicate with the chairman via intermediating persons. In contrast, the chairman may address the worker any time, if he likes to. Therefore the social distance $d(C, W) \neq d(W, C)$, if one defines as distance the number of intermediating persons necessary to establish a contact (cf. Klüver 2000; Milgram 1967; Watts 1999). Therefore social spaces seem to be characterized by asymmetrical metrical relations too.

The same experience is often made in physical space which usually is the prime example for spaces with a symmetrical metric. Everybody who has done walking in the mountains knows of course that the walk from point A in a valley to point B on a summit is much longer than the inverse walk. To be sure, in geometrical relations $d(A, B) = d(B, A)$, *but for the walker* these distances are not the same, in terms of exhaustion, time and energy. Even more striking are the experiences of distance when sailing on a sea or lake. If a sailing boat has to go from A to B and the wind is blowing in the direction from B to A then each sailor knows that of course d(A,B) is much larger than d(B,A). In the first case one has to cruise against the wind and, therefore the distance,

$$d\,(A, B) = \sqrt{2 * d\,(B, A)}.$$

As in the case of the mountain walker $d(A, B) = d(B, A)$ in geometrical terms but for the sailor the distances are largely different. The knowledge that the geometrical distance between A and B is the same as the distance between B and A is not much worth to the sailor, in particular if he has in addition to consider strong currents on the way from A to B. Therefore the *practical* experience of physical space often tells us that the physical metric is *not* symmetrical and that the symmetrical metric relations of mathematics, physics or land survey are an abstraction that is of not much use for the problems of daily life.

At least since the famous distinction of Bergson between physical time and phenomenological time cognitive scientists have gotten used to the fact that the experience of time is not necessarily the same as the homogeneous time concept of physics and mathematics – on the contrary, it is usually quite different. Our little examples demonstrate that the experience of space may differ in the same respect from the homogeneous and symmetrical concept of space theoretical science is used to. Cognitive and social spaces, so it seems, are usually not characterized by a symmetrical metric; therefore it would be an important task for mathematicians to analyze the characteristics of spaces with asymmetrical metric. To put it into a nutshell, spaces that are a product of practical, cognitive, social and/or emotional experience usually must be characterized by mathematical relations that differ from the abstractions of mathematical geometry and physics. The asymmetrical metric of our conceptual space obviously is just one example of more general aspects.

Finally we may now return to the relation and the distinction of meaning and information. We said above that one can construct cases where the meaning of a message is roughly the same for two communicators but the degree of information is different. Consider for example a message from a sender C with concepts X and Y that activates a particular semantic network S for the receiver A and let us assume that S is roughly the same for a second receiver B. Then the degree of information would be the same for A and B if and only if d(X,Y) is the same for both activated networks. It is easy to imagine examples where this is not the case: consider two experts in classic Greek literature A and B, A being an elderly male professor and B being a younger female professor with a strong bias for feminism. The networks are roughly identical with respect to the concepts, i.e. their number and designations. The male professor has his male heroes like Hector, Achilles and perhaps the clever Ulysses; accordingly he has strong connections between Ulysses and Achilles. The female professor on the other hand tries to reconstruct the whole story from the women's point of view, i.e., she concentrates on Penelope, Andromache and of course Helena. Therefore her connection, e.g., between Ulysses and Penelope are stronger than those between Ulysses and Achilles. The meaning of a sentence containing Ulysses and Achilles is nearly the same for both; the degree of information is in this case quite different. Accordingly easy is it to construct messages with a different meaning but the same degree of information, which we leave to the readers.

We have developed this model of information in such detail because the model must allow to analyze it in computer experiments, i.e., to implement it into suited computer programs and to do experiments with them. For a general theoretical sketch of the "meaning of information" the basic definition with which we have started this subchapter would be quite sufficient. But, as in the natural sciences, a theory of communication that is suited to be tested in computer experiments and to be compared with empirically known communicative processes has to be formulated in such detail. If the methodical procedure that we described at the end of the previous subchapter shall obtain significant results then detailed definitions and algorithms are unavoidable.

This detailed definition for the computation of the informational degree is developed in particular for symbolically coded messages, i.e., in the most cases of human communication verbally coded messages. But this definition can, of course, also be applied to messages that are not symbolically coded, for example the perception of something to eat and drink as in the case of Vladimir. Certainly, e.g., the perception of fruit juice in a drugstore will generate some specific meaning for the respective observer, e.g., a possibility to quench one's thirst. Yet probably other associations will be generated , e.g., the remembrance of other situations when fruit juice was available, other kinds of non alcoholic drinks and so on. This process of the generation of mediate meanings was described in the preceding subchapter. Accordingly, the information degree of the respective message can be computed the same way as in the case of symbolically coded messages. Therefore, in all cases where not only one specific meaning is generated by a message but also an according association field the detailed definition can be applied. It is just necessary to define an association field the same way as we characterized a semantical network, i.e., mathematically as a weighted graph.

One of the main functions of communicative processes is without doubt the generation of mutual understanding as the basis and the necessary condition for the continuation of each single communicative act. The definitions we developed in the last two subchapters also allow at least a preliminary definition of understanding, which is valid in particular in the medium of symbolically coded communication. With this we shall conclude these basic considerations.

Consider a message like "after the Greek's smuggling of Ulysses' horse into Troy Aeneas fled with Laertes to Italy". If the receiver of this message is educated with respect to the Homeric epic poem he is able to "understand" the message even if he does not know the name of Laertes. But if he knows "Ulysses", "horse", Troy" and "Italy" the receiver is able to connect "Laertes" with the other concepts that are part of his semantical network. Understanding in this case means that the message can be integrated into the semantical network of the receiver and that the reception of the message enlarges the network. In more formal terms understanding means that the message is integrated as a sub graph into the receiver's network. In contrast to this example Lady Edgeware in the sketched detective novel apparently was not able to understand a message like "the judgment of Paris caused the Trojan war" because her only network containing "Paris" consisted of concepts like "high fashion", "Chanel no. 5" or "Dior". Not only did her network not contain concepts "like "war" or "Ulysses" but she was in addition not able to connect these concepts with those of her semantic net. These examples lead to the following definition:

A sender A and a receiver B understand each other if all the concepts of A's message are either a) a sub graph of the network of B, that is the disjunction of the message and B's network is equal to the message; or, b) only a subset of the concepts of the message are a sub graph of B's network, but the concepts that are new for B can be connected with other concepts of his network and the whole message becomes a sub graph of B's enlarged network. If the receiver is able to do that is of course a question of his learning biography: the original network of B and that of A had to be rather similar at the beginning of the conversation in order to enable B to "learn" from A, that is to take over the new concepts in the way just described. A of course cannot know if B did in fact understand him. Only if B answers with a message that belongs to the same semantical network of A's first message then A will perceive that B understood at least some parts of A's message.

If, e.g., a female sender A says to B (a man) "I love you" then perhaps B will activate an association field with concepts like "sexual intercourse", "suited opportunity for making love", "danger of Aids" and the like. If B responds "I love you too" then A perhaps will generate an association field like "common apartment", "marriage", "children" and so on. Then A will ask "when shall we marry?" and B will realize that they completely misunderstood each other.[19] Writers of love stories will know how to come out of this situation of misunderstanding.

To put it into a nutshell, understanding means the exchange of sub graphs of the respective semantical networks and in particular the ability to change and enlarge the networks via the process of communication. Of course, condition a) includes the possibility that B knows all the concepts of the message but that the concepts are connected in other ways than in A's network. For example, B may have wrongly believed that Laertes was the father of Ulysses. In this case B may be willing to correct his connections. We shall see in computer models described in chapter seven that such a willingness is by no means a matter of course but that it depends on different social factors. The general definition of understanding will also play an important part in several computer models of communication described in the following chapters.

3.3. A COMPUTATIONAL MODEL

In order to make these general considerations on algorithms and equations to generate attractors of meaning and to compute the information degrees of messages a bit more concrete we show a first model. Note that this example is just for visualizing purposes and that general results obtained with an extended model based on this simple one will be given in chapter seven.

---

[19] We are quite aware of the fact that this distribution of association fields follows a rather traditional conception of gender roles: men think about sex, women about marriage. The question if things are different today we leave to the readers.

The model consists of an interactive neural net (IN) that represents the semantical network and thus the cognitive system of a receiving communicator. The messages are given to it as three-dimensional vectors, consisting of three concepts. The network generates particular point attractors or attractors of periods larger than 1 and computes the information degree of the messages according to the equations given in the preceding subchapter.

An IN is a so called recurrent network which means that principally all units can be connected with weight values $w \neq 0$. Although it is possible to implement learning algorithms into an IN this type of network usually is used the way that the user has to construct the weight matrix himself, i.e. the matrix containing the values of the connections between the units. To be sure, the connections between the different units of an IN may represent very different relations. In this case we used the IN to represent semantical relations between the different concepts. The "activation flow" between our units, i.e. the artificial neurons, is determined by the linear activation rule, namely

$$(3.3.1) \quad A_j = \sum A_i * w_{ij}$$

that we mentioned in chapter 2. A_j is the activation value of the receiving neuron j (the equivalent to the state of a cell in a CA), A_i are the activation values of the sending neurons i, and w_{ij} is the weight value of the connection between a sending neuron i and a receiving neuron j. There is some evidence for the assumption that our brain uses at least in several cases of information processing just such "summing" procedures (cf. McLeod et al. 1998).

For the interpretation of the following network imagine a student of computer science who has just passed a course on the programming language JAVA, one of the presently most used programming languages. After the finishing of this course parts of his cognitive system may contain a semantical network like this:

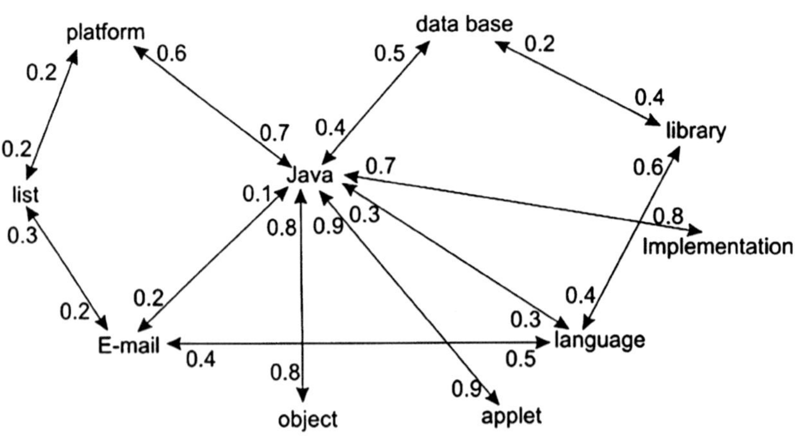

The semantical network demonstrates that the concept JAVA is at the center of the network, not only because it has connections with $w \neq 0$ to and from nearly all other concepts but also because the weight of the connections are comparatively large. The respective strength of the connections are to be interpreted as the "associative strength" between concepts, i.e. the strength of activation of the concepts when receiving a certain message. As we said in the foregoing subchapter the values of the weights determine the order in which the concepts are associated. We assume this semantical network to be quite realistic because it was constructed for us by a student who had just learned how to write computer programs in JAVA.

An IN is started by "externally activating" one or several of the artificial neurons. Before a specific run of the IN all activation values of the units i are $A_i = 0$. External activation means that some of the units j get an activation value $A_j > 0$; the initial external activation values are then sent via the linear activation rule through the whole network. Note that the recurrent topology of an IN makes it sometimes difficult if not impossible to generate stable states, i.e. point attractors, because each unit can be directly connected with each other unit.

Let us first consider the computation of the information degrees of different messages. When the receiving IN gets the message "(Java, applet, language)" the network starts with the first concept, in this case Java. The receiver this way "knows" that the sender will speak about Java. According to the procedures described in the preceding subchapter the receiving system generates a vector of expectation, which is in this case the vector "(Java, applet, implementation)". The expectation vector is generated by starting with "Java" and afterwards by selecting those two concepts whose connection values are the two greatest with respect to Java. According to the equation for computing the degree of information and taking into account the fact that the first two concepts are the same in the received message and the expected message the degree of information of this message, is $I = 1 - 0.7 * 0.3 = 0.79$. The next message "(Java, list, implementation)" is measured by the expected message "(Java, applet, implementation)" and it has the information degree of $I = 0.82$. In this case the chain of concepts between "applet" and "list" had to be chosen at random because there are two chains between these concepts of the same length. The selected chain in this case is "applet", "Java", "e-mail", and "list". The vector of expectation is in both cases the same because the receiving network always starts with the first concept of the factual message and generates its vector of expectation from this "starting concept". Therefore, each message with the first concept "Java" will generate the same vector of expectation, because in each case the program will chose the two concepts with the strongest connections from "Java". The reason for this rule is, as was mentioned above, that the first concept of a message defines the theme about which the sender will communicate and about which the receiver has to generate his vector of expectation.[20]

[20] This special IN was implemented by Eric Schmieders, who also performed the computation of the information degrees.

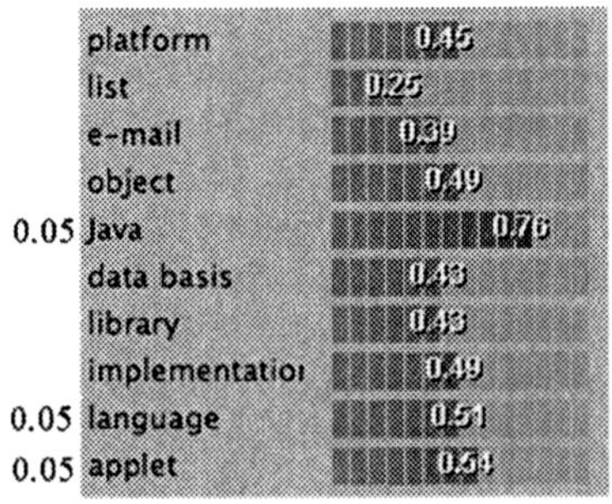

Figure 2. Point attractor generated by the message (Java, applet, language)

Accordingly, messages with other first concepts, that are theme defining concepts, generate other expectation vectors. For example, the message "(library, platform, language)" generates in the receiving system the expected vector "(library, language, data base)" and the received message has an information degree I = 0.85. The message "(data base, list, Java)" generates the expected vector "(data base, Java, library)" and has the information degree I = 0.88.

Per se, of course, the computation of the degree of information is not very important. Yet we shall see in later applications of this model how the factual development and outcome of communicative processes may depend on the information degree of messages for a receiver.

The same model can be used for the generation of meaning and in particular the dependence of meaning on the learning biography of a receiver. We take again the semantical network of the computer science student and "send" it the first message, i.e., "(Java, applet, language)". The reception of a message means with this model that those units are externally activated with a numerical value of 0.05, which represent the concepts the sent message consists of, in this case the units "Java", "applet", and "language". After computing the degree of information the IN starts its runs and generates after 19 steps a point attractor; figure 2 and the following figures show the final state of the IN where the length of the beams represent the strength of the final activation of the respective units.

The figure shows the strong final activation of the unit "Java", which is due on the one hand to the external activation of this unit and on the other hand to the central position of "Java" (see above) in the semantical net. "Applet" and "language" are also rather strongly activated because of their external activation. An interpretation of this attractor, therefore, is that the meaning of the message is a strong association between the three sent concepts and in this sense the meaning is in accord with the message. We may see these three units as the immediate meaning of the message. The other units are activated too but not to the same degree as the first three. An obvious interpretation is that in very densely connected networks several other concepts are immediately associated with the sent concepts and that we see not only the immediate meaning but mediate meanings too. We believe that in this aspect the model is in accord with association processes known from our everyday experience, i.e., the model is empirically valid to a high degree.[21] In the terms of the preceding subchapter on meaning we can summarize that the meaning consists of the three sent concepts and the mediate meanings in form of the associated concepts. In this sense the semantical network apparently represents an association network as defined above.

Now consider the meaning of a second message, namely "(list, library, language)". The according point attractor that the IN generated after 21 steps is shown in figure 3:

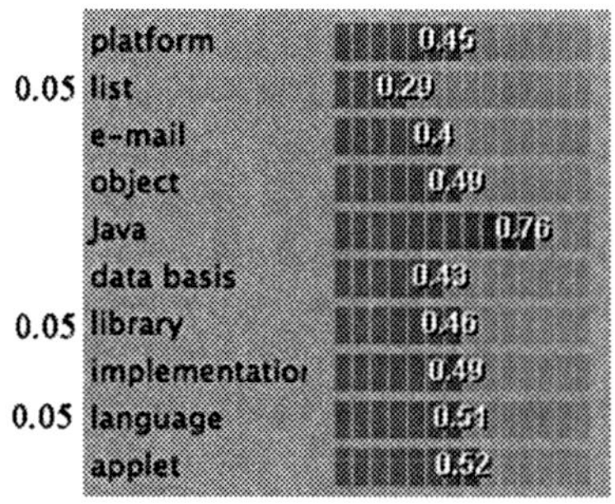

Figure 3. Meaning of the message (list, library, language)

One sees that again the unit "Java" is strongly activated, much more than the other units. Despite the fact that "Java" was not a part of the message the meaning of this message obviously is centered around the concept "Java" again. That seems a bit strange on a first sight because "Java", in contrast to "language", was not externally activated. In particular the attractor is nearly the same as that of the first message, although the message contained different concepts. One can interpret this attractor that the second message means the same for the receiving system as the first, despite their conceptual differences.

A similar observation can be made in a lot of cases when one analyzes the respective expectation vectors. For example, the message "(platform, e-mail, object)" generates the expectation vector "(platform, Java, list)", $I = 0.87$; the message "(platform, language)" with $I = 0.7$ generates the expectation vector "(platform, Java)". Messages in this model may contain three or two concepts. In other words, in many cases of messages the receiving system expects a message containing "Java" regardless of the "theme" of the message, i.e. its first concept. It

[21] We confirmed this belief by asking several students to give us their associations when hearing messages like those above. In all cases the students immediately associated a lot of such concepts although of course not exactly those that the network associated.

seems as if the receiving network very often expects that the sender will "speak" about "Java" and that the receiving system is "surprised" if the sender does not. "Surprised" means that the information degree in these cases is frequently rather high, i.e., the message is unexpected to a high degree and therefore contains much information.

These on a first sight strange results are of course due to the topological dominance of "Java" in this particular semantical network in the sense described above. Other messages that also did not contain the concept "Java" obtained very similar results, that is final point attractors with the significant highest activation value of "Java". Therefore, one could suspect that this result is a typical artifact of the model, generated by the specific characteristics of it. Yet on a second sight these results are not so strange as they seem to be. In cognitive psychology numerous cases are reported where humans always associate the same meaning regardless of the factual messages. That is for example the case with persons who have strong prejudices with respect to certain human minorities, e.g. in the case of an anti-Semitic bias, where all social events are reduced to the influence of Jews. One may say that the application of the famous Rorschach association inkblot test in such cases is based on the assumption that such a fixation on certain concepts occurs very frequently. In other words, people who tend to see the world only from one very selective point of view may be characterized by a semantical network where one concept is dominant in the same sense that "Java" is dominant in our example and that all messages will be associated with a meaning that has the dominant concept at its center. Therefore, the results of our network are not strange at all but refer to – and explain – a lot of cases known from cognitive psychology and everyday experience.[22]

When we speak of "prejudices" and refer to the example of anti-Semitism we certainly do not mean to suggest that all cases where the meaning of a message is centered around a certain dominant concept are problematic cases like those of strong prejudices or even pathological ones as in the example of the young man who saw himself as Don Juan (see footnote 22). The example of the student with Java as the center of a network about programming languages is harmless enough. Speaking in terms of cognitive psychology and in particular those of Piaget the example of "Java" must be seen as a classical case of "assimilation", that is the interpretation of different messages or perceptions respectively in terms of one dominant "schema", as Piaget called it. Assimilation processes of that sort are very common. They are not only a necessary part of the cognitive development of a child but, as we mentioned before, necessary phases of cognitive orientation. The assimilation by one single schema is by itself not problematic but only if assimilation is done with the same schema in very different and thus often inappropriate cases. Assimilating different messages, e.g. to the dominant schema of "Java" demonstrates, in this example, only a successfully passed course on that programming language.

---

[22] In a well-known movie "Don Juan DeMarco" Marlon Brando as a psychotherapist applied the Rorschach test to a young man (Johnny Depp) who believed to be the original Don Juan. To be sure, "Don Juan" always associated "sex" or "attractive women" with the inkblots regardless of their appearance. This associative fixation on sex is, as is well known, theme of countless jokes and stories.

We compared the example above with the attractors of another semantical network with the same units but with different weighted connections. In contrast to the network shown above the connection weights were distributed in a more equal fashion; in particular the unit "Java" was not more in such a dominant position. One can imagine that our second network represents another programmer who knows several programming languages, including Java, and who talks about Java with the first programmer. The attractors with respect to the two messages are given in the next figures.

The differences to figures 2 and 3 are obvious. In figure 4 "Java" is still strongly activated but only because of its external activation at the beginning of the simulation. "Language" and "applet" are approximately as strongly activated as Java and "library" too. The semantical network of our fictitious second programmer does not contain "Java" as the dominant concept but as one among other equal important ones. The difference with respect to the second message (cf. Figure 3 and 5) is even greater: "Java" is activated in only a medium fashion; high activation values belong to the externally activated concepts "language" and "library", as is to be expected with such a network.

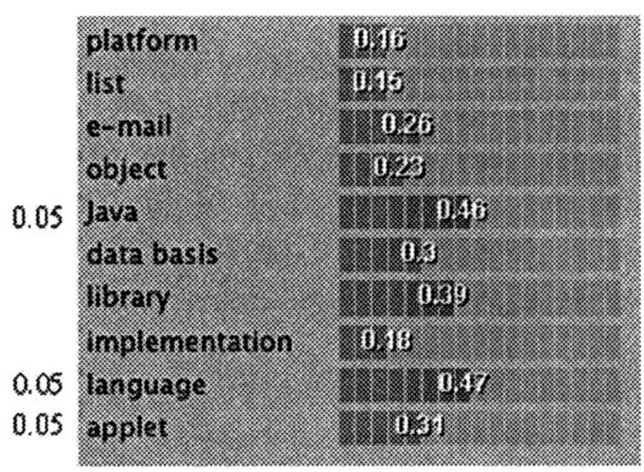

Figure 4. attractor of the message (Java, applet, language)

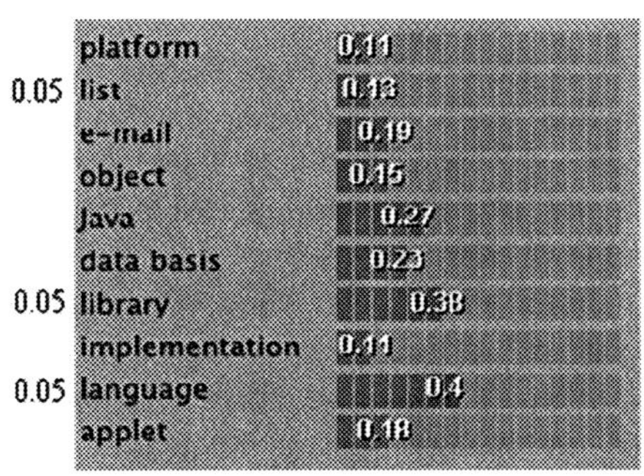

Figure 5. attractor of the message (list, library, language)

Because we shall show several experiments done with an extended version of this model in chapter seven we discuss it no further. After all, it was just our intention to demonstrate how to translate the mathematical and theoretical considerations of the last two subchapters in computational models, or in other words, how to perform an operationalization of these concepts. But before we finish this chapter on basic concepts we have to introduce another one concept, the third and last.

3.4. RELEVANCE AND EVALUATION OF MESSAGES

In everyday language not only "meaning" and "information" are frequently used in a synonymous fashion but also "relevance". A message is said to be "meaningful" if the speaker wishes to say that it is important or relevant for him; the same is often the case when a speaker calls a message "very informative". But as we have, in the tradition of Shannon and Weaver, to distinguish between "meaning" and "information", we also have to distinguish between these two concepts and the concept of "relevance". In particular we have also to define this concept in terms of complex systems, i.e., in terms of dynamical semantic or neural networks respectively.

Consider again a cognitive system that consists of different semantic or neural networks. When this system receives a message or signal it generates the meaning(s) of the message and computes the degree of information the way just described. Such a message might be very meaningful in the sense that a large association field is generated by it; the message might also have a high degree of information because it contains not expected contents. But nothing is said by these characterizations of the message about the *relevance* it has for the receiver.

By "relevance" we want to characterize, according to the everyday understanding of this concept, if a message has *practical consequences* for the receiver and if so, by which degree. A message like "in the Andromeda Galaxy a supernova has exploded" may have some meaning for an educated layman, i.e., he will generate several attractors in an association field that contains concepts like "galaxy", "supernova", "stars", "milky way" and so on. The message might also have a rather high degree of information, because perhaps the receiver did not know that the concepts "supernova" and "explosion" belong together – they should have been strongly connected but were not in his network. But despite the high information degree and the elaborated meaning the message is not very relevant for the receiver because this message has no practical consequences at all for his own life. He just receives it and will probably soon forget it.

A professional astronomer on the other hand will attach much more meaning to this message and perhaps not such a high degree of information because he probably expected the message. But in many cases such a message has a high degree of relevance for him because it has consequences for his professional life. In other words, he will perhaps feel anger that he did not make the discovery himself, he will try to confirm the message by making his own observations, he will get in touch with other colleagues and so on. The message has a high degree of relevance because it causes him to some reactions – emotions and practical actions. In order to model this difference between meaning and information on the one hand and relevance on the other we have to enlarge our former model. Information and meaning are processed by networks that generate attractors and association fields. The relevance of a message must now be represented by another part of the whole network our cognitive system consists of. This can be illustrated by a former example, that is Vladimir, the dog of Pavlov (see above 3.1.).

When Vladimir learned to associate the bell's sound with the signal "food" he generated an according attractor. But this attractor alone is just the systemic representation, i.e., the meaning of the signal of the bell. To produce saliva the brain has to be connected with other parts of the organism, i.e., the saliva producing parts, whatever they may be. The attractor (of the bell) therefore acts as a generator or activator respectively for the saliva producing parts of the organism. The attractor state, therefore, of the brain's sub-network "processing of bells" activates via its connections to the other parts of the organism the production of saliva *according to the strength of the connections;* other states of this sub-network in contrast do not activate the production parts.

By generalizing this little example we can define the degree of relevance the following way:

We call that part of the whole cognitive system that processes the message in form of the generation of meaning and the computing of the information degree the *cognitive net* (CN). The CN is connected with another sub networks or just layers of units that we call the action part (AP) of the cognitive system. According to the connections between CN and AP some attractors will activate parts of AP and cause this way different actions of the whole system while some attractors will not.

Apparently a message is relevant for the cognitive system if the CN transmits its attractor state to the AP and otherwise not. If the AP gets an activation by a particular attractor of the CN then the AP will generate an attractor itself. This particular attractor of the AP we call the *content of relevance* of the message because this attractor causes the actions according to the message. For example, after the conditioning processes of Vladimir the content of relevance of the signal "bell" was quite different from the same message before the conditioning processes – producing saliva or not.

The *degree of relevance*, i.e. the degree by which one relevant message A is more relevant than another relevant message B, is dependent on the norms or values of the whole system. For example, for most humans the value of staying alive is certainly higher than the value of finding good entertainment. Therefore, the message "there comes a dangerous animal" has a higher degree of relevance than the message "there is a new and interesting movie at the cinema". We may safely assume that in living systems exists a hierarchy of values that define the degrees of relevance of different messages. Some of these values animals and humans have obtained as part of their biological heritage; other values have to be learned, i.e., they have to be placed at the correct place in the hierarchy of values during processes of socialization. The latter is especially the case with cultural values, i.e. values that are valid for one particular culture but not necessarily for other cultures.

Yet the degree of relevance is not only dependent on the values of the respective system but also on the state the system has obtained at the time of the message. Consider again an organism with a high value of "food". If the organism is hungry at the time when a signal "food available" arrives, the signal will have a high degree of relevance. But if the organism is satiated, then the signal will have not much relevance; other signals, for example "potential sexual partner" will bear more relevance. These considerations lead to the following definition:

The state of the receiving system CN is represented by a numerical value s with $0 \leqslant s \leqslant 1$, for example "hunger". According to the construction principles of artificial neural networks the connections between CN and the action part AP will be "weighted", i.e., they are also represented by a numerical value w with $0 \leqslant w \leqslant 1$. The strength of the connections – the "weights" – represent the value(s) the received signals have for the system. The degree of relevance dr of a message is then defined as

$$(3.4.1) \quad dr = s * w.$$

For example, let us assume that "food" has a very high value, e.g. 1. The state of "hunger" is accordingly represented by a value $s = 1$, that is, the system's orientation is directed towards food. The degree of relevance of the signal "food available" is $dr = 1 * 1 = 1$, or in other words, the system will act because of the high degree of relevance. If on the other hand the system is satiated, then its state is with respect to "hunger" $s = 0$, which obtains the degree of relevance *for the same signal* as $dr = 0 * 1 = 0$. The system will not act at all.

If there are more than one connections between CN and AP then the value of dr will be computed the usual way characteristic for neural networks, i.e.,

$$(3.4.2) \quad dr = s * \sum w_i$$

for the different connections i.

If the system gets several different messages at the same time, then it will "compute" the dr of all messages and will act according to the message with the highest degree of relevance.

The definitions of the content and the degree of relevance immediately show that relevance must be analytically distinguished from meaning and information, as the example of the astronomer already demonstrated. A message then may be understood as a three-dimensional construct that is characterized by a certain meaning "me", degree of information "di" and a certain content and degree of relevance "dr": a message "m", therefore, must be understood as m = (me, di, dr).

When we represent as before the message by a vector that operates as input to a cognitive system then the cognitive system is principally able to generate a certain meaning, to compute the degree of information, to generate actions by transmitting the attractor of the CN to the AP, and thus determining the content and degree of relevance. To be sure, to do this in a successful manner the cognitive system had to learn (a) to generate the "correct" attractors, if the system was not been "born" with it, (b) to construct the "right" connections within its association field in order to understand the communicative processes it takes part in, and (c) to connect the CN the "right" way with the AP in order to react adequately to different messages. Yet the problem of learning will be dealt with in later chapters.

CHAPTER 4

THE SOCIAL DIMENSION OF COMMUNICATION

According to the universal modeling schema (cf. Chapter 2) and to the general definition of communication that we introduced in the first chapter communicative processes may be understood as dynamical networks that are embedded in social frames, and that both generate and are generated by certain cognitive dynamical processes. The concept of "social frame" means that the social interaction rules of communicative processes are not only dependent on the specific situation but also on the general structure(s) that characterize a particular society. This is a truism if one puts such an assertion in this global way, but it is far from trivial how to transform this statement into a mathematically describable social analysis of communicative processes.

Social analysis is often done without taking into regard the cognitive processes of the respective social actors. In particular, frequently in studies of social phenomena no individual actors are taken as the basis of the processes but "collective actors" like institutions or firms. The success of such restricted studies shows that indeed social processes can not seldom be understood on a level *sui generis*, that is by just analyzing social actions and interactions determined by the specific rules that are valid for the respective domains of analysis. In such cases we may still speak of communicative processes when we analyze the respective social interactions but we have to note that this is a rather restricted form of communication. But because such restricted assumptions are frequently useful in order to methodically "reduce the complexity of the problems" (Luhmann 1984) as far as the problems allow, we shall start our task how to model communicative processes by concentrating on the social dimension only. The according concentration on the cognitive dimension will be done in the next chapter. In other words, we shall in the first steps dismantle the whole complexity of communication into the social and the cognitive dimension respectively and shall in the succeeding steps recombine these two dimensions – together with the semiotic dimension – to models of communication proper, i.e., models that contain all three dimensions. It seems obvious, at least for us, that there is no other methodical way to capture such complex processes as communication. Yet this procedure is certainly not new but a fundamental characteristic of modern science in general. To quote Luhmann again (Luhmann 1984), analysis, i.e. dismantling, and recombination are the methodical cores of science in contrast to other forms of thinking.

In order to demonstrate how processes of social interactions can be modeled by the Soft Computing modeling techniques we described in chapter 2 we shall give some examples of the possibilities of these techniques by applying them to group dynamical processes. These processes, i.e. the dynamics of certain social groups are generated by interactions determined by simple social rules. But despite the apparent simplicity of these examples it is important to note that rather fundamental characteristics of social systems can be studied by analyzing group behavior. In a certain sense these examples show some of the building bricks for complex models of communication.

4.1. THE MODELING OF SOCIAL INTERACTIONS

One of the classical methodical instruments in the fields of social network analysis is the use of so called socio-matrices or Moreno-matrices respectively (Freeman 1989; Moreno 1934). A socio-matrix is basically nothing else than a formal description of certain relations between the members of a social group. Yet it is also possible to apply this technique to greater social fields, e.g. firms or institutions.

Consider a social group of four members who know each other to a certain extent. Each group member has some emotional relation to the other three, for example "liking", "disliking", and "neutral". When we designate the members by a, b, c, and d and represent the respective emotions by 1 for "liking", −1 for "disliking", and 0 for "neutral", we can represent this emotional structure by, e.g., the following socio-matrix:

	a	*b*	*c*	*d*
a	0	1	−1	0
b	1	0	1	0
c	1	1	0	1
d	0	1	−1	0

The matrix shows that a is neutral towards himself, does like b, dislikes c, and is neutral with respect to d. In other words, the first line of the matrix shows the emotions of a towards the other members, the second line those of b and so forth. Note that in all places of the main diagonal of the matrix, i.e. the emotional relations a person has towards himself, there is a zero. Methodically that means that for the analysis of the emotional group structure it does not matter how a person likes himself or not. In the examples described below we shall always operate with such a restriction. To be sure, that restriction is not necessarily valid in cases of, e.g., therapeutic communities where the self-feeling or self-appraisal respectively of the community members may be a crucial factor. But for our examples this restriction is sufficient.

To be sure, the values of a socio-matrix need not represent emotional relations. It is always possible to represent other forms of social or personal relations. For example, one model of communicative processes that is described in chapter seven the socio-matrix used there represents degrees of similarity between the group members. In addition, it is not necessary to use only such a "ternary" representation, i.e., to use only three values. If one wishes to represent the values more differentiated one can always chose real numbers, e.g. in the interval between −1 and 1.

A socio-matrix represents a group "structure", i.e. a web of relations between the members. In the terms introduced in the second chapter the matrix can be seen as an expanded adjacency matrix that defines a certain topology of the group. But by itself the socio-matrix gives no insight into the possible or even probable dynamics of the respective group; in order to obtain such insights it is necessary in addition to define certain rules of interaction.

Suppose again that the socio-matrix represents the emotional group structure. Then we can introduce a general rule of interaction, derived from the classical work of Homans (1950) on "The Human Group". To put it into a nutshell, one of his basic principles is that each group members prefers to interact with other members he likes than with those he dislikes. In more formal terms one may express this principle by saying that a member A prefers to interact with B, if he likes B; if that is for certain reasons not possible, the next choice of A will be an interaction with C, if his emotional attitude towards C is neutral. In other words, each group member tries to select other members according to his own preference of interaction.

Together with Rouven Malecki we translated this general principle of Homans into a formal model, namely a cellular automaton (CA) (see chapter 2) with the following rules:

a) The cells on the grid of the CA represent the single group members; the states of the cells represent the emotional state of the members, i.e. their individual feeling of well being. A cell with the state s = 0 represents an empty space that can be occupied by a "member" cell. The feeling is dependent on the specific sub group in which each group member is situated; while the whole group is the set of all non empty cells on the CA-grid the particular sub group is represented by the Moore-neighborhood of a cell.[1]

b) The "emotional state" of each cell is computed by taking into account the emotional relations of the cell in the center to the cells in the Moore-neighborhood; the state is just the arithmetical mean value of the relation values of the cell towards its neighbors. A variant of this rule also takes into account the emotional values of the artificial members in the Moore-neighborhood with respect to the cell in the center. In that case both mean values are simply summed. Empty cells in the Moore-neighborhood are counted as cells with low negative values (with respect to the center cell). In other words, an empty cell is worse for the well being than a cell to which positive or neutral values are attached, but better than a neighbor cell with the attachment of negative values.

c) The general rule for each cell is to seek a neighborhood in which the emotional state of it can be optimized. In order to do this each cell is testing its enlarged

[1] The Moore neighborhood of a cell consists of the eight adjacent cells on the grid, namely the four cells on the sides of the square cell and the four cells on each corner.

Moore-neighborhood if it would offer a better neighborhood.[2] That means that the program computes for each cell the emotional state values of each place in the enlarged Moore-neighborhood. If the results are better than the emotional state in the original position and if the according cells are empty then the cell moves into the new position. A variant of this rule enables the cell to check each cell on the whole grid if there are positions that would give better values.

d) Usually the cells representing group members are distributed at random on the grid; the same is done with empty cells. The program starts with the computing processes for the first cell on the top line. Because the CA is constructed as a two-dimensional torus, the Moore-neighborhood consists of the according cells on the lowest line of the grid, the cells on the top line, the cells on the line below, and the cells on the column on the right side of the grid.

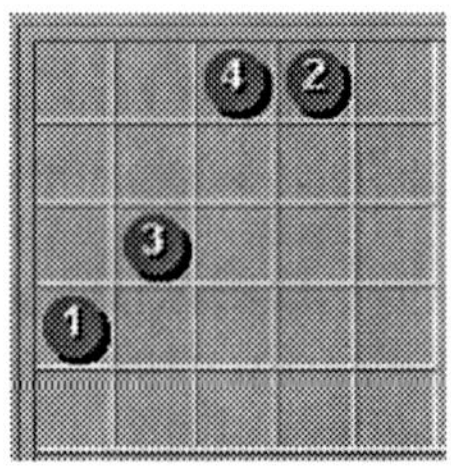

Figure 1. Moreno-CA with cells distributed at random

The program stops if the whole system reaches an attractor, preferably a point attractor, or if a certain number of runs did not generate an attractor.

The reasons for these rules are rather obvious: The principle of Homans presupposes that each human actor is interested in his own well-being and that he prefers emotional states of well-being to others. In this sense Homans is a partisan of a rational choice approach insofar that he thinks of social actors as beings who always look for the best choice in action situation (cf. Fararo 2001). The CA-rules just translate that basic assumption into the formalism of a suited CA. In addition, we introduced the presupposition that the well-being of group members mainly depends on the direct social neighborhood, that is a particular sub-group. That is why the program computes the emotional state of a cell in dependence of the Moore-neighborhood and not of the set of all cells.

---

[2] The enlarged Moore-neighborhood consists of the cells of the Moore-neighborhood and the cells adjacent to the cells of the Moore-neighborhood. One easily verifies that the enlarged Moore-neighborhood contains $8 + 16 = 24$ cells. A general recursive formula for additional enlarging of a Moore-neighborhood is given by $n + 1 = 4(n + 2) + 4 = 4(n + 3)$, if n is the number of enlarging processes.

The rule of the relation value to an empty cell is based on the assumption that most people prefer being alone than being in the social neighborhood of someone whom one does not like. To be sure, there are certainly humans who are an exception to this rule, i.e., who prefer even the neighborhood of someone whom they dislike than being alone.[3]

The task of the program is to predict the differentiation of a social group into different sub-groups. A point attractor of such a system means that the group has stabilized, i.e., each group member has found the best social position that is possible in the according group. Of course, it is possible that the group does not reach an attractor state, at least not a point attractor. We shall deal with this possibility below.

The program that we call in honor of Moreno the Moreno-CA was frequently empirically validated. One example of the prediction of a real group shall be shown in some detail.

A student of us performed a little social experiment with a group of children in the age of 10 and 11 from a school at Dortmund (western region of Germany). He asked them to describe their feelings towards the other children and obtained that way a socio-matrix of the group.[4]

He then asked them to go to a strange class room and to chose places as they liked. He recorded their respective positions in the room and inserted their socio-matrix into the Moreno-CA. The factual positions of the children and the prediction of the CA are shown in the following figures:

Figure 2a and 2b.

[3] This may sometimes be the reason that married couples stay together although they only quarrel and dislike each other.

[4] Because it is a bit problematic to directly ask the children they were asked to tell if they would like to share a room with the other pupils at a summer camp, if they would not care to share a room, or if they would refuse to share a room with particular pupils.

Figure 2a shows the real outcome of the social experiment, figure 2b shows the prediction of the CA. The Moreno-CA of course could not predict the "geometrical" positions of the children, i.e. if for example pupil 7 would sit himself on the left or the right side of the room. The CA should – and could – predict the relative positions of the children with respect to the others.

A comparison of the two figures demonstrates that the Moreno-CA was able to predict the factual positions of the children rather precisely. Nearly all children form a special subgroup with the exception of pupil 5 who is definitely an outsider in this group. The program accurately predicted his isolated position that he also chose in reality. The only error of the CA was with respect to pupil 3 who in reality placed himself besides the outsider 5. Yet there was a melancholy reason for the behavior of pupil 5 that the teacher of the class told the experimenter: pupil 3 was known to her for his tendency to annoy the outsider 5 in order to win an applause from the other pupils. Therefore, the behavior of pupil 3 was due to a particular (negative) social character that could not be prognosticated by the Moreno-CA. Note that the program, of course, was not meant to predict just the sitting positions of the pupils when entering a strange class room but that these positions are a visualization of the differentiating of the whole group into certain subgroups. According to the principle of Homans we assumed, which the teacher confirmed, that the children would form social clusters with respect to their liking and disliking other children. Therefore, it is safe to state that the children would not only chose sitting places according to Homans' principle but that they would act in the same way in other – and more important – situations like the formation of learning groups, choosing team members at football and so on.

This satisfactory validity of the program with respect to predictions was tested several times under different conditions, e.g., in a summer camp with children of different cities, in high school classes and in a hostel for adolescents of socially deviant behavior. Despite the differences of these social experiments in several aspects the program in most cases demonstrated that the differentiation of a group into sub-groups on the basis of the values of the according socio-matrix can be predicted with a sufficient degree of precision. These and other results convinced us that our methodical procedure is quite valid in regard to empirical analysis.[5] We shall demonstrate such combinations of empirical research and computer simulation with respect to the observation of communicative processes in later chapters.

The practical use of such programs is obvious: every teacher, group psychologist, superior of a team and so on has to know how the group he is responsible for is differentiated, for example if there are outsiders, stars (whom all others will choose) etc. A socio-matrix alone is very often not sufficient to predict such differentiating

[5] These observations were performed by Dominik Kalisch for his BA-thesis and by Matthias Hermann for his MA-thesis.

processes, in particular if the according group is rather large. Simulation programs like the Moreno-CA give more detailed and precise insights into the behavior of the group. We developed a variant of the Moreno-CA for the usage in the mentioned hostel for deviant adolescents in order to predict the degree of aggressiveness of subgroups if the adolescents are left alone. The aim of this program is to prevent the formation of subgroups with too high degrees of aggressiveness. We were told by the teachers responsible for this hostel that the formation of such subgroups is a severe social problem in the hostel and that they hope to get help from our programs. First results indicate that the hope of the teachers is not in vain.

For methodical reasons, i.e. to minimize the danger of artifacts produced by the logical structure of the program we additionally used a certain neural net, i.e. a Kohonen feature map (KFM) for the same task. A KFM is a neural net that performs its learning processes in a "non supervised" way. This means that a KFM does not get immediate feed back from its environment as it is the case with supervised learning nets.[6] Non supervised learning is a self-organized process insofar as the neurons of the net – the artificial units – are "clustered" according to their values of activation. By a so called "winner takes all" principle the network forms clusters of neurons or groups of neurons. We used a so called Ritter-Kohonen network (Ritter and Kohonen 1989) that operates on the basis of a "semantical matrix" and has the task to construct ordering structures from a set of information. A little example by Ritter and Kohonen may illustrate this procedure.

	eats-flesh	mammal	flies	lays-eggs	herbivore	big
lion	1	1	0	0	0	1
duck	0	0	1	1	1	0
cat	1	1	0	0	0	0
eagle	1	0	1	1	0	0
horse	0	1	0	0	1	1

This matrix again reminds of the mentioned adjacency matrix and must be understood in a similar fashion. A 1 in the matrix signifies that the respective animal has a certain characteristic, e.g. a lion certainly eats flesh and is a mammal. A 0 of course signifies that the animal does not have the respective characteristic – a lion does not fly and a horse does not eat flesh. The task of the network is now to cluster the concepts of the animals according to the similarity of their characteristics.

[6] Supervised learning nets usually orientate their learning processes to a given "target vector". The difference between the factual output of the net and the target vector is the measure for the degree of the necessary changing of the network.

A result is, for example, shown in figure 3:

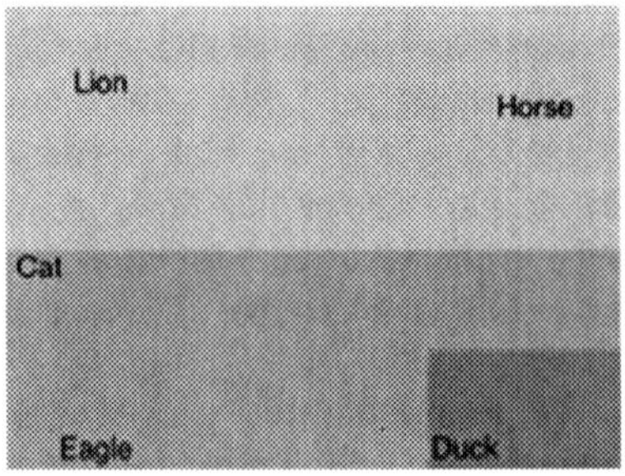

Figure 3. the clustering of animal concepts

In other words, the KFM generates an explicit order from data where the order is "hidden", i.e. only implicitly contained.

For the prediction of group processes we used the socio-matrix of a particular group as the semantical matrix. Each group member is then represented by a certain vector, e.g. member $5 = (1, 0, 1, -1)$, that is nothing else than the according row of the socio-matrix. The vector represents the emotional values of the particular member with respect to the other members, in this example the four other members (we omitted the values of the main diagonal of the matrix for the reasons given above). The task of the self-organizing neural net now is to cluster the group members with respect to the relative similarity of their vectors. Because the vectors represent the feeling of a particular member towards the others we wanted to see if the according clustering of the members by the network would produce similar results as the simulation by the CA. Note that the CA simulates a dynamical process, i.e. the interactions of group members; the KFM in contrast generates a geometrical order by using the implicit structure of the socio-matrix.

A very interesting result was obtained by using the socio-matrix of the school-class with the outsider no. 5 and the pupil no. 3 with the questionable character. Remember that the CA was not able to predict the unfriendly behavior of no. 3. In figures 4a and 4b we compare the factual outcome of the social experiment (left) with the result of the Kohonen network (right).

We see that the KFM predicts the formation of a large sub-group with no. 5 as an outsider. In this respect the KFM indeed generates nearly the same result as the CA. But we also see that the pupil no.3 is placed by the KFM rather near to no. 5, which is in difference to the result of the CA and which is also more in accordance with the factual behavior of no. 3. It seems that the KFM has "discovered" in the socio-matrix a hidden mixed feeling of no. 3 towards the outsider. Perhaps, but this is just a speculation, no.3 and no.5 have the chance to become friends in the long run although they did not like each other at the time of the analysis. Literature, movies and everyday experience are full of such examples.

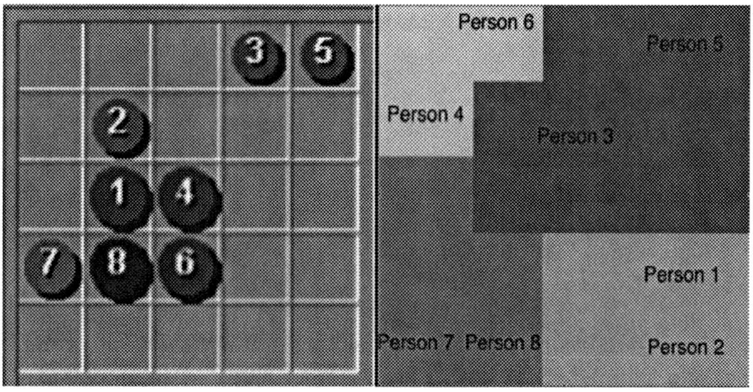

Figure 4a and 4b.

In a lot of test runs with very different socio-matrices we confirmed the fact that in most cases the CA and the KFM generated very similar results, although of course not always identical ones. Because the algorithms of the CA and the KFM respectively are very different, these results were by no means expectable. Therefore, one has to ask how these correspondences can be explained.

In the second chapter we introduced the concept of the topology of a system, that is the set of relations between the system's elements. The topology determines if certain elements are able to interact. In addition the rules of interaction determine how the elements interact, if they do so. In our social and computer experiments obviously the topology is the determinant factor: the socio-matrix represents the "emotional structure" of the respective groups and the socio-matrix also is the common basis for both types of models. Therefore, despite the differences between the algorithms of the models the results are similar because nothing else than the topology of the groups is taken into account. In the case of the CA the topology determines the behavior of the cells, i.e. if they associate or try to avoid one another. In the case of the KFM the same topology decides if and how similar two members are, when they are represented by their vectors. Because two vectors are similar if the members roughly are similar in liking and disliking the same persons – as it is the case with pupils 5 and 3 –, it is a necessary consequence of the topology that the KFM obtains very similar results as the CA. We shall come back to the topology of social systems and its influence on the dynamics of systems from a very general point of view at the end of this subchapter.

The representation of the system's topology in a socio-matrix exhibits another important aspect about the dynamics of a certain social group. A stabilization of the group means that the group has reached an attractor state; in the case shown above it was a point attractor. Yet, as we mentioned, it is by no means a matter of course that a group reaches a point attractor. Consider the following example of a simple group consisting of three members A, B, and C. Let the socio-matrix of this little group be

	A	B	C
A	0	1	−1
B	1	0	−1
C	−1	−1	0

Apparently this group has no problem to reach a point attractor, for example a state A B C, that is a state where A and B are together and C is in an outsider position like the pupil no. 5 in the example above.

Now assume the matrix to be

	A	B	C
A	0	1	−1
B	−1	0	1
C	1	−1	0

A likes B and wishes his nearness, unfortunately B dislikes A and tries to avoid him. Accordingly B wishes the nearness of C who in turn wishes to avoid B and searches the nearness of A. Consequently, if everybody looks for an optimal position (Homans' principle) then no point attractor is possible. If A goes to B, B goes away and so on.

A comparison of the two matrices immediately explains the reasons for the different behavior in the two cases. The first matrix is characterized by so called symmetrical relations: the feeling of B towards A is the same as that of A towards B and accordingly the feelings towards C. In contrast the second matrix is characterized by asymmetrical relations, i.e. the emotional values v of two persons X and Y are given as $v(X, Y) = -v(Y, X)$. Therefore, the little example can be generalized, as we found out in several experiments:

If a socio-matrix contains many asymmetrical relations – about 50% or more –, then the group will reach no point attractor but only attractors of period 2 or larger. On the other hand, a group will always reach a point attractor if the number of symmetrical relations is significantly larger than 50% . If the number of asymmetrical relations is about 40% , then the group will need a rather long preperiod before it reaches a point attractor. As the number of symmetrical or asymmetrical relations respectively is a topological feature of the group we see again the importance of the analysis of topological structures.

Before we discuss this aspect in a general way we demonstrate another possibility of predicting some characteristics of a group by the use of a socio-matrix. This time we use for a model an "interactive net" (IN), a special type of neural networks that was used in subchapter 3.3. Because we use this network type in other examples as well we repeat once more the general description of IN.

An IN is a so called recurrent network which means that principally all units are connected with weight values $w \neq 0$. Although it is possible to implement learning algorithms into an IN, this type of network usually is used the way that the user has to construct the weight matrix himself, i.e. the matrix containing the values of the connections between the units. To be sure, the connections between the different units may represent very different relations. In subchapter 3.3. the weighted connections between the units, representing particular concepts, represented the strength of semantical relations between these concepts. In this case we used the IN to represent again a certain social group and via the values of the socio- matrix the emotional relations between the group members. The "activation flow" between our units, i.e. the artificial neurons is determined by the linear activation rule, namely

$$(4.1.1) \quad A_j = \sum A_i * w_{i,j}$$

that we mentioned in chapter 2. A_j is the activation value of the receiving neuron j (the equivalent to the state of a cell in a CA), A_i are the activation values of the sending neurons i and w_{ij} is the weight value of the connection between a sending neuron i and a receiving neuron j. In contrast to the Moreno-CA, where we had to introduce different rules of transition, in the case of the IN it is sufficient to use just one general rule of interaction for all neurons regardless of their specific activation value or their topological neighborhood.

The representation of a specific group, for example of four members a, b, c, and d, and their emotional relations by an IN is simply

	a	*b*	*c*	*d*
a	0	1	−1	1
b	1	0	1	−1
c	−1	1	0	0
d	1	−1	0	0

if the values of the matrix are those of the socio-matrix. That means that we construct the weight matrix for our particular IN by using the values of the socio-matrix. In order to obtain certain simulations and by that predictions of the behavior of the group one "externally" activates one or all neurons, i.e. the neurons get a certain numerical value, usually a real number between 0 and 1. Then the succeeding activation values of the neurons are recursively computed by the formula (1) above. The program stops if a point attractor has been reached, i.e. if the activation values of the neurons do not change any more, or if other criteria are fulfilled. For illustration purposes we show the graphic visualization of this IN, i.e. its attractor state after an external activation with value = 0.1 for all units.

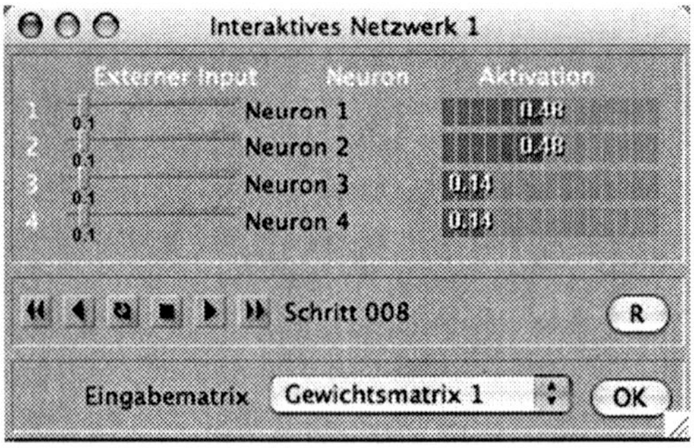

IN in a stable state

The task of the IN for this group simulation is the following: Each member of the group has a certain feeling *with respect to the whole group* – he feels well, he is unhappy, he is indifferent and so on. It is obvious that the individual behavior of the members is at least partially dependent on the feeling the members have with respect to the group. For example, members of a working team will not work at their best if they feel unhappy with respect to the team; the same situation is well known from pupils whose learning success often depends on the "climate" of the class, i.e. how well they feel as members of a certain school class. Therefore, it is often quite important to know such facts about the group. The task of the IN is to predict on the basis of the socio-matrix these feelings of all group members. This is done via the activation values of the neurons in their final state, that is when the IN has reached a point attractor. If, for example, the possible activation values are in the interval from 0 to 1, then the final activation value of a neuron of 0.3 means that the according member is not feeling very well, whereas a value of 0.8 means that the feeling is very good.

Note that there is an important difference to the Moreno-CA. The cells of the CA compute their emotional states only with respect to their Moore-neighborhood, i.e. to a specific subgroup they just have as their immediate social milieu. The neurons of the IN compute their activation states with respect to the whole group.

The operation of such an IN is best shown via an example where the empirical validity of the simulations – and predictions – were tested by two of our students. The respective group was a high school class at Dortmund (Western part of Germany), consisting of 31 pupils at the age from 16 – 18 years. Because of the size of the group – and the according IN with a weight matrix of $31 * 31 = 961$ values – we do not in detail show the IN but just report the results.

The empirical procedure was of course slightly different: the construction of the socio-matrix was done again by questionnaires; in addition each pupil was individually asked about his/her emotional state with respect to the whole class. The questionnaire's scale ranged from 1 = "very poor" to 4 = very well". The simulations were done with an external activation of all units with the same activation value of 0.05. On the left side is the prediction of the IN, on the right side the result of the comparison of the IN-prediction with the result of the survey.

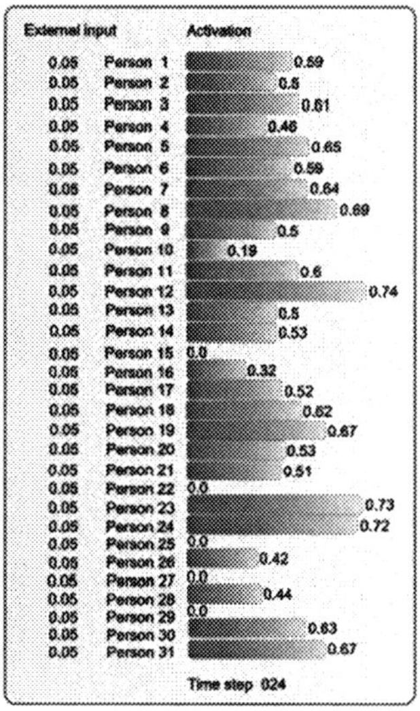

Emotional state →	very well	well	average	poor
Number	19	11	1	0
Correspondence	10	10		
Minimal deviation	5		1	
Strong deviation	4	1		

Results:

The right table shows that in only four cases the IN-prediction strongly differed from the empirical results, that in five cases there was only a slight deviation and that in all other cases the IN rather accurately predicted the emotional states of the pupils.

Apparently the prognosticating validity of the IN is very satisfactory, with the exception of the four deviant cases: Yet a careful analysis of the socio-matrix soon gave a probable explanation: The four "deviant" pupils obviously were not aware of the fact that they were disliked by nearly all other pupils. An additional questioning of these youths confirmed that hypothesis. Because they were in error with respect to their "objective" standing in the class and the IN used of course the factual socio-matrix the two students who had performed the empirical questioning and the simulations with the IN commented that "not the program was in error but the humans".

According empirical validations of the IN nearly always obtained the same results: Apparently the individual feeling of a group member with respect to the group is to a large extent determined by that particular topology of the group, which is represented by the socio-matrix. It is even possible, by the way, to analyze a group with respect to the question, if a particular member should be given an outstanding position in the group, e.g. as a speaker for the whole group. To do this an experimenter activates not all units together but only one at a time. Then there are three possibilities:

a) The IN does not reach a point attractor but only an attractor of period 2 or larger. In this case the respective member is not able to stabilize the group; he/she should not be given a special position.
b) The IN reaches a point attractor but only one with rather low activation values. In this case all other members should be analyzed the same way. If there are members whose external activation obtains better results, i.e. generates a point attractor with larger final values, then these members should be preferred. If there are no better members – better in this respect –, then the member should be given only a position with low authority.
c) The IN reaches a point attractor with high final values. The respective member could be selected for outstanding positions.

We tested these additional possibilities of IN-application too and got interesting results. In most cases members of the respective groups confirmed and/or agreed to the propositions of the IN. In one case we applied the IN to a handball team from the *Ruhrgebiet*, an industrial region in the West of Germany. The program demonstrated that only in one case the IN could reach a point attractor, but that one with rather high values. A questioning of some team members had the result that this team member was in fact the elected team captain. Apparently the IN is also able to give some assistance in such decision problems.

For a general result of these experiments we obtain that the topology of a group determines factual behavior *and* the individual well being. To be sure, these simulations are "only" simulations of social interactions and not of communicative processes if we understand communication in the complex way defined in the preceding chapters. Yet the topology of a group that is represented by such a socio-matrix as in these examples is, of course, always the result of preceding communicative processes. That is why it is possible to get satisfactory simulation results by concentrating only on the social dimension, that is social interactions. In particular, the examples of the IN-simulations demonstrated that it is in addition possible to predict the "inner" feelings of group members by just having a socio-matrix at our disposal and to give advices about group decision problems.

As a final remark to this subchapter it should not be omitted that frequently participants of the described empirical surveys and social experiments simply could not believe that the programs could predict not only their behavior but also their emotional state of mind. Some even spoke of something like "witchcraft" that the programs are able to perform.

In an important sense one can understand the socio-matrix of a certain group as a steering device that determines the dynamics of this group. Because communicative processes are of course always processes that depend on and are a part of the dynamics of the specific group we shall in later models use the methodical instrument of the socio-matrix for the modeling of more complex communicative processes than those just described. That is why we demonstrated the possibilities of predicting group behavior by using the socio-matrix of the group and by inserting its values into the simulation programs. Although the processes just described are only comparatively simple versions of social processes we shall see that they are the basis for the modeling of complex communicative processes.

In a strict sense of speaking a socio-matrix exhibits *structural* characteristics of a group and does not explicitly give information about *dynamical* features of this group. Yet in particular the considerations on the proportion of symmetrical and asymmetrical relations in a group demonstrated that such structural aspects can explain the dynamical behavior of the group, i.e. if the group trajectory generates point attractors or only attractors with longer periods. Conversely, the dynamics of a group can exhibit those structural features that generate the observed behavior. In other words, if one represents the structure of a group in a topological or graph theoretical way then the old and venerable dichotomy between social structure and process or dynamics respectively loses its importance. Structure and process are certainly not the same but they can be looked at as two sides of the same coin. Describing a social or communicative system in a structural or a dynamical way is obviously nothing else than looking at the same thing from two different but logically equivalent points of view.

4.2. SOCIAL TOPOLOGY AND COMMUNICATION: AN EXAMPLE OF OPINION FORMATION

Before we discuss the problem of a social topology in general we give an example of the modeling of "simple" communicative processes. "Simple" means that we still do not take into account the whole complexity of communication but just the results of communicative exchange processes. In other words, we describe in this example only the formation of certain opinions in dependency of the social positions of the actors. The exchange of certain opinions is assuredly an example of communicative processes and fortunately one that can be analyzed with rather unsophisticated means. That is of course also the reason why social surveys on the opinion and the change of opinion of, e.g. voters or consumers can be undertaken without great methodical problems.

The analysis of opinion formation by using CA-models has already some tradition (cf. e.g. Nowak and Lewenstein 1996) and goes back to the classical study of Schelling (1971) on social segregation. The use of CA-models for this question has great advantages because one can use the position of the cells on the grid as representations for the social milieu of the social actors that are represented by the cells. In other words, a CA generates something like a "natural topology" by placing the cells on the grid and even a metric: If one defines the distance between two cells x and y as the minimal number of cells between them, including the target cell – we may call this set of cells the minimal chain between x and y –, then it is easy to see that this definition obtains indeed the classical conditions for a metrical space. For readers who are not acquainted with these concepts we add the according definition:

A metrical relation is defined as a numerical value d with

(4.2.1) (1) $d(x, x) = 0$;

(2) $d(x, y) = d(y, x)$ and

(3) $d(x, z) \leq d(x, y) + d(y, z)$ (triangle inequality).

A little example may illustrate the metric of a CA; the symbols represent cells on the grid of this example CA:

x	1	2	3	4
5	6	7	8	9
10	11	12	13	14
15	16	y	17	18
19	20	21	22	13

Apparently the distance between the cells x and y is $d = 3$, the distance between y and 4 is $d = 3$ too and the distance between cells 19 and 3 is $d = 4$. One immediately sees that conditions (1)–(3) are fulfilled.

The mathematical concepts of CA-topology and CA-metric are important for the purpose of modeling processes of social interaction and communication because they allow to define in a precise sense concepts like "social nearness" and "social distances":

A rather natural metrical relation d can be defined for social systems the following way: $d(x, y) = n$, if $n - 1$ is the number of persons that are necessary for the two persons x and y to interact, according to the social rules that determine the actions of x and y. For example, a worker is not allowed to directly interact with the chairman of the board; it takes several persons like secretaries, personal assistants and so on to make an interaction possible. By defining $d(x, x) = 0$, we apparently obtain a relation of a social metric. $d(x, y) = 1$ means that x and y can interact without intermediating persons. We define this social metric by taking over an idea from the "Small World Problem" by Milgram (1967; cf. also Watts 1999). In other words, by translating the mathematical concepts of metrical relation into those of social action theory it is possible to understand social spaces as particular cases of metrical spaces. By using CA-models to represent such social spaces it is apparently possible to immediately transform certain social relations into formal, i.e., spatial relations between the units of the model. But note that according to the remarks in chapter 3 on cognitive, emotional and/or social spaces the condition (2) is not always fulfilled and that frequently such spaces are characterized by an "asymmetrical" metric.

For the modeling of processes of opinion formation the meaning of "nearness" and "distance" is rather obvious: The nearer two persons are in the social sense of the word, the more the persons will be able to influence each other, that is to persuade the other with respect to one's own opinion, and vice versa. To be sure, persuading usually is a symmetrical process in the sense that if A tries to influence B, then B will try the same with respect to A. This symmetry of such communicative processes is also taken into account by the particular topology of a CA-grid: Remember that the CA-relation "cell A is in the neighborhood of cell B" automatically implies the relation "cell B is in the neighborhood of A". That is why we spoke of CA as formal models with a symmetrical topology.

In real social situations the process of persuading must not be, of course, a purely symmetrical one. The result of single persuasion processes usually depends on the respective rhetorical abilities of the communicators, the social status, certain personal characteristics like charm and so on. It is easily possible to capture such deviations from the assumption of symmetrical processes in a CA-model too. But if one wishes, as we did, to model processes of opinion formation by communicative interactions for large social groups, i.e. 100 members and more, one can assume that such individual deviations can be neglected because they neutralize themselves in the statistical average. Therefore, we constructed the following model by using only symmetrical relations.[7]

The model OPINIO (derived from the Latin word for opinion) is a stochastic cellular automaton that uses as principal geometry a Moore neighborhood. The cells are in one of nine different states that represent different political opinions. A cell in the state 1 represents an extreme left wing position; accordingly the state 9 represents an extreme right wing one. The basic assumption of this model is as simple as the Homans principle of the models of group dynamical processes: each individual prefers a social milieu – a social neighborhood – where most of the other individuals are of the same or a similar opinion and each individual dislikes being in a social milieu where most of the others do not share one's own opinion. This assumption is very similar to the assumption of the well known segregation model of Schelling (1971): Schelling simulated the formation of ghettos with a CA-model by assuming that people prefer milieus consisting of other people who are similar to them in relevant respects and they tend to leave such milieus where this condition is not fulfilled. Schelling could demonstrate with this model that it is not necessary to assume ideological or racial prejudices in order to explain the formation of ghettos or urban communities with strict homogeneous populations.[8]

According to this basic assumption an artificial individual in our model, i.e. a cell in a certain state, has two basic options of action if the average opinion of its social milieu strongly differs from its own one: a) The individual can change its opinion, that is it lessens the difference to the average opinion of its milieu by increasing or reducing its state by 1. b) It can "move", that is like the cells in the Moreno-CA described in the preceding subchapter; it can search for another milieu where the difference to its own opinion is significantly lower that in its original Moore neighborhood. If the cell has found a Moore neighborhood where the difference of the average opinion to its own is lower than in its actual neighborhood, measured by

---

[7] We confirmed that assumption by experimenting with an enlarged model that contained also asymmetrical relations, distributed at random on the CA-grid. The results were not significantly different from those of the model that consists only of symmetrical relations.

[8] The simulations of Schelling did certainly not prove that no factors of, e.g. racial prejudices are involved in the formation of ghettos. But they demonstrated that it is not always necessary to assume such strong causes like particular prejudices when trying to explain processes of segregation. It is always useful to look for simpler explanations before one assumes deplorable attitudes like racial prejudices. Schelling, by the way, became a Nobel laureate in economics for these and other works in 2005.

a certain threshold, then the cell places itself in that Moore neighborhood, providing that there is at least an empty cell in this new neighborhood. The original position in the first neighborhood then becomes an empty cell.

The stochastic components in this CA-model are on the one hand a certain probability if the cell reacts at all, that is if the cell simply accepts being in a neighborhood with mainly individuals of other opinions or if the cell reacts. If it reacts the second stochastic component on the other hand is the option of choosing between opinion changing and moving. This option is defined by a probability parameter that determines with which probability the artificial individual either moves or changes its opinion. The OPINIO-CA offers the varying of this parameter, i.e. a user can decide if the probability of moving should be larger than the other or vice versa. In particular it is possible to insert different values of the probability parameter for the different cell states. The reason for this possibility is the assumption that people with radical opinions tend to prefer moving to opinion changing in contrast to people with moderate opinions, i.e. cell states from 4 to 6. The experiments, however, whose results are shown below were mainly performed by using a parameter value of 0.5 for all states and for both cases. In many experiments we found out that different parameter values do not have much influence on the outcome, at least not in large groups. "Large" means in this model several thousands cells; we show results of experiments with 4000 cells.

OPINIO is again a typical bottom up model in the sense that the rules and the determining effects of the two probability parameters are strictly locally defined. An individual only orientates itself with respect to its local Moore neighborhood. Therefore, the formations of (political) opinions that are representative for a whole "society", that is the whole population of several thousands cells is a classical case of the emergence of global phenomena out of local interactions.

To be sure, OPINIO does not take into account other decisive factors of the formation of political opinions like certain policies of the respective government, sudden incidents like, e.g. the events at 9-11-01 at New York and Washington, or the economical state of the society. It only considers purely social factors, i.e. the outcome of the mutual influencing processes of the members of a particular community. Yet despite this restrictedness of the model some results are astonishingly similar to well known empirical phenomena.

Figure 5 shows an initial state of the whole system; the different cell states are nearly equally and at random distributed on the grid. The single line besides the grid represents the numerical distribution of the different cell states. On the left and right side of the line the extreme political positions are represented; the moderate positions are represented in the middle section of the line.

The second figure shows the resulting state after 100 steps.

Figure 6 shows two interesting aspects that can also be found in social reality. On the one hand even after only 100 steps a significant trend to moderate positions can be seen. The different cell states are not equally distributed any more but, as the line on the side of the grid demonstrates very clearly, the number of cells being in "moderate" states has become much larger than the number of cells with

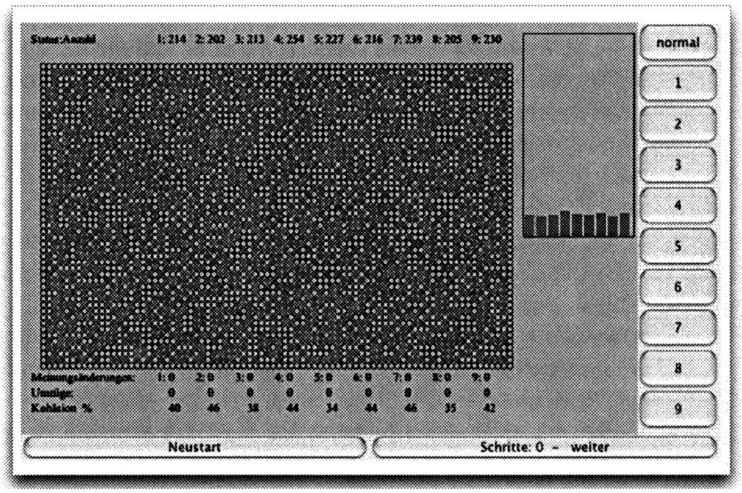

Figure 5. initial states

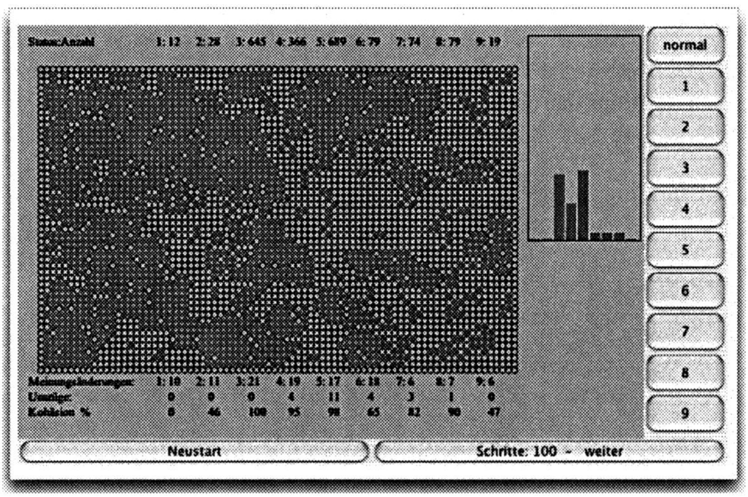

Figure 6. after 100 steps

"extreme" states. In political reality, at last in societies of the "Western type" like the USA or Germany, this dominance of moderate positions is recognizable by the political dominance of rather large political parties – in Germany for example the Social Democrats and the Christian Democrats –, which define themselves as representatives of the "political middle".

The fact that OPINIO is able to model such processes of the emergence of dominant moderate positions is due to the rule that the cells measure the difference of their own state to that of their Moore neighborhood by computing the arithmetical mean of their neighborhood cells states and by subsequently computing the difference to their own state. It is rather evident that an orientation to mean values favors the formation of "mean" positions. Remember that the changing of a cell state always means the increasing or lessening of the state by 1; as the cell with the changed state is itself a neighborhood cell of the cells in its Moore neighborhood these cells will accordingly react. Only in the rather seldom cases where extreme positions are dominant in the respective neighborhoods the center cells will change their state in the direction of more extreme positions. The apparent similarity of the results of OPINIO with social reality hint at the possibility that "real" processes of opinion influencing may contain such a mechanism, i.e. the orientation of social actors to mean positions in their social milieu – one may also call such an attitude an orientation to the mainstream.

On the other hand the figure shows a similar process of clustering as the experiments of Schelling have demonstrated. People with different opinions segregate, i.e. they form large groups containing only members with equal or similar opinions. According to the dominance of moderate opinions the largest clusters are formed by individuals with "middle" positions. The "radicals", that is cells with extreme low or high state values only survive in isolated subgroups. Such effects are also well known in socio-political reality; in extreme cases the representatives of radical opinions even tend to form secret subgroups that are hermetically isolated from the mainstream of society.

When continuing the simulation another additional mechanism becomes effective:

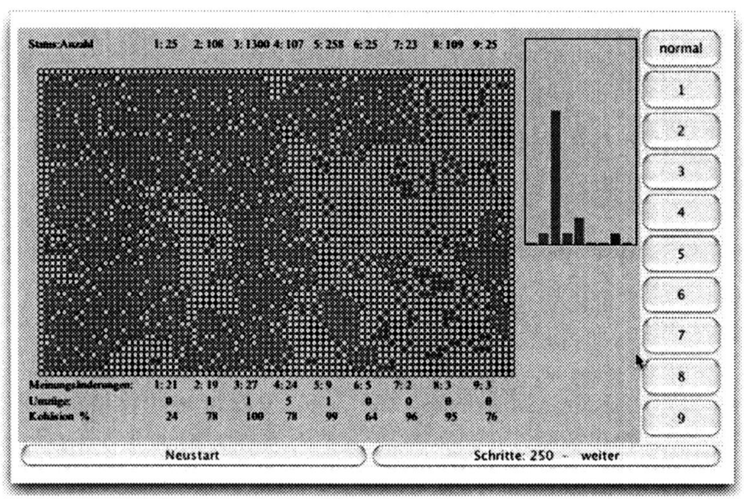

Figure 7. after 250 steps

The moderate opinions still are dominant but the distribution of moderate positions is now centered on one cell state; in political terms one may call this state as a social-democratic position, i.e., a moderate left position. This concentration on one particular cell state is due to a so called "Matthew-Effect": "For whosoever hath, to him shall be given, and he shall have more abundance; but whosoever hath not, from him shall be taken away even that he hath." (Matt. 13, 12)

The Matthew- Effect, whose importance for social processes was first discovered by Popper and Merton, can be understood as a special form of positive feed back: Small advantages in an initial state and in the successive states of the system's trajectory tend to be permanently increased until after sufficient time the advantages have become dominant for the whole system. The local rules of transition of the OPINIO-CA do not, of course, favor one particular state but only the formation of moderate positions in general. Yet in the course of the simulation the clusters of the moderate left positions have generated in a certain stage of the simulation – to be more exact, after about 150 steps, – some clusters of this position that were a bit larger than the other moderate clusters. This initial advantage was enough to let this position become dominant. Other simulations with different initial spatial distributions of the cells on the grid resulted in the dominance of moderate right positions. But nearly always the simulations produced such results due to Matthew-Effects, either in advantage of moderate left or right positions.

Despite the fact that Matthew-Effects can be observed in political reality too – a lot of undecided voters tend to vote for the party, which in their opinion will be the winner –, in contrast to OPINIO such processes do not go on forever. Very often voters become conscious of such effects and change their opinion and voting behavior because one party should not become too strong. OPINIO does in this aspect not completely capture socio-political reality. By careful studies of the simulation runs one discovers an additional effect, i.e., the emergence of so called "local attractors" (see above chapter 3.1). Local attractors are subgroups of elements that form a stable configuration, i.e. it does not change any more, although the system as a whole changes, being not in a point attractor state. In the case of OPINIO such local attractors are formed by the isolated small clusters at the top edge of the grid:

The local attractor groups emerge after 280 time steps (figure 8); one sees in figure 9 that the local attractors remain stable even after 600 runs. This permanent existence of the attractor subgroups is of course due to their isolation from the other clusters; that is why these subgroups, consisting of "radical" cells, are able to maintain their extremely different opinions – extreme with respect to the mainstream. In social reality such local attractors also are a well known phenomenon, meaning social subgroups or sub communities respectively that try to maintain their different subculture by isolating themselves from the mainstream of society. One rather famous example for such an isolated subculture are the Amish in Pennsylvania.[9] It is not an unimportant insight with respect to the capabilities of OPINIO that it is able to generate even such effects.

---

[9] The Amish became known to a general public by the cinema movie "Witness" with Harrison Ford.

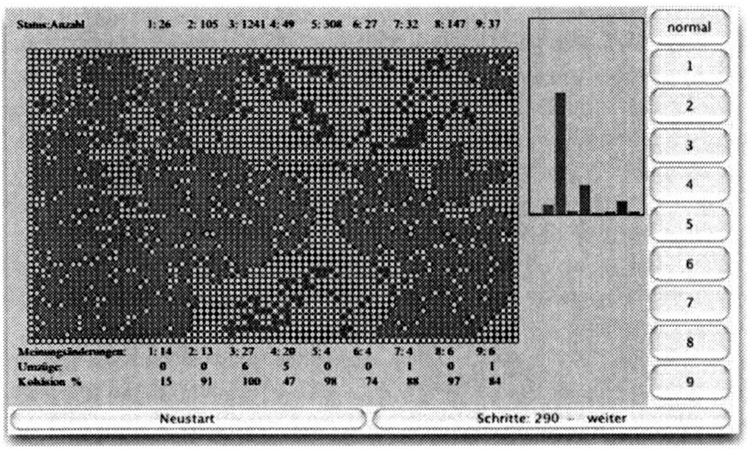

Figure 8.

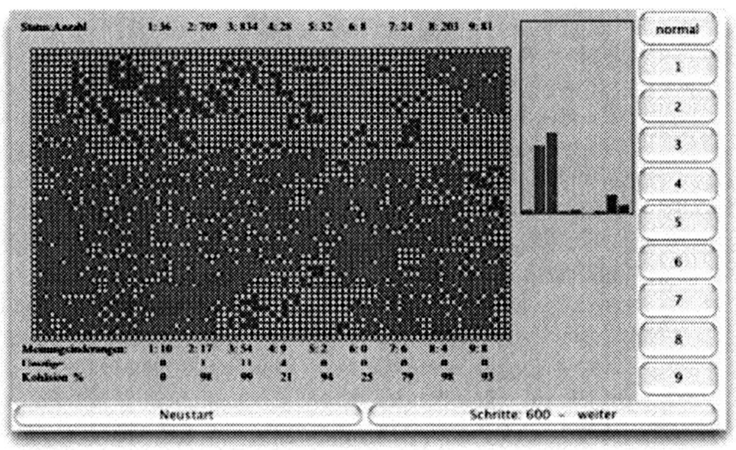

Figure 9.

OPINIO models, as we said in the beginning of this subchapter, just the social dimension of communicative processes and does not take into account the internal cognitive processes that are the "subjective" basis for opinion formation and/or opinion changing. This restriction expresses itself in the model by representing the artificial individuals just as "finite state machines", i.e. as black boxes that change their state or their geometrical position on the grid according to their respective social milieu. In the sense of learning theories one may say that the individuals are treated in a behaviorist fashion like the dog of Pavlov we mentioned in chapter 3. Yet the fact that OPINIO is able to reproduce effects that are well known from social reality demonstrates that it is principally possible, at least for questions like opinion formation, to methodically treat human beings just like that. Of course, such a methodical approach has its limits as we could see when discussing the Matthew-effect. That is why a complete modeling of communicative processes has to take into account the internal cognitive processes as well as the social rules that determine communicative situations.[10]

It is possible to enlarge the formal techniques of OPINIO in at least two different aspects. On the one hand OPINIO uses the geometry of the CA only in a very simple fashion, i.e., a single cell takes into account only the adjacent cells of its Moore neighborhood and ignores the rest. According to the consideration about social geometry/topology at the beginning of this subchapter the influence of more distant cells should be taken into account too. This could be done, e.g., by also computing the arithmetical mean of the additional cells of the enlarged Moore neighborhood; call this *mv*', and the mean of the cells of the Moore neighborhood *mv*. Then the total mean with respect to the center cell could be computed as

$$(4.2.2) \quad \frac{mv + mv'/2}{2},$$

when we take into account that the additional cells of the enlarged Moore neighborhood have only weaker influence on the center cell, in this formula apparently only half of the influence of the cells in the Moore-neighborhood. The defining of the influence of the enlarged Moore-neighborhood is, to be sure, quite arbitrarily and can be changed. First experiments with this enlargement of OPINIO demonstrated that for large groups the effects are not very different from those reported.

Another more interesting enlargement is the introduction of so called fuzzy algorithms into OPINIO. We omit the technical details because an introduction into Fuzzy Logic would transcend the purpose of this book. It is sufficient to say that the basic idea is the following: The opinion of an individual cannot always be represented by a certain integer as in OPINIO. A voter is not strictly a partisan of a certain party but favors, say, the Christian Democrats in Germany "more or less". In other words, his state of mind is not a distinctive value with "either that or that", but rather "fuzzy": In some aspects he favors the moderate right but in other aspects he prefers the moderate left. This is probably the reason why many voters are undecided even a short time before elections. The concepts of Fuzzy Logic and Fuzzy Set Theory allow to represent such undecided states of mind, in particular by representing the states of the CA-cells by fuzzy numbers. If a fuzzy OPINIO that has been already constructed generates different results for the model

[10] One may even say that sociology as a science independent from psychology is only possible because such restricted approaches as the one of OPINIO are sufficient for a lot of important questions.

we described above will be seen because the experiments with this model are still in progress.[11]

4.3. THE EMERGENCE OF SOCIAL ORDER BY COMMUNICATIVE PROCESSES OF TYPIFYING

The examples that we demonstrated in the last two subchapters all referred to social situations and social processes where certain social rules determined the respective social dynamics. "Rules" of course do not necessarily mean officially fixed rules like laws or institutional regulations but rather informal regularities of social behavior like the principle of Homans or the preferring of social similarities. Yet what about situations where there are no obligatory rules at all and where the individual actors have to generate such rules for themselves? It is possible to model such situations too and to analyze these processes of common rule generation in the respective models.[12] But let us first consider the problem of the origins of social order from a more theoretical point of view.

In a certain sense the social sciences are divided according to the specific anthropological assumption they are based on: On the one hand there are the partisans of the conception of *homo oeconomicus*, as Dahrendorf named this approach. Man is a rational and egoistical being who acts in each situation according to the best strategy he has calculated. On the other hand there is *homo sociologicus* who is social by following the social rules that are important and valid in a certain situation. As these terms suggest, *homo oeconomicus* is one of the most important and basic assumptions in the economical and part of the political sciences; *homo sociologicus*, of course, is the basis for many theoretical approaches in sociology and cultural anthropology.

The anthropological assumptions that are connected with *homo oeconomicus* were not invented but most influentially expressed by Hobbes who first formulated the question of the emergence of social order in terms of this paradigm: How is social order possible in a world full of egoists who only try to maximize their respective profits? Not his famous answer survived, i.e., the order enforcing state as a *Leviathan*, but his starting point and the formulation of the question. In this sense Hobbes may be called the founding father of those Rational Choice (RC) approaches that share his rather pessimistic assumptions about man and that are prominent in economics, political, other social sciences, and game theoretical attempts to explain the possibility of social order.

One of the *methodical* advantages of RC is the fact that, since the invention of mathematical game theory, RC models can be expressed in a mathematical way. Therefore, many of the attempts to found mathematical social sciences upon action theories were influenced by the RC paradigm. In particular, it seemed possible

---

[11] In a recent textbook on "Soft Computing", written in German, we describe the structure of a deterministic version of OPINIO and that of an according fuzzy CA. First experiments with those three types of CA show different forms of behavior. See Stoica-Klüver et al. 2006.

[12] This model is described in more detail in Klüver et al. 2005.

to deal with the problem of Hobbes in a precise fashion, i.e. to demonstrate in a mathematical way the "conditions of possibility" of social order, to vary a famous term of Kant. Paradigmatic for these attempts is the analysis of social dilemmas via computer simulations, in particular the studies with respect to the Prisoner's Dilemma (PD). These dilemmas, with which already Parsons dealt (Parsons, 1968), are all based on the problem how to act best in a situation where different strategies of action are possible.

Among other difficulties with the RC approach there is the most important objection that RC in general is not very realistic. To be sure, people often do act in an egoistical way and they often look in a rational fashion for the best strategies with respect to a certain problematic situation. In this sense Homans (1974) defines behavior "as a function of its payoffs" (Fararo, 2000, 221) and social behavior as an exchange process. But the concept of *homo sociologicus* implies that social actors are social because they orientate their behavior to certain social rules and in particular that they generate rules in cases where there are still none. The famous "crisis experiments", for example of ethnomethodology, clearly demonstrate the shock people receive if common social rules are deliberately disregarded (cf. Garfinkel, 1967). Human beings are not only used to certain social rules as the appropriate social order for particular situations but they also need them in order to get along in a world with a sometimes overwhelming complexity.

Vanberg (1994) summed up the arguments why man is at core a social being, i.e. a rule following individual:

Because man is in a biological sense a deficit being (the *Mängelwesen* of Gehlen (1956)) with only few instincts human beings have to form social rules and institutions in order to get a relieve from the burden of constantly having to make new decisions. It is much easier to follow well established rules of behavior than to think anew in each new situation and it is often better to apply rules that have been successfully tried in the past than to try new and often problematic strategies of action.

In addition, social actors are able to gain some "social capital" (Bourdieu) this way. If they are known to respect social rules then others will trust them at least with respect to these rules and will act accordingly.

RC is certainly not wrong but insufficient and it must be completed by other theoretical approaches that explain *how* social order emerges. The arguments of Vanberg and other scholars clearly demonstrate *why* the emergence of social order is profitable and therefore evolutionary plausible. But nothing is said about the *how*; the attempts to explain social order by long-term profits from iterated action situations are apparently not enough. Therefore, we have to look in other theoretical directions, that is to the classical studies of the ontogenesis of subjective identity on the one hand, namely G. H. Mead (Mead, 1934) and the construction of social order via processes of typifying (Berger and Luckmann, 1966) on the other.

As is well known, Mead characterizes the process of the acquisition of social competences via the distinction between "I", "Me" and "Self". "Self" as the goal of socialization is a permanent interplay of I and Me: I is the spontaneous, "natural" component of the personality, Me represents the "socialized" component, i.e. the acceptance, understanding and internalization of social rules and norms. The most important part of this ontogenetic process of identity acquirement is the growing capability of the child to distinguish between concrete individuals – *the significant other* in the terms of Berger and Luckmann – and the *generalized other* (Mead), i.e. other persons as occupants of certain social roles. For example, as long as the child only knows its own mother, the concept "mother" is identical with the concrete person of the own mother, the significant other. If and when the child learns that there are other mothers then the child becomes able to perform the distinction between the individual persons – its own mother, the mother of the best friend – and the social role of "mother". In the terms of Berger and Luckmann the child generates certain types, i.e. social roles, by distinguishing between purely individual characteristics that are peculiar to certain individuals and "social" characteristics, namely the characteristics of a particular social role. The generation of (social) types then is the abstraction of individual characteristics and the concentration on common social aspects. *In nuce*, the child becomes socialized by the successful construction of social types and in this sense by the generation of rules of interaction that depend not mainly on individual characteristics of the respective other but on social ones which the other has in common with people of the same social type. A teacher must be treated according to the role of teacher, regardless of particular differences in personalities.

Berger and Luckmann generalized these insights of Mead to the general process of the establishment of social order: Social order is the result of mutual typifying processes of at least two interacting actors. Social rules emerge via "habituation", i.e. via the iterative application of the same action strategies the actors have successfully used during previous interactions. "Successfully" refers to the fact that like in RC the actors try to make the best of the action situation. But unlike in RC-approaches the actors do not simply try to maximize their profit but they try to obtain rules of interaction that can be accepted by both actors. To be sure, dominant persons will have more influence on the result of the interactional process than weaker ones. Therefore, this process of establishing mutually obligatory rules of interaction is not necessarily symmetric in the sense that the actors always will treat another as equals. The emerging social order may be a hierarchical one. Yet the task for both actors is the same in the beginning: they have to perceive the other and have to try some forms of action that in the end will be accepted as social order. This process of mutual adjustment of behavior can be summarized in the following way:

Imagine the first meeting of two persons A and B who have the problem to develop some kind of social order, that is specific rules of interaction. The first meeting of Robinson and Friday is such a case because both did not know each other and both were forced to establish a particular social order, as they could not leave the island. A and B are both estimating the other and try to develop an action strategy that suits the specific actor and that is accepted by the other. In other words, both try to act according to their own interests but both have to take into regard the reactions of the other. In the end of such a process of mutual adjusting and adaptation A and B establish some form of interaction, that is they establish a simple form of social order by having developed certain rules of interaction. According to Berger and Luckmann, social order like institutions must be understood as the result of such processes of "exchange" (Homans), i.e., as the result of the mutual adjustment of the respective behavior.

When other actors join this initial social group then the process of mutual adjustment has to be repeated. Yet after a certain time, newcomers to a group with an already established social order will be typified by the members of the group: The newcomers will be classified as belonging to the same (social or personal) type as some members of the group and will be accordingly treated. The "objectivation" (Berger and Luckmann) of the social order, subjectively constructed by the first members of the group, is a result of distinguishing between group members as concrete individuals and their social characteristics as occupants of certain roles *as* group members – high or low in the hierarchy and so on. In this sense social types are nothing else than social roles in the classical meaning of this concept, namely "generalized expectations of behavior" and conversely appropriate cases of the application of certain rules of interaction. The parallel to Mead's considerations is obvious.

Berger and Luckmann did not transform these basic ideas into precise models and did not develop it in detail. Yet in our opinion this approach is very well suited to overcome the shortcoming of RC approaches without losing their advantages. The mutual adjustment is, of course, driven by the wish to get along with the other in a way most satisfying for oneself. In this sense RC is still valid because the adjustment processes follow a rational strategy. But the outcome is not just cooperative behavior with expectations for a long run but certain *rules of interaction* that remain valid even after a period of separation. In particular, the combination of certain rules to social institutions allows the distinction between an individual person and the social role this person occupies. The computational model that we now present captures the basic aspects of these processes of the emergence of social order.

When transforming the general considerations of Berger and Luckmann into a computational model we made the following assumptions:

A certain social actor has a specific "personality", i.e., he has some personal characteristics that allow to identify him and to recognize him again when meeting him after a time. These personal characteristics are in the case of human persons features like size, sex, age, intelligence (as far as this can be perceived), certain personal manners like a specific way to speak and so on. In the case of robots, to take another example, such characteristics can also be physical attributes like size or form; the characteristics may in addition be certain competences like physical strength, abilities to move in a certain landscape etc.[13] Internet agents, to give

[13] In a cooperation project with a scientist of NASA, Maarten Sierhuis, we are just trying to apply this model to the problem of robotics, i.e., to implement robots the capability to generate social order of interaction between robots and human operators (cf. Klüver et al. 2004).

another illustration, may be identified by features like a specific knowledge base, certain computing capabilities, a particular degree of autonomy and so on. The actions of the respective actors or agents respectively are dependent on the personal characteristics, although not in a fixed way.

The actors have a general learning capability: They are able to recognize their own mistakes and to correct their behavior accordingly. These learning processes are performed by varying an "internal structure" of the actors that transfers the personal characteristics into particular actions. In the case of human beings one can describe this internal structure as a kind of self-image. It is a truism that individual social actions in a particular situation are a result both of a certain personality and the image a person has of himself. To be sure, the actions in a social situation are also determined by the respective social rules; but the specific manner these rules are executed depend on these two personal factors. Social learning in the sense that one has to adjust one's own behavior according to the other actors or agents one meets is the changing of the self-image in order to generate adequate forms of social action.

The most fundamental assumption is that at the first meeting of two actors the *mutual* learning process must take into account a) the two personalities of the actors, b) the own actions and the actions of the other as a reaction to one's own actions and c) the necessity that both actors or agents must be content with the result of the mutual adjustment. In this sense the establishing of certain social rules of interactions is always a compromise between the different personalities and the according interests.

The general model of artificial actors or agents, as we will name them in the following descriptions, with these capabilities is this:

Each agent consists of two different artificial neural nets (NN), the action net (AN) and the perception net (PN). The combination of two networks enables the agents to perform two different tasks, namely the generation of suited rules of interaction on the one hand and the recognizing of "acquainted" agents after a time on the other hand. In addition, the perception network also performs the process of "typifying".

a) The action network

The action network whose task is the generation of adequate rules of action is a multi-layered feed-forward network: The activation flow between the artificial neurons as units of the net is only directed from the input layer via the connecting intermediate or "hidden" layer(s) to the output layer. That means mathematically that only the upper half of the weight matrix of the network is of importance; the second half below the main diagonal can be neglected. The most important rule is the linear activation rule that determines the "flow" of activation between the artificial neurons

$$(4.3.1) \quad A(j) = \sum i w_{ij} A(i)$$

if A(j) is the activation value of the receiving neuron j, A(i) the activation values of the sending neurons i and w_{ij} are the weight values between the sending neurons i and the receiving neuron j. At present we are experimenting with action nets of different architecture, i.e. different numbers of layers. Below we will sketch the architecture and results from a network with three layers, i.e. an input layer, an output layer and a hidden layer. According to our experiments similar results can be obtained by using networks with only two layers, i.e. without a hidden layer. The input layer of the action network represents the personality of the particular agent, written as a vector $X = (x_1, \ldots, x_5)$; the five dimensions are – at present – arbitrarily chosen. During the training processes of the AN the X-vector of each agent remains constant, that is, the network always gets the same input.

The output layer $Y = (y_1, \ldots, y_5)$ represents components of action like the selection of certain words, miming, gestures, keeping a certain distance, being respectful and so on in the case of human actors. In the case of robots, for example, the Y-vector, that is the action vector, would contain components like coming near, asking for something, obeying an order – or disobeying – and the like.

The weight matrix of the AN represents the internal structure of the agents or the *self-image* respectively. In our experiments we usually restrict the connections in that way that only the weight values between the components x_i and y_i are

(4.3.2) $w_{ii} = 1$ and

$w_{ij} = 0$ else.

A two-layered action net can be visualized as
Agent A

$$\begin{array}{ll} \text{AN}: & (x_1, x_2, x_3, x_4, x_5) = X_A \\ & \;\downarrow \;\;\downarrow \;\;\downarrow \;\;\downarrow \;\;\downarrow \qquad \downarrow \\ & (y_1, y_2, y_3, y_4, y_5) = Y_A \end{array}$$

The simulations start with five agents A, B, C, D, and E, each of them containing an action network of the described feed-forward type and a perception network (see below).

When A for the first time meets B, both have to evaluate the other, that is they have to mutually find a behavior Y_A and Y_B that is suitable for oneself and for the other. Both A and B start with random weight matrices with the described restrictions.

A starts – with its AN – with a vector Y_A and B with Y_B. "Starting" means that the ANs gets their respective X-vectors as input, that is the X-vectors of their own personalities, and generate via the linear activation rule an according Y-vector as their (first) actions.

Both actions are then evaluated by the formula

$$(4.3.3) \quad \delta = 1 - \frac{|(X_A - X_B)|}{|(Y_A - Y_B)|}$$

The basic idea of this formula is that when establishing rules of behavior between two persons both the personalities and the respective actions must be mutually taken into account. A orientates himself to B and vice versa. The mutual task of A and B is to minimize δ , i.e., to approximate the quotient to 1. In other words, the actions must be proportional to the respective personalities.

A behavior that is satisfying for both is reached *when the relation between the personalities is nearly the same as the relation between the actions.* The reason for this definition is that a person tends to act rather "strongly" in those characteristics where he is good or even superior in relation to others; in turn, other agents accept this type of action if they perceive that the first agent is indeed superior in this respective aspect. To be sure, an agent may be in error whether he is indeed good in some aspects. Then the mutual adjusting process forces the agent to correct his internal structure – the weight matrix – at least in this aspect.

If this is the case, i.e., if the first actions are not satisfactory, the well-known delta-rule is used for the changing of the internal structure of both agents:

$$(4.3.4) \quad w_{ij}(t+1) = w_{ij}(t) \pm \eta(t_i - a_j)o_i = \eta o_i \delta j$$

where w_{ij} (t) is the weight value between the units i and j at time t and accordingly $w_{ij}(t+1)$ the new value at time $t+1$, η is a so called learning rate, i.e. a measure for the changing of the weight value, o is the output of the unit j at time t and finally δ is the size of the "error", i.e. the difference between a target_i (t_i) value and the factual value of the respective unit that is computed by equation (4.3.3). The delta-rule is a common learning rule in the case of supervised learning, i.e. if the network computes its error by "knowing" the difference between its own output and a desired one, that is a target value.

Obviously the learning situation for A and B is one of a *moving target*, i.e. the adjusting processes of A depend on the adjusting processes of B and vice versa. This is not the usual learning process of supervised learning because normally the target vector is constant. Therefore, it was not obvious when starting the experiments with the networks that they would be able to converge. Yet in most cases they do. The well known experiments of Axelrod (1987), by the way, analyze a similar situation of moving targets. Our results confirm that not only genetic algorithms, which Axelrod used, but also rather simple neural feed-forward networks are able to master such a situation.

In the end, that is defined by a minimized δ, A and B have developed vectors Y_{AB} and Y_{BA}, i.e. action vectors with respect to one another. These vectors are social rules in the sense "if A meets B, then A acts according to the vector Y_{AB}" and vice versa.

Now this process of establishing rules of interactions is repeated with the other agents. As a final result we have a social group where each agent is connected with each other agent by a specific Y-vector Y_{NM} for two persons N and M.

The set of all Y-vectors, i.e. the 20 respective rules of behavior is the social order of this group, generated by the perception and evaluation of the other agents. The Y-vectors are ordered in a manner described below; the result of such an ordering is a social order where the relations between the agents form a certain kind of social hierarchy. The particular form of course depends on the different personalities of the initial agents that is, the agents of the "primordial" group.

Note that these rules are still just valid with respect to one pair of agents. The rules are not general in the sense that they are valid for different persons or pairs of persons respectively. This needs another process, namely the recognition and typifying of known and new agents by the perception network.

Another evaluation possibility, by the way, is obtained by a geometrical representation of the X- and Y-vectors in the according planes they generate.[14] The evaluation formula described above can also be computed via the angles of the two pairs of vectors:

$$(4.3.5) \quad \frac{((X_1 * X_2) / |X_1| * |X_2|)}{((Y_1 * Y_2) / |Y_1| * |Y_2|)} = \frac{\cos(X_1, X_2)}{\cos(Y_1, Y_2)}$$

and

$$(4.3.6) \quad \delta = 1 - \frac{\cos(X_1, X_2)}{\cos(Y_1, Y_2)}$$

Experiments done with this formula obtained similar results as with the other equations; this is a strong indicator for the fact that our results are not artifacts due to the particular forms of evaluation.

For illustrating purposes we show one of our prototypes.[15] It is a three-layered feed-forward network with only three X- and Y-components. One typical training run obtains the following results (figure 10 and figure 11).

The networks must be understood the following way: The first line above represents the X-vector of the respective agent; the next line forms a so called hidden layer and the last line below represents the respective action. The weight values between the lines are the representation of the self-image of the agent. Because in the mutual training processes the weight matrices of the nets are adjusted, not only the actions but also the self-image of the agents have to be corrected. The networks are of the feed forward type, i.e., the activation flow between the neurons only goes from the first line above via the hidden layer to the last line below. This last line has the function of an output layer.

By comparing the respective X- and Y-values of agents A and B one sees that indeed the action components in the Y-vectors correspond to the values of the according X-vectors. The criteria of convergence, defined above, are obviously fulfilled.

[14] This formula was proposed by Jörn Schmidt.

[15] The implementation was done by Ulf Ackermann and Moritz Balz.

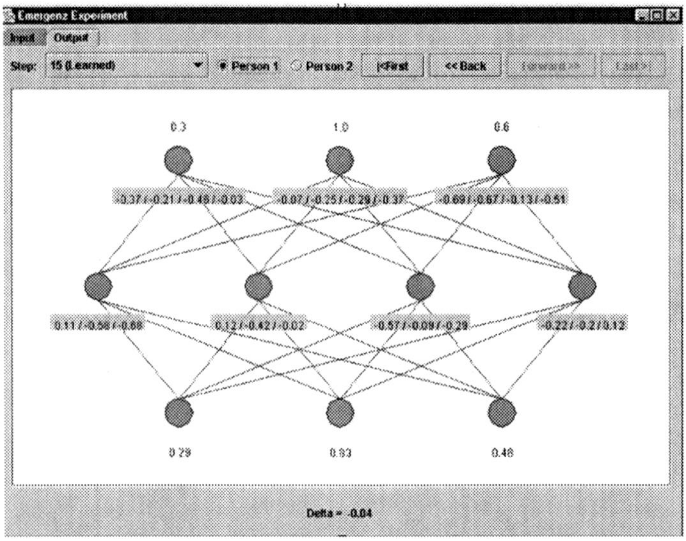

Figure 10. Learning result of person 1. The top layer is the personality vector of person 1. Each personal component is coded in the interval from 0 to 1

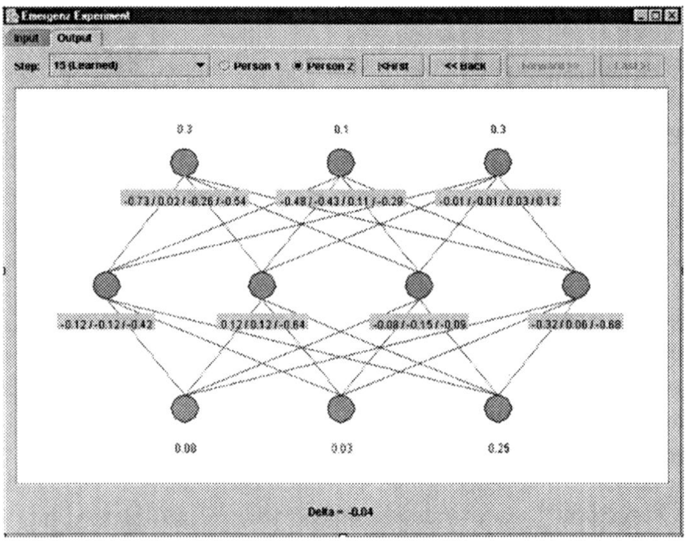

Figure 11. Learning result of person 2

b) The perception network PN

The PN is a hetero-associative net with two or more layers. The input layer of the PN of a person A is the X-vector of a person B, which the person A meets. The output layer is the Y-vector of A with respect to the person B.

PN of actor A:

$$
\begin{array}{c}
X_B \\
\downarrow \\
Y_{AB}
\end{array}
$$

Y_{AB} is again the action vector of A with respect to person B.

A and B mutually generate action vectors Y with respect to one another, as was described above. These vectors are rules of interaction insofar as A and B always both act according to their Y-vectors when they meet again. When these rules are established, the PN_s of both agents are trained to associate the X-vector of the other agent B with the own vector Y_{AB} (in the case of A); the same is the case after A has established a mutual rule with C, D and E. A then has 4 rules at its disposal that are "stored" in its PN via the training processes of associating a certain X-vector with the corresponding action vector.

"Hetero-associative" means the training with respect to a pair of different vectors. We use two different kinds of hetero-associative networks as PN. The first type is a feed-forward network, similar to the action network but with usually three or more layers (again depending on the size of the vectors). The training is done by using the back-propagation rule, one of the most powerful learning rules in neural networks:

$$
(4.3.7) \quad \delta_j = \begin{array}{l} f'_j(net_j)(t_j - o_j) \text{ if j is an output unit} \\ f'_j(net_j)_k(\delta_k w_{ik}) \text{ if j is a hidden unit} \end{array}
$$

The back propagation rule is basically just a generalized delta-rule.

The second type of PNs is a so called bi-directional-associative network (BAM). Its training is done in a quite different way, i.e. by using a certain form of matrix- and vector multiplication. Two vectors V and W are associated by multiplying X with a matrix M, obtaining

$$
(4.3.8) \quad V^*M = W
$$

Conversely, we obtain

$$
(4.3.9) \quad V^*W = M
$$

with $m_{ij} = v_{ij}{}^* w_j$ for the respective components of the two vectors and the matrix. (Technical details can be looked up in any textbook on neural networks. Note that * does not mean the usual matrix multiplication.)

If after establishing this order A meets B again (or C or D), then the PN of A is able to recognize B by taking his X-vector as input and by generating the according action vector Y_{AB} as output. A thus remembers B and is able to act according to the established rule.

When A meets a new person F, there are two possibilities:

a) F is not similar to any member of the group (*in the perception of A*!). In this case the PN of A will not recognize F; A and F will have to establish specific rules of behavior according to the procedure described above.

b) F is similar to a member of the group, say D.

Then the PN of A will generate the vector Y_{AD} when receiving the X-vector of F. In this case F will be perceived by A *as the same type as D*, although F is not identical with D (F is another person or agent respectively).

When A acts with Y_{AD}, F has to adjust his own Y-vector with respect to A; the adjusting process is not mutual but only the task of the newcomer F. The reason for this is the consideration that members of an already established group only typify a newcomer, whereas the newcomer has to adjust his behavior with respect to all members of the group.

Now the rules of interaction become *general* rules in the sense that they are valid not only for a particular agent B but also for all other agents that belong to the same type as B. In sociological terms, the rules are valid for all agents that belong to the same social type, i.e., that occupy the same social role. But that is just one possibility of interpretation. In any case, the agents now are able to typify, i.e. to abstract from individual peculiarities of other agents and to perceive them as representatives of a certain type.

A second example

The complete process just described can be demonstrated by another example.[16] We started with a group of five actors 4, 3, 2, 1, 0 with the respective X-vectors; this AN again has one hidden layer.

Actor 4: X-vector = (0.0, 0.6, 0.3, 0.0);
Y-.vectors with respect to
Actor 0 = (0.0, 0.4, 0.0, 0.3, 0.0)
Actor 1 = (0.0, 0.3, 0.2, 0.0, 0.0)
Actor 2 = (0.0, 0.6, 0.5, 0.2, 0.0)
Actor 3 = (0.0, 0.0, 0.6, 0.2, 0.0)

Actor 3: X-vector = (0.3, 0.2, 0.0, 0.1, 0.6);
Y-vectors with respect to
Actor 0 = (0.2, 0.1, 0.0, 0.1, 0.5)
Actor 1 = (0.0, 0.1, 0.0, 0.0, 0.0)
Actor 2 = (0.3, 0.1, 0.0, 0.5, 0.0)
Actor 4 = (03, 0.4, 0.0, 0.0, 0.6)

Actor 2: X-vector = (0.1, 0.3, 0.1, 0.6, 0.6);
Y-vectors with respect to

Actor 0 = (0.0, 0.0, 0.0, 0.2, 0.4)
Actor 1 = (0.0, 0.3, 0.0, 0.0, 0.1)

[16] Implemented by Simon Cohnitz

Actor 3 = (0.1, 0.2, 0.1, 0.0, 0.0)
Actor 4 = (0.1, 0.3, 0.0, 0.5, 0.6)

Actor 1: X-vector = (0.3, 0.1, 0.5, 0.4, 0.5);
Y-vectors with respect to
Actor 0 = (0.1, 0.0, 0.1, 0.3, 0.1)
Actor 2 = (0.2, 0.1, 0.4, 0.2, 0.0)
Actor 3 = (0.0, 0.0, 0.5, 0.3, 0.1)
Actor 4 = (0.3, 0.0, 0.1, 0.1, 0.5)

Actor 0: X-vector = (0.5, 0.3, 0.9, 0.8, 0.9)
Y-vectors with respect to
Actor 1 = (0, 2, 0.2, 0.2, 0.1, 0.1)
Actor 2 = (0.2, 0.0, 0.3, 0.1, 0, 1)
Actor 3 = (0.0, 0.0, 0.2, 0.1, 0.0)
Actor 4 = (0.2, 0.1, 0.3, 0.1, 0.1)

Y-vectors mean, as described, social rules of interaction. The group is socially structured in the sense that each actor knows how to behave towards another actor when meeting him again. This is done by the PN. In addition, as we already mentioned, it is possible to generate a social structure of the group in the sense that the group members are placed into a social hierarchy. This done by comparing the different Y-vectors the actors have generated for each other actor. If Y_{ij} designates the Y-vector of actor i with respect to actor j, then the social position P_i of actor i in the group is computed by

$$(4.3.10)\quad P_i = \frac{(\sum_i |Y_{ij}|)}{4}$$

In other words, the relative position of i is determined by the arithmetical mean value of the length of the Y-vectors. The reason is that the more dominant the *actions* of an actor are with respect to the other actors, and if they agree upon this dominance – that is the case in our model –, the more high is his ranking in the group. Visualized as a network the social structure of our group becomes

with the P-values for our actors

$P_4 = 0.62$; $P_3 = 0.51$; $P_2 = 0.46$; $P_1 = 0.51$; $P_0 = 0.35$.

The positions of the actors obviously are not very strictly differentiated in a stratified way.

Now an actor 5 was added to the group with the X-vector = (0.4, 0.1, 0.0, 0.1, 0.6).

The other actors had to typify him in order to insert him into the group and to generate X-vectors with respect to him. The results of the typifying processes were as follows ("type 3 etc." means that the new actor is typified as the same type as actor 3):

Actor 4 typifies 5 as one of type 3; the according Y-vector of 4 = (0.0, 0.0, 0.6, 0.2, 0.0)

Actor 3 typifies 5 as one of type 1 with a Y-vector = (0.0, 0.1, 0.0, 0.0, 0.0)

Actor 2 typifies 5 as type 3; Y-vector = (0.1, 0.2, 0.1, 0.0, 0.0)

Actor 1 typifies 5 as type 3; Y-vector = (0.0, 0.0, 0.5, 0.3, 0.1).

An exception is actor 0 who was not able to typify 5, that is to associate him with one of the other actors. The reason for this different behavior of actor 0 in comparison to the other actors is that of course each actor has a different weight matrix in his PN because each actor had to learn the four others, but not himself. The learning task and the result in form of weight matrices is different for all actors. Therefore, it is not to be expected that the actors always agree upon typifying. In this case the actor 0 has to interact with 5 via their mutual ANs. We see that the typifying result of actor 3 also is not the same as those of actors 4, 2, and 1. The reason is that actor 3 was not trained with his own X-vector while actor 5 was generated as a slight variation of actor 3. Actor 3, so to speak, was not able to recognize the similarity between himself and the newcomer. The other actors, with the exception of actor 0 could do this because they were trained with the X-vector of actor 3.

Experiments with this model, performed by Simon Cohnitz, obtained the following general result: the perception networks are able to typify newcomers with a percentage of about 0.8, if the X-vectors of the newcomers differed not "too much" from those X-vectors with which the perception networks of the members of the primordial group were trained – provided the original group is not larger than ca. 10 members. "Too much" means a difference of 0.4 or more in all components of the new X -vector with respect to all X-vectors of the original group members. The experiments also demonstrated that the typifying results became more general, i.e., more different actors became typified as the same type, the larger the group became via newcomers. This is exactly what human actors do: the more people they become acquainted with the more general become the types the people are attached to. In this sense the model is validated by everyday social experience. To be sure, the perception network does not distinguish between "personal" types, depending on personal characteristics, and "social" ones, depending on social roles, status etc. But this distinction can be easily implemented into the model.

At present we are experimenting with different possibilities how to place a newcomer if the former group members do not totally agree upon typifying him. One can imagine a majority vote, which would place in our example the newcomer 5 into type 3. If such solutions are satisfactory is a question of the empirical validity of this model. Further studies in this direction seem necessary.

Following the theoretical foundations of Mead and Berger/Luckmann it is apparently possible to construct models of the emergence of social order that do not have the shortcomings of RC. To be sure, the model is highly idealized in the sense that it does not claim *literal* empirical validity. It describes, so to speak, the mathematical essence of the emergence of social order via the processes of mutual adjustment of behavior, social learning and typifying. Yet there can be no doubt that these processes are the basis for all constructions of social order by real persons and not the abstract egoistical and rational entities of most RC-approaches. In particular the model allows to define in a mathematical way concepts like social types and processes of typifying. The methodical way of analyzing phylogenetic processes by looking to the according ontogenetic ones seems a fruitful approach not only in linguistics but in the social sciences too. In addition, the model is a very general one. Therefore, applications of this model are not only possible for research in the social and communicative sciences but also for robotics and probably Internet agents. In this sense the social sciences could stimulate other more technical disciplines.

On a first sight this model seems to have not much to do with communication. But if we remember the general definition of communication given in the first chapter one immediately sees that the establishing of social order is done by communicative processes: the interaction between the different actors consists of sending signals, i.e. performing certain actions that are received by the other actor – the receiver. The receiver evaluates the signal and answers with an own action; the first sender becomes a receiver. The meaning of these signals are a point attractor of the receiving actor, i.e. the answer in form of an action. This is quite literally the pragmatic definition of meaning by C. S. Peirce. Via the evaluation processes both sender and receiver are forced to adjust their self-image; accordingly the respective meanings of the signal change as long as no mutually accepted social rule of interaction is established. In other words, the establishing of social order is done by special mutually evaluated communicative processes that generate meaning by sending certain signals.

In contrast to the models described in the two preceding subchapters the communicating actors are not treated as black boxes like the cells in the different cellular automata. The weight matrix of the action net represents an internal self-image of the actors that has permanently to be adjusted according to the success of the actor's actions. In addition, the perception net represents the memory of the actors and therewith the ability of remembering and typifying. Therefore, this model is nearly a complete representation of the complex process of communication: both social and cognitive aspects are taken into account. We shall describe similar models in the next chapters.

4.4. SOCIAL DIMENSIONALITY AND COMMUNICATION: THE THEORY OF SOCIAL DIFFERENTIATION

Communicative processes are embedded, as one might say, in social situations that are characterized by specific rules. These rules determine the behavior of the communicators and define the social dimension of the respective communication. In order to formulate a precise, that is a mathematical theory of communication it would be favorable to define a measure for social situations with respect to the impact of the according social rules on the embedded communicative processes. Such a measure can indeed be derived from certain well established theoretical assumptions about the evolution of societies, namely the well known theory of social differentiation. Therefore, it is necessary to reconstruct this theory for the purpose of our analysis.

The theory of social differentiation goes back to Herbert Spencer and was reformulated in terms of social systems theory, e.g., by Luhmann (1984) and Habermas (1981, II). The core of the differentiation theory is that the evolution of all societies, if it occurs at all, takes place in three stages of different forms of social differentiation. The first stage is the so called segmentary differentiation that is characteristic for early tribe societies. "Segmentary" means that the fundamental form of social structure that determines all social interactions is the differentiation of these societies in social "segments", i.e., rather autonomous parts of the society that are defined by kinship relations. The social identity of a member of such a tribal society is primarily defined by his belonging to a certain segment, i.e., a clan. Note that these clans are consisting of people who are either by common ancestors or by marriage directly or indirectly kindred. The social segments the tribal society consists of are rather equally entitled, although there is often one clan who is a bit more prominent than the others. Usually a member of this clan is the occupant of the role of chieftain for the whole tribe. Differentiations inside the clans are mostly orientated to biological differences like sex, age, or other physical characteristics.

Most of the known societies remained in the stage of segmentary differentiation or in a transition form of so called "stratified, tribal societies". Those societies that evolved into the next stage via the transition form generated the new social structure of stratified differentiation. This term means that now another additional form of structuring evolves that allows the distinction between socially "higher" and "lower" persons. In other words, with the emergence of stratified differentiated societies social classes or social strata respectively evolved that determined the social position of the individuals. The belonging to a certain clan or family was still important but in addition the placement of this family in one of the different classes defined that status of the individual, i.e., its social identity. Classical examples of these stratified class societies (Eder 1976) were the ancient cultures of, e.g., China, Egypt, Rome, Medieval Europe and the Islamic societies of the Middle Ages. In contrast to the early tribal societies these new forms are characterized by a fundamental social inequality with its well known negative consequences. In the words of Habermas (1981, II), these new societies gained in the dimension of systemic steering capacity, i.e., action capacity, and lost in the dimension of social peace.[17]

It is important to note that the emergence of a new form of social differentiation had not the effect that the old form(s) vanished. On the contrary, the new forms gave the respective societies an additional form of differentiation with the remaining of the old forms. These were, so to speak, inserted in the new forms, as one can see in the case of the combination of segmentary and stratified differentiation. The main form became the differentiation into vertically ordered classes; inside the classes the segmentary differentiation remained in form of kinship, that is families or clans. The feudal wars in Medieval Europe among the noble families about the position of the king are a well known example for the continuous importance of segmentary differentiation, embedded in the new form of stratified one.[18]

The transformation from segmentary differentiated tribal societies to stratified class societies happened only seldom, as we remarked. Historians are still debating how many such higher evolved societies occurred in history, but as far as we know most scholars agree that there were not more than approximately twenty cases. The transformation to the next – and until now last – state of social differentiation, namely that of functional differentiation, happened even only once in history, i.e., at the beginning of the European Modern Times at approximately 1500 AD. Due to different social factors that cannot be explained in this study (cf. Klüver, 2002) in modern Europe another form of social differentiation evolved, that is the emergence of functional social subsystems. These subsystems, of which the most important ones are economy, i.e., modern capitalism, policy, and science, are characterized by a certain societal function, which is their reason of existence, and by a functional autonomy. The last term means that these subsystems operate according to a special systemic logic that cannot principally be influenced by their social environment.

Take for example the functional subsystem of capitalistic economy. Its societal function is, of course, the material reproduction of society, i.e., the production and distribution of all those material goods that are necessary for living, including a living in luxury. In the Middle Ages the economical logic was vastly influenced by, in particular, religious norms, e.g., the norm of a "fair profit" or the prohibition of financial business for Christians. Modern capitalism is, among other features, characterized by the absence of such norms. The capitalistic subsystem of modern societies only operates according to the maxim of profit maximizing and this maxim cannot be disputed by the environment of the economical system. The operations in functional specialized subsystems are only evaluated according to the success these operations generate. The same characteristic is valid for, e.g., the scientific subsystem whose function is the production of new knowledge. The logic of these operations, i.e., the scientific methods and theories, cannot be influenced by the

[17] The permanent class struggles between Patricians and Plebeians in ancient Rome are one of the most famous examples of the social unrest in these societies.

[18] Shakespeare's plays about the continuous struggles between the feudal families of Lancaster and York are still the best illustration of these feudal wars of which we know.

environment of science. In this sense these functional subsystems are "functionally autonomous".[19]

As in the case of the emerging of stratified differentiation the old forms of differentiation did not vanish when functional differentiation evolved (cf. e.g. Hondrich, 1987). The vertically placed social classes or strata respectively still exist – and that means social inequality. But they are not longer characteristic for the basic structure of a modern society because they determine the social position of an individual only with respect to a certain subsystem. The question is meaningless if a medical doctor belongs to a higher class than a qualified computer programmer from, e.g., Microsoft. Because their social professions belong to different subsystems only within these subsystems can the question of "higher" or "lower" be decided. As the doctor is in a higher position than a nurse, the programmer is in a higher position than a care-taker.

The importance of segmentary differentiation has lessened but this form did not vanish either. To be sure, the importance of families for the definition of a social status and social identity is not very great. But other types of segmentary differentiation have emerged that are again placed inside the functional subsystems, i.e., they are not decisive for the whole society. The economical subsystem, for example, is segmentary differentiated in specific branches of production and within these branches in firms; the scientific subsystem is segmentary differentiated in scientific disciplines, universities and other institutions of research; the political subsystem is segmentary differentiated in political parties and so on. In modern societies, therefore, we have a combination of three different forms of social differentiation with the functional one as the basic form that characterizes the whole society and with the older two forms as social structures that are decisive for the respective subsystem.

Another important distinction must be mentioned. A social actor usually belongs to only one subsystem in the sense that he is able to act, mainly by occupying a certain professional position, in an active manner. A medical doctor as an active member of the medical subsystem is only able to do this in this subsystem, and he is not able to socially act in an active manner in, e.g., the educational system.[20] Yet the doctor has the right to "passively" participate in each other subsystem. For example, he participates as a consumer in the economical system, he participates as a voter in the political subsystem, and he does the same as the client of a lawyer in the legal subsystem. Accordingly a lawyer is able to actively act in the legal subsystem, he participates as a patient in the medical subsystem and so forth. In other words, the functional differentiation of modern societies has as one important consequence the fact of "universal inclusion" (Luhmann, 1984): Each member of

[19] That is of course not to say that these systems are isolated from the whole society or that they are independent from other subsystems. Science for example needs the financial subsidy from the economical and the political subsystem. The subsystems are functional autonomous but they are not self-sufficient.

[20] We exclude some special cases like university professors who do both research and teaching.

such a society, regardless in which subsystem he actively operates, has the right to universal participation in all other subsystems. Therefore, an individual is either in an active role, like a medical doctor when curing patients, or in a client role like the patients. Luhmann (loc. cit.) states that each situation is determined by occupants of active roles and occupants of complementary roles like lawyers and clients, teachers and pupils, doctors and patients.

Before we refer these general theoretical considerations to our subject of communication, we have to translate these theoretical insights into more mathematical terms (for details see Klüver, 2002; Klüver and Schmidt, 1999b):

One can visualize a segmentary differentiated society as a line that is divided in distinct parts by the respective segments. Each individual belongs to exactly one segment. Because this type of differentiation is the only one by which the whole society is structured and because, as we said, the segments are principally equal one can understand these societies as a one-dimensional space with the segments as disjoint subsets.

The addition of the stratified differentiation can be understood as the unfolding of a second dimension, i.e. a vertical one. The distinction between classes and by that the placement of the individual class members as "higher" and "lower" transforms the one-dimensional spaces of tribal societies into spaces of two dimensions, that is a plane. Finally, the emerging of functional differentiation transforms these two-dimensional spaces into three-dimensional ones, that is spaces which are mathematically equivalent to the three-dimensional space of our perception. In this sense we can understand societal evolution as the successive unfolding of social dimensions.[21]

When speaking of differentiating structures or dimensions of social spaces we use, strictly speaking, terms of top down modeling, that is description terms for the whole social system we speak of. According to our preference of bottom up models, which we explained in the second chapter, we have to translate these "global" terms in those of local processes. Sociologically speaking such a translation means the according introduction of terms of social action theory.

Let us first consider the meaning of physical spatial dimensions for our form of perception. The three spatial dimensions allow us to "categorize" (Kant) each object or event according to the distinctions "before – behind me" (first dimension), "above – below me" (second dimension) and "left – right of me" (third dimension). In other words, the structuring of the space of perception as a three-dimensional space allow us to distinguish different objects and events by their distinction with respect to one or all dimensions.

Now consider the first dimension of segmentary differentiation. One the one hand a particular segment determines the social identity of each individual and on the other hand it defines a boundary between those individuals to whom a

[21] There is an interesting parallel to this idea of the unfolding of dimensions. Recent physical theories, in particular the so-called super string theory, describe the first phases of the evolution of the physical universe as the unfolding of three spatial and one temporal dimension (cf. Greene 1999).

certain individual belongs and those individuals that are "strange", i.e., who do not belong to one's own social group. For a particular individual, therefore, segmentary differentiation means the distinction between "strangers" and "people of the same kin" or "people who belong to me". The segmentary differentiation can thus be interpreted as the identification of all people one meets according to that basic difference of "strange – belonging to oneself".[22]

The second dimension of stratified differentiation is of course the distinction between "socially higher than oneself – socially lower – or socially equal". Therefore, societies with both segmentary and stratified differentiation allow the identification of any individual by placing him in a square matrix, i.e. a two-dimensional grid, perceived from the perspective of a certain individual X:

	strange	*familiar*
higher	*ind.A*	*ind.B*
lower	*ind.C*	*ind.D*

Thus individual A is strange to X but socially higher, individual D is familiar to X and socially lower and so forth. For the sake of simplicity we omit the cases of social equality.

For translating the "local" meaning of the functional differentiation as a third dimension into the social perception of a particular individual one has to remember Luhmann's principle of universal inclusion (see above). Each social individual in a certain action situation either occupies an active role, e.g., via his particular profession, or he is in a client role, that is a passive one. Therefore, functional differentiation means the introduction of the third distinction "active – passive" and that allows the identification of each person in this dimension.

Keeping in mind that in modern societies all kinds of differentiation are valid, we can represent each individual by a triple (X, Y, Z), X being either "strange" or "familiar", Y being "lower" or "higher" or "equal" and Z being "active" or "passive". If we follow contemporary social systems theory by assuming that these three types of differentiation structurally describe a modern society in a complete manner then we can assume that in particular the social dimension of communicative situations can be completely described that way (see below).

We transformed these considerations into a computational model, namely a cellular automaton, which is optimized by a genetic algorithm (for details cf. Klüver, 2002: Klüver and Schmidt, 1999b). The research question was two-fold: On the one hand we were interested in the problem why the unfolding of the second and third dimension happened only seldom and in the case of functional differentiation only once. On the other hand we wished to know if the insight of

[22] Cultural anthropology has discovered overwhelming material how social rules of interaction operate in such cases – how to interact with strangers, how to interact with people of the own clan and last but not least how to construct rules for making strangers „a bit more familiar", for example by marriage or trade (cf. e.g. Habermas loc.cit.).

Habermas (loc.cit.) could be confirmed in a formal model that higher stages of social evolution generated in all known cases an increase of steering capacity as well as an increase of social unrest. Is this perhaps a necessary consequence of the unfolding of an additional dimension?

To cut a long story short, we were able to answer both questions by combining them. The basic assumption of the model is that a social system measures its success in two "dimensions" (not to be understood as the social dimensions defined above): On the one hand a social system is dependent on its steering capacity, i.e., its capability to deal with problems that can be defined as environmental demands – for example changes in climate, natural resources, competition with other societies and so forth. On the other hand a social system must maintain some form of social order and rest: A society that is in permanent disorder by civil wars, class struggle and other forms of political unrest is hardly successful in one of its main functions, i.e., to guarantee safety, stability and emotional familiarity to all its members. Therefore, we had to assume that on the one hand the steering capacity is increased by the introduction of additional social dimensions; history confirms that. On the other hand we had to assume that societies try to maintain social order, which may be in opposition to the goal of maximizing the steering capacity. For visualization purposes we show the figure of one simulation that demonstrates a "successful" evolution, i.e., the unfolding of all social dimensions:

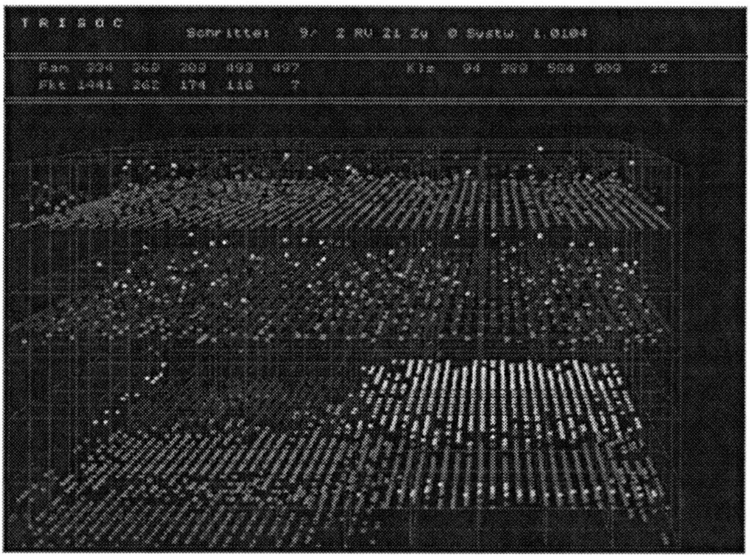

Figure 12. Three dimensions of social differentiation

Figure 12 shows the three dimensions of social differentiation, where each level separately represents one dimension. The lowest level shows the social relations of the social actors, each represented by a single cell, with respect to segmentary differentiation; the middle level accordingly shows the relations with respect to the stratified differentiation, and the highest level those with respect to functional differentiation. The strength of these relations is represented by the geometrical nearness of the cells on the CA-grid: the nearer two cells are the more closely their social relations are and vice versa. The state of the cells represent different social roles the actors are occupying.

The basic assumption of the model is that the generation of certain social roles means the institutionalization of according forms of division of labor and that the occupants of social roles are performing their tasks better than such individuals who operate in an unspecialized manner, i.e., who do not occupy a certain role. In consequence of role generation the steering capacity of the system increases, i.e., its capability to deal with "external" problems, that is problems posed to the system as environmental demands. Yet because the generation of new social roles brings some kind of unrest into the society, e.g., the emergence of social inequality, traditional social ties between the individuals lose their strength and as a consequence social rest will decrease.

The figure demonstrates that on the lowest level and also on the second level the social integration with respect to these forms of differentiation decreased indeed. There are many empty cells between those cells that represent social actors, which means that the social distances between the actors has become rather great. The system obviously paid for its success in unfolding all three dimensions with loss of social integration. Such a process is, for example, well known with respect to "modern", i.e., three- dimensional societies: It is hardly possible to enumerate all the critical authors who deplored the loss of traditions and the increasing social distance between social actors in these societies.[23] Because in all simulations such phenomena of increasing social distances could be observed we may safely assume that these are indeed a necessary consequence of social evolution.

Our numerous simulations also demonstrated that the unfolding of two or even three dimensions only seldom occurred. In most cases the system obtained no more than an initial unfolding of the second dimension and never generated the third one. This result is in accord to history, i.e., the emergence of "stratified tribal societies", which remained in this stage of evolution. Even cases of social regression could often be observed: the system began to unfold the second dimension but not only stopped this process but even went back into the stage of just segmentary differentiation. Such cases of social regression are also well known from history; one of the probably most famous cases is that of the Mayan societies that for reasons still not fully discovered regressed from the stage of stratified differentiation back to the initial stage of just segmentary differentiation.

---

[23] A famous exception to such critical interpretation of modern societies are Marx and Engels who in their "Manifesto of the Communist Party" (*Manifest der kommunistischen Partei*) rather early observed – and prognosticated – these processes and accepted them as a necessary consequence of social progress. In fact, they even welcomed them.

Mathematically speaking the main reason for the behavior of our artificial society and probably also of "real" societies is the fact that such systems have to orientate themselves to two goals at the same time. These goals are, as mentioned, the maintaining of social rest and order on the one hand and the increasing of their steering capacity on the other hand. Because these "internal" and "external" goals are in some sense opposing the systems have to solve a classical optimization problem. Increasing one goal value means the decreasing of the other and vice versa. Apparently in real societies as well as in our artificial model the actors prefer to live in a social world of rest and familiarity. Only if the environmental problems become so great that the old ways are not sufficient any more then people will accept social change and the according unrest.

The evolution of human societies is one of the most complex problems of contemporary science and we shall not discuss it here any more (see Klüver 2002). Our subject, after all, is the analysis of communication. We mainly introduced the concept of social dimensions because we think that we can derive a theoretically confirmed measure for the social context of communicative processes by using this concept. This is the subject of the next subchapter.

4.5. THE SD-PARAMETER

Before we define the "social degree" (sd) parameter some methodical preliminary remarks are necessary:

Communicative processes between human actors always occur in a certain social context and are partly determined by it. That is of course a truism. Yet the social rules that characterize the social context do not totally determine the communicative behavior of the communicators. In most cases the rules leave a space of freedom for the communicators with the consequence that the factual communicative processes also depend on individual factors. One of these factors we named the cognitive dimension of communication and we shall deal with it in the next chapter. But certainly there are additional factors like the emotional state of the communicators, disruptions by other humans and events in the environment of the factual communication. Therefore, a mathematical measure for the social context that will be expressed by the concept of the sd-parameter is no guarantee for an exact prediction of factual communicative processes: it does not take into account the individual factors just mentioned. When we use the term of "measure", we mean just that it is possible to classify communicative situations by their sd-values in a sociological sense. In addition, the sd- value of a certain communicative situation allows to determine the degree of complexity the according communicative processes can *principally* generate. If we remind of the definition of (dynamical) complexity given in the second chapter we postulate that the sd-parameter can predict the *principal* complexity of behavior or dynamics respectively that the specific social context allows. It is a question of the mentioned additional factors if the communicative processes are realized in the most possible complex manner or if the communicative process only generates a kind of simple dynamics. In this sense the sd-parameter is akin to the ordering parameters that we described in chapter 2.1. Therefore, one may call the sd-parameter a communicative ordering parameter. The impact of certain sd-values on the communicative dynamics will be given via a hypothesis of the determination of cognitive processes (of the communicators) by the sd- values of the social context:

The lower the values of the sd-parameter are the greater is the degree of complexity of the resulting communicative processes and vice versa. "Complexity" of communicative processes must be understood, according to the general definition of communication, as a) complex interactive dynamics of the interactive system, b) complex cognitive dynamics as a result of the interactive dynamics, and c) a complex dynamics of the whole process as a resulting interdependency of the interactive and the cognitive dynamics. This hypothesis will below be explained in more detail.

The definition of the sd-parameter relies upon the characterization of social systems as three-dimensional social spaces, described in the last subchapter. To be sure, we described early societies as social systems with only one dimension as a "global" characterization of these societies. Yet looking at communicative processes from a micro point of view it is easy to see that in practically all communicative processes all three dimensions have to be taken into account, regardless of the type of societies. One can understand this by assuming that the dimensions of stratified differentiation and that of functional differentiation are in these societies effective on a micro level but not on the macro level of the whole society. By reminding of footnote 21 we can say that these dimensions are only unfolded on small (social) distances but not on large ones. According to this concept of three-dimensionality we define the sd- parameter as a linear combination with respect to the three dimensions.[24] In other words, a specific value of the sd-parameter is given by the sum of the particular values in the three dimensions.

a) Consider the first dimension, i.e., that of segmentary differentiation. When we translate that concept into the distinction between "familiar" and "strange" and when we take into account that two persons in a factual communication are not either familiar or strange but "more or less" familiar or strange respectively then it is easy to imagine that two communicators can be characterized in a communicative situation by their respective degree of belonging to the same social segment. Take for example two communicators who both are interested in football but not to the same degree.[25] Let us say that A is very interested in football; he regularly goes to football games and is a fan of a certain club. The degree of A as a member of the social segment "football fan" can be measured as e.g. 0.9, if we measure this degree $sd_{A_{seg}}$ in an interval $0 \leq sd_{seg} \leq$

---

[24] The term "linear combination" names the mathematical technique of representing a vector in a vector space. For example, a three-dimensional vector $v = (x, y, z)$ can be represented as $a^*x + b^*y + c^*z$, if a, b, and c describe the proportions of v with respect to the unit vectors (1, 0, 0), (0, 1, 0), and (0, 0, 1)

[25] "Football" is used here in the European meaning of the term; US-readers can understand it as "soccer".

1. sd_{seg} means of course the segmentary dimension of the sd-parameter. The other communicator B is interested in football too, but only to a lesser degree. He sometimes watches games on television and reads about these games in the Monday edition of his newspaper, but not always, and he does not care about a particular club. Let us say that the degree of B is $sd_{B_{seg}} = 0.2$.

When A and B meet to discuss football then obviously the communication will not last long or, in other words, the communicative process will not generate a complex dynamics. B knows not very much about the present state of the national football league (in Germany the *Bundesliga*) and he is not very interested to discuss a subject for a longer time that holds only minor interest for him (remember the definition of relevance in chapter 3). Yet B knows enough to follow A's eager remarks about certain players and the particular club of which A is a fan. Therefore, the conversation can continue for some time, although not very long.

If one tries to combine the values of A and B as one numerical value as a measure of the communicative situation, then of course different techniques are possible. We use a very simple one, namely the (absolute) difference. It has the advantage that it takes into account the individual values of both communicators under the assumption that the factual communicative process is determined by a compromise between the two individual values, i.e., a compromise between the respective interests the communicators have to discuss this subject. The sd-value for this specific situation is then

$$(4.5.1) \quad sd_{seg} = |sd_{Aseg} - sd_{Bseg}| = 0.7,$$

which is a rather high value. Accordingly the cognitive and communicative dynamics will be a comparatively simple one.

If there are three or more communicators involved the general definition for the segmentary dimension of the sd-parameter has to take into account that the social degree of the situation is determined by all communicators. There may be, in our football example, communicators with great interest in this subject, others with a medium one and those with only little interest. We can say that these communicators are characterized by different degrees of belonging with respect to the social segment "football". The simplest way to define the sd-value for more than two communicators is, of course, the arithmetical mean for each pair of communicators A and B. Thus we obtain

$$(4.5.2) \quad sd_{seg} = \Sigma_i sd_{iseg}/n = \Sigma_I \, |(A - B)_I| \, /n$$

if there are n pairs of communicators involved.

Note that the value of sd_{seg} is not constant for certain communicators but varies according to the subject of the communication or the according social segment respectively. In our football example the sd-value is rather high because of the great interest of A and the little interest of B for the segment "football". But if we assume that both communicators have a great interest in chess and that both rank with sd_{seg}-values of about 0.8, the communication will become rather complex, if external factors will not disturb it.[26]

b) In the second dimension the social communication context is, of course, measured by the vertical distance between two communicators. If we measure the social position of one communicator A with respect to that of the other communicator B, then it is possible to define a "stratified measure" sd_{st} by the degree in which one communicator is able to influence the other via its social position. If for example communicator A has with respect to communicator B the value $sd_{Ast} = 0.9$ and B has $sd_{Bst} = 0.3$ (with respect to A) then A's influence on B can be measured again as the difference between the two individual values, in this case obviously $|0.9 - 0.3| = 0.6$. As we again obtain a rather high value the interpretation is that A can "force" B to accept a certain theme and to act accordingly. Consider for example the communicative case between a sergeant and a private in an army. The sergeant usually gives orders and the private's answers contain seldom more than "yessir". Such a communication can be defined as a very simple one because the private will not generate complex cognitive dynamics. Accordingly the sd-value is quite large.

Note that these values are defined by the respective social positions, i.e., the social status of the communicators. Individual factors like rhetoric abilities are not taken into account because the sd-values "only" measure the social structure of the communicative situation.[27]

In the case of more than two communicators we characterize the whole situation again via the arithmetical mean for all sd_{st}–values with respect to all pairs of communicators. Thus we obtain the general definition for the stratified dimension

$$(4.5.4) \quad sd_{st} = \Sigma_i sd_{ist} / n,$$

if there are n pairs i of communicators.

In other words, the smaller sd_{st} is for a given situation the more socially equal are the communicators and vice versa. Note that the restriction for the segmentary dimension (cf. footnote 26) is not necessary for this dimension. It is only the social difference that counts regardless if the communicators have high or low sd-degrees in the vertical dimension.

---

26 Obviously this definition has a special weakness: If both communicators are not interested in a specific subject, that is if their degrees of belonging to a certain social segment are small or even zero, then the difference of their sd-values will be small too and the complexity of their communication should be great. That is an absurd consequence if none of them wishes to talk about the particular subject. But in such a situation no communication would occur at all or the communicators would chose another subject in which at least one of them is interested. Therefore, the definition above and the general hypothesis assume that at least one of the communicators has a significant high degree of belonging.

27 In a course on communication science several students seriously believed that in a situation like that of the sergeant and the private it should be possible for the private to argue if he must accept the order. These students obviously did not understand the "objectivity" of social constraints.

c) For the definition of the third dimension of the sd-parameter it is useful to take an example where the communication is determined by the distinction of active and passive roles or, in the terms of Luhmann, the distinction between the occupant of an action role and the occupant of a client role. Consider the case of the communication between a medical doctor and a patient. Let us assume that both communicators are socially approximately equal, e.g., the doctor and an engineer as his patient. In this case the situation is characterized by $sd_{st} = 0.1$ or even $sd_{st} = 0$ (if both have positional values that are nearly equal then the according sd_{st}-value is very small). Both the doctor and his patient belong to a high degree to the same social segment, in this case the domain or subsystem respectively of medicine – the doctor because of his profession and the patient because of his strong interest in getting cured. Therefore, the sd_{seg}-value also is rather small. The main difference between the two communicators certainly is the amount of knowledge on the subject of illness, because the doctor is an expert in this field and the patient an interested layman. The same consideration is valid for all communications between occupants of action roles and those of client roles.

By generalizing these considerations about any communicative situation, i.e., not only those that are characterized by the difference between action and client roles, it is plausible to measure the sdf-value of a communicative situation as the difference of knowledge the two communicators have with respect to the subject of the communication – in this case a medical communication about the possible disease of the patient. For the sake of simplicity one may think of such knowledge as a set of according concepts and their relations, i.e., as a semantical network. We shall come back to the concept of semantical networks in later chapters; here it is sufficient to remember the examples of semantical networks that we gave in the third chapter. Mathematically speaking such networks can be defined as subsets of a set $C \times C$, if C is the set of all concepts one communicator has at his disposal on a certain subject. In other terms, semantical networks are sets of ordered pairs of concepts. If we call a certain semantical network Nw, then $Nw \subseteq C \times C$.

The definition of the sd_f-value of a certain communicative situation can be done the same way as the definitions for the other two dimensions, namely as the difference of knowledge between the two communicators. That difference in turn can be represented by the difference between the respective networks.

If we assume for our medical example that the medical network(s) of the doctor that it contains about 100 concepts with respect to the probable type of disease of his patient and if we further assume that the according network of his patient, who has informed himself a little about that particular disease, consists of ca. 20 concepts, then the difference between the doctor and the patient with respect to that subject is 80 concepts or as a measure in the interval between 0 and 1 the difference is 0.8.

According to this rather high value it can be assumed that the communication will be rather simple, i.e., the doctor explains his own assumptions about the illness and the patient will – usually – accept the diagnosis. Note that "simple" does not necessarily mean that the conversation will take not much time because with some patients the doctor will need some time to persuade them with respect to his diagnosis and in particular his therapy.

Yet for some technical reasons that are not important here, the simple arithmetical difference between the size of the networks is not suited for computing the sd-value in this dimension. Therefore, in contrast to the definitions of the other two dimensions we use instead the quotient of the two numbers of size.

In general the sd-value for the functional dimension can then be defined for two communicators A and B as

$$(4.5.5) \quad sd_f = 1 - |Nw_A| \,/\, |Nw_B|,$$

if $|Nw_A|$ designates the set theoretical power of the network of communicator A, i.e., the number of concepts of the network, and if $|Nw_A| \leq |Nw_B|$.

In the case of more than two communicators we take again the arithmetical mean of the sdf-values for all pairs of communicators. Thus we obtain the general definition

$$(4.5.6) \quad sd_f = \Sigma_i \, sd_{if}/n,$$

if there are n pairs i of communicators.

This definition of the sd-value in the functional dimension must also take into account the case where no communicator has much knowledge with respect to the particular subject and hence the difference between them is rather small. In this case there are two possibilities: either the communicators do not communicate at all about this subject, which means no communicative dynamics occurs. Or the communicators talk a lot without knowing much but without perceiving that fact either. In everyday experience one perceives such situations not seldom. If that is the case then our general hypothesis is again valid, i.e., small sd-values generate complex dynamics. It is not important that such conversations would seem fairly absurd to an external observer. The term "complex" dynamics does not take into regard the content or the sense of the communication.

Note that as in the case of the segmentary dimension the sd-value in the functional dimension depends on the particular theme of the communication. The doctor and his patient may be both interested in football and may even be fans of the same club. In that case their knowledge would be approximately equal and accordingly the sd-value in the functional dimension would be very small.

Remember that we defined the whole sd-parameter as a linear combination of the particular parameter values with respect to the three different dimensions. The reason for this definition is simply that we represent a communicative situation or its social context respectively as a part of a social space that in turn is mathematically defined as a vector space.[28] We mentioned above that the representation of vectors is

[28] In chapter three we defined "degree of information" as the difference of two vectors by using the same mathematical terminology.

usually done via the formation of a linear combination. By following this established technique we simply have to sum up the different values given by the equations (1), (4) and (6). For normalization purposes we again take the arithmetical mean and obtain

$$(4.5.7) \quad \mathrm{sd} = \Sigma_i \mathrm{sd}_i/3.$$

The sd-value obviously is the smaller the smaller the differences are between the communicators with respect to the different dimensions and vice versa. If sd = 0, the communicators are in all practical aspects equal, i.e., they belong to the same degree to the respective social segment, their social positions are equal too and they have approximately the same knowledge on the particular subject at their disposal. If sd = 1, the opposite holds: the communicators belong to distinct segments, they are placed in a hierarchical order with the effect that only one communicator can influence the other and only one communicator has at his disposal some knowledge about the subject of the communication. To be sure, such a situation is not very probable because one can hardly imagine why such totally different persons would communicate at all, in particular if they belong to different segments. Therefore, in reality the extreme cases will be with sd-values that are very large but unequal to one.

When one remembers the hypothesis mentioned above of the impact of sd-values on the communicative dynamics it is rather plausible that high sd-values indeed generate only simple dynamics. If two communicators are very different with respect to a) the social segments they belong to, they have not much in common to discuss. Accordingly only simple cognitive processes will be generated by the communicative situation and the conversation will not take much time. If two communicators are very different with respect to social status, then the communicator with higher social status will frequently give only orders or will expect that the other accepts his own remarks because of the difference in status. The communication will generate again only simple cognitive dynamics and accordingly only simple forms of interaction.[29] Finally, if the difference in knowledge between two communicators is very great then the communication will be only simple. A medical doctor just tells the patient his diagnosis and gives certain advice for therapy. The patient may think a lot about the diagnosis with respect to his own life but these cognitive processes usually do not determine the dynamics of the communication between doctor and patient. Again, high values generate simple dynamics. It is easy to think about converse examples with low sd-values.

Extreme cases with very high sd-values are typical for all kinds of hierarchically structured organizations like the army, prisons, or authoritarian churches – "totalitarian institutions", as Foucault named such forms of social order. An example is

[29] To be sure, there are often situations where the communicator with higher social status will offer the other a situation of equality, e.g. if a manager meets his young assistant at a bar. But the communicator with the lower status will always know, at least if he is socially intelligent, that this equality is rather dangerous for him and must not be taken too literally.

the above mentioned communication between a sergeant and a private that consists only of commands by the sergeant and the "yessir" by the private. It is easy to see that in all dimensions the sd-values are extremely high, with the exception of the first dimension, i.e., the belonging to the same social segment of the army. But even in that case the degree of belonging is different, at least in armies like that of Germany: The sergeant usually is a professional soldier with an according high degree of belonging to the army, the private has only to serve for a short time and accordingly his degree of belonging is much lower. Very small values of the sd-parameter are in contrast typical for situations with symmetrical relations. Social organizations that are characterized by mainly symmetrical relations may be named as "democratic", although not only in a political sense but also with respect to the distribution of knowledge and the according competences.

If one accepts the theoretical assumption that each social situation is completely characterized by its three-dimensional frame (Luhmann loc.cit.), then the sd-parameter also completely characterizes communicative situations, as far as the social context determines the situation. Yet empirically real communicative processes are in a social sense not only determined by their sociological characteristics, as we mentioned in the beginning of this subchapter, but by another important factor, that is social practice. Consider the difference between the two following communicative situations:

Situation 1: A pair of (young) lovers is sitting on a bench in a park on a beautiful summer evening (perhaps they are talking about the evening star as in chapter three). According to the results above the situation is characterized by a sd-value near 0, because the lovers are nearly equal in all important *social* aspects. As they have all of the evening for themselves and nobody is pressing them it is easy to imagine that the conversation between the lovers can go on and on, interrupted only by interactions of a non verbal kind. In particular one can imagine that the loving pair speaks about all topics that are of common interest to them or even only to one of them. Thus the lovers generate a communicative process that not only lasts quite long but in addition causes rather complex cognitive processes.[30] This is a situation according to a low value of the sd-parameter.

Situation 2: Two owners of a small software firm are discussing if they should accept the buying offer of a big firm. The owners have to make their decision within the next hours, which is not much considering the importance of the decision they have to make. The sd-value of the situation is again very low, if one assumes (a) that the two partners belong to the same social segment, i.e., the firm, to the same degree, (b) that they are social equals, and (c) that their knowledge about their firm and the consequences of their respective decisions also is equal. In these aspects the situation is socially and mathematically the same as situation 1. But the communication and the underlying cognitive processes in situation 2 will be,

---

[30] "Complex" means here again, as usual in this book, long trajectories of interaction and cognitive processes. It is not assumed that the conversation of the two young people necessarily contains a lot of cognitively difficult topics.

of course, much simpler than in situation 1 because the two owners have not much time, that is they have to act in a rather short time. One can imagine that they will just discuss the negative consequences if they do not sell and what conditions they could get if they try to bargain with the big firm. Therefore, despite the low sd-values in the social dimensions the resulting communicative dynamics will be comparatively simple.

These two examples demonstrate that the communicative dynamics is not only dependent on the respective sd-values of the social context but also on the time the communicators have at their disposal before they have to act in a specific manner as a result of the communication. Luhmann (loc. cit.) made a well known distinction between communication and action by defining action as the closure of communication. In the two examples such actions as a closure may be the decision to sell the firm or, in the case of the lovers, to go to bed together. The lovers have all the time before they decide whether they go to their sleeping room or not; the owners have only few time before they have to act.

If we generalize these examples then it is apparently necessary to introduce an additional factor to the previous definition of the sd-Parameter. The time the communicators have at their disposal is not an individual factor but it also is a social characteristic of the communicative situation. The two examples above illustrate that point: It is a social characteristic, at least in Western societies, that economical decisions have to be made rather quickly and that social actors in the subsystem of economy have to take this rule into account. It is again a social characteristic of situation 1, at least also in Western cultures that, e.g., the families of two lovers have no right to interfere (if the lovers are adults, of course) and to leave the lovers as much time as they wish. We can name this time factor as ta – "time to act" – and define $0 \leq \text{ta} \leq 1$. $\text{ta} = 1$ means that the communicators have as much time at their disposal as they wish, notwithstanding the fact that all communications can last only finite time. $\text{ta} = 0$ means that the communicators have practically no time at all before they have to act; the above example of the communication between the sergeant and the private is such a situation because the private has immediately to carry out the orders of the sergeant.

Apparently the time factor cannot decrease the social values of the sd- parameter. In the most favorable case, i.e., $\text{ta} = 1$, only the social characteristics of the situation determine the complexity of the communicative process. In all other cases, i.e., $\text{ta} < 1$, the impact of the time will decrease the degree of complexity of the communication. In the extreme case of $\text{ta} = 0$, only accordingly extreme simple forms of communication will be possible. Therefore, it seems plausible to add the ta - value to the "real" social sd-value of a situation, that is to enlarge the respective sd-value by (1 – ta). Because for normalization purposes the whole sd-value of a situation should be measured in the interval between 0 and 1 we can define the "enlarged" sd-parameter sd_{en} as

$$(4.5.8) \quad \text{sd}_{en} = \text{sd} + (1 - \text{ta}), \text{ if } 0 \leq \text{sd}_{en} \leq 1,$$

$$\text{sd}_{en} = 1, \text{ if } \text{sd} + (1 - \text{ta}) > 1.$$

The interpretations of the respective values of this enlarged parameter remain, of course, the same, namely that high values generate only simple communicative dynamics and vice versa. The examples given in the last section illustrate this. To be sure, it is often rather difficult to measure ta in the case of empirically real communicative processes, yet in many communicative situations at least plausible guesses can be made. This is in particular the case in situations with extreme ta-values.

When one remembers that communicative processes consist of messages sent, received, and measured by their degrees of information and relevance, and when one takes into account that besides the characteristic of the social context – the sd-parameter – meaning, information, and relevance also determine the process of communication, then it immediately becomes evident why a formal theory of communication is difficult to achieve. To make matters even more complicated we still have to consider another communicative aspect, which is in an abstract way also a social characteristic of communicative processes. We shall discuss it in the next subchapter.

In order to make these general considerations a bit more concrete we show a computational model that simulates the impact of the sd-parameter on the according cognitive processes. By doing this we anticipate in a certain sense the subject of the next chapter, namely the logic of the cognitive dimension of communication.

The model consists of an Interactive Neural Network (IN) that we already described in the preceding sections. Each unit of the IN represents a certain concept, that is the IN represents a particular semantical network of a specific communicator. A "message" that is sent to this communicator consists, as in the examples of chapter 3.3, of three concepts (A, B, C) and by this message those three units of the IN are externally activated that represent the concepts of the message.

The impact of the sd-parameter means for the receiving IN that certain concepts of the IN are "blocked", i.e., the connections from and to these concepts get the weight value $w = 0$. The activation flow in the IN that is started by the reception of the message does not reach these units. In other words, the IN behaves as if these units do not exist. The reason for this arrangement is the assumption that, e.g., high sd-values mean for a receiving communicator that he does not associate as many concepts with the message as his association networks would normally allow, but that he can activate only a part of his association nets. If for example the mentioned sergeant barks an order then because of the high sd-value of the situation the private only associates some unfriendly thoughts and tries to get away as fast as he can. The private does certainly not reflect on the social structure of an army, about the societal necessity of armed forces in general and/or the advantages of pacifism. The same private would perhaps produce such general associations in a situation with low sd-value, for example during a discussion with his comrades. Therefore, the private behaves as if these association nets of him do not exist in a situation with high sd-values.

When it receives a message the IN "computes" the sd-value of the situation. For the simple experiments we did with this IN the sd-value was implemented as a system's parameter, namely the values sd = 0, 0.2, 0.5, and 0.8. Each sd-value means for the IN that an according percentage of the units is blocked: sd = 0.n blocks 10 ∗ n% of the units. For example, an IN with 20 units has 4 units blocked if the sd-value is 0.2, an IN with 30 units has 10 units blocked in the case of sd = 0.33, and so on.

Because we assume that the semantical networks of human receivers first associate those concepts that have the strongest connections with the concepts of a message and only later those concepts with weaker connections, the IN selects for blocking those units that have the weakest connections with the units of the message. To be more exact, the IN computes the weight values of all connections from the "message units" to the other units and selects those units X for blocking that are characterized by

$$(4.5.9) \quad w(A, X) + w(B, X) + w(C, X) \leq w(A, Y) + w(B, Y) + w(C, Y),$$

for all units Y of the IN with the exception of the message units A, B, and C.

If there are more than one unit to be blocked then, of course, first the unit X with the lowest connection value according to formula (9) is selected, then the unit with the next lowest value and so forth.

Our experiments were done with networks consisting of 10, 15, 20, and 30 units; the sd-values were those mentioned above. The main results of these 16 experimental series are briefly summarized:[31]

In general the networks with blocked units behaved in a similar fashion like smaller networks that consist of just as many units as the larger IN had not blocked. That is of course not very astonishing as the human example of the private shows. sd-values larger than zero mean for artificial and human receivers that only some parts of their associative potentialities are able to operate. Yet as an interesting result we obtained that the final activation values of the not blocked units decreased the higher the sd- values were (the blocked units, of course, remained in an activation state of zero). Networks with 30 units, for example, could only activate the message units when the sd-value was 0.8. In other words, the networks behaved as if high sd-values blocked the *whole network*, not only the blocked units. In more human terms one can say that high sd-values mean for a receiver that he is only able to accept the message and repeat it. The quoted "yessir" of the private can be understood this way because it is nothing else than a confirmation of the message. This behavior is not the same as that of smaller networks whose units are not blocked at all.

To be sure, these simple experiments are not much more than an operationalization of the considerations about the sd-parameter. Yet the similarity of the behavior of these networks with everyday experiences of the impact of social situations on the cognitive processes of human receivers is striking. The situation of a university examination, for example, is certainly one with a very high sd-value. The inability of many candidates to answer questions about themes they "actually"

[31] The experiments and the implementation were done by Alexander Bendel.

know a lot about can be interpreted just this way: some parts of their semantical networks are blocked and even the not blocked parts can only be activated in a very low manner. It is no wonder that such candidates are literally unable to answer even very simple questions. It may be that our IN-model is even more realistic than we originally thought.[32]

As a final consideration we can note that the sd-parameter obviously is a kind of meta parameter which we mentioned in chapter 2. The changing of the topology of the respective IN apparently is a special case of changing rules of interaction by some measure. We shall see the impact of this meta parameter more in detail in another model in chapter 7.

4.6. SEMIOTIC PRODUCTION RULES

In the first chapter we mentioned the formal similarity of our theoretical frame with the famous sign model of Morris (1970). Our reflections on meaning and information in the third chapter can be considered as an analysis of the semantical dimension of sign systems, reformulated in terms of (mathematical) complex systems theory. The definition of the sd-parameter certainly belongs to the pragmatic dimension of the sign model because the social rules expressed in the values of the sd-parameter determine the sign mediated process of communication. We did not deal with the syntactical dimension of the model of Morris and shall do this in the following considerations. Yet again some methodical preliminary reflections are necessary.

The well known distinction that was accentuated by Morris between the pragmatic, semantical, and syntactical dimensions of signs suggests that these dimensions are independent aspects, i.e., the values in one dimension can vary independently from the other dimensions. In particular, one can assume that the origin of the dimensions of certain sign systems also independently occurred in the sense that the pragmatic use of a sign system is determined by other criteria than the syntactical relations between the signs on the one hand and the respective meanings that are "attached" to the signs on the other hand – "attached as an abbreviation for our definition of meaning. Such an assumption would be only partly true, as the following considerations will demonstrate. The structure of a sign system, i.e., the topological relations between different signs and the according production rules how to generate sign complexes out of single signs, is not independent from the pragmatic use of these sign systems – at least not in the radical sense the concept of "dimensions" may suggest. Therefore, the following reflections on semiotic production rules belong as well to the pragmatic aspect of Morris' sign model as to the syntactical one. In this sense, and of course not only in this, the analogue between the model of Morris and our theoretical frame is not more than a heuristic device, although a rather useful one.

---

[32] As there are many candidates at such examinations who get not blocked that way it is always necessary to take the "human factor" in account: the sd-value of a communicative situation does not determine the processes of each individual the same way.

The reflections on the sd-parameter demonstrated in what way a communicative process is dependent on the social "value" of the situation. In other words, the social context of a communicative process determines the social rules of communicative interaction insofar this process is part of "the social construction of reality" (Berger and Luckmann 1966). Yet a society is not only characterized by its social structure, i.e., the social rules in the sense defined in the preceding chapters, but also by its "culture", i.e., the valid knowledge and in particular the structural organization of this knowledge (Habermas 1981 II; Geertz 1973). A society, whose world view is based on the religious conception of a divine creator culturally differs to a great extent from another society where scientific theories about the origin of the universe are in this respect the "valid knowledge". Therefore, a society must always be understood as a two-dimensional ensemble of a) social rules that form the social structure, and b) a certain knowledge, by which the members of this society are able to express themselves and in particular to communicate about particular themes (Klüver 2002). Communication about certain subjects is possible if and only if the communicators share a common culture that determines the use and the meaning of the used symbols. In addition, the common culture also determines the syntactical rules, i.e., in what way certain signs or symbols respectively must be combined in order to generate "well formed formulas", to use the famous expression of Chomsky (1966). Because these different aspects all are originated in and determined by a specific culture as one dimension of the according society we deal with the subject of semiotic rules in the chapter on the social or societal respectively dimension of communication.

By applying these theoretical considerations to the more concrete problem of communication we obtain that the dynamics of a communicative process and its development in general is not only determined by the social structure of its context, i.e., by the sd-values of the proportion of the different social roles the communicators are occupying. The themes of the communication as a part of the culture common to both communicators are of high relevance too and in particular the "contents" of the communicative acts play a decisive role for the succeeding or failing of communication. Contents of messages are mainly transmitted in form of symbols, as far as human communication is concerned. To be sure, not only since the famous study of Watzlawick et al. (1967) the importance of non verbal communication as the form of analogous communication is well known. But as non verbal signals have also to be attached in a correct manner to the discrete symbolic form of communication, it seems that semiotic rules, i.e., rules that determine the production of sign complexes, must be taken into account too.

To put it into a nutshell: The contents of messages are subject to certain rules nearly the same way as the social rules of interaction determine the communicative behavior of the communicators. Therefore, when we take into account such rules we have to analyze them as rules that are relevant for the syntactical dimension of sign production as well as for the pragmatic one, i.e., the usage of those symbols and non symbolic signs that are of relevance in a certain communicative situation. To be sure, syntactical rules in the sense that Morris defined that concept are not the same as pragmatic rules that tell us how to use certain signs according to certain contents. But in both cases, as we shall see, the rules determine the production and generation of sign complexes, symbols or non symbolic signs. That is why we analyze both types of rules under the common heading of semiotic production rules, that is those rules that belong to the semiotic dimension of communication. As the usage of signs in both aspects is culturally determined, we can understand this particular analysis as the analysis of the cultural dimension of communication, in contrast to the socio-structural dimension of society that was defined by the sd-parameter.

Consider now at first the sign complex “the dog the man is biting”. Each speaker of the English language will immediately understand the semantical content of this “sentence”, although it is not “well formed” in the sense of Chomsky – English, after all, is a SVO-language (subject – verb – object). Because it is known from comparative linguistics that other syntactical structures than SVO exist in other languages (cf. e.g. Pinker 1994), the syntactical rule for the production of well formed formulas for English sentences is not an absolute universal characteristic of language but a cultural construct that originated some when and for unknown reasons as a heritage from the Indo-European primordial language. Yet despite the fact that this rule was violated in the example the understanding of this sentence is possible without problems for a speaker of English. In this case the violation of a certain production rule could occur without disturbing the process of communication, at least with respect to the mutual understanding of the communicators. The only possible consequences could be that either the hearer of this bad formed formula will think of the speaker that he is too stupid or uneducated to generate grammatically correct sentences or that the hearer will correct the speaker.

Now consider a sign complex like “$x(f, y)z = .$” By all customary mathematical standards this formula is quite meaningless because of the violation of syntactical production rules. A trained mathematician will probably guess that the speaker had something in mind like “$f(x, y) = z$” but he cannot be sure; a formula, e.g., like “$f = (x, y, z)$” makes sense too in some mathematical contexts. The only communication that can occur after the sending of the first formula will be a question of the receiver about the “true” formula. In this case the understanding of sign complexes is obviously nearly totally dependent on the correct usage of the syntactical production rules.

By comparing these two examples another very important difference must be taken into account. It is quite easily possible in a conversation on “man biting dogs” to talk about dogs in general, to extend the topic to the living conditions in big cities with their problems for animals and children, to discuss subsequently problems of children’s education and so on. In other words, such themes like dogs and related topics allow to extend the discussion to literally all themes the communicators are interested in. There are no sharp boundaries between the different fields of concepts. To be sure, this is the case with nearly all themes of everyday communication and it is a characteristic for such conversations. But if one takes communications in the field of the humanities, for example discourses on German literature of the 20th

century, then it is remarkable to see which different topics can be combined and generated by starting a conversation, e.g., at the subject of the early poems of Bert Brecht. In a quite "natural" fashion it is possible to speak about the tradition of the laborer's movement, the history of German emigrants, the rise and fall of the societies of "real socialism" and so forth. In this sense the topics of discourses of the humanities are rather similar to those of every day communication: they allow the extending of initial themes to very broad fields, that is all those topics that can be associated with the initial theme. It is a question of time – see the enlarged sd-parameter – and of the individual interests and knowledge capacities of the participants how far such extensions are developed. But there are no strict boundaries that define which topics belong to the initial subject and which not.

Mathematics is, as was to be expected, the other extreme. Not only are the syntactical rules much more important in order to guarantee the mutual understanding of the communicators, but the different topics are much more sharply separated. A conversation on number theory, e.g., may not be extended into the field of multi-dimensional non Euclidean geometry, if the communicators do not deliberately decide to do that. In addition, it is literally impossible to go from number theory to problems of education or politics. Mathematical topics are strictly defined and are accordingly strictly separated from all other subjects, even if both communicators are interested in certain other subjects. It takes a common "meta communicative" decision of the communicators (Watzlawick et al. 1967) to change a mathematical topic and to switch the communication to other mathematical topics or to non mathematical ones.

One can characterize this distinction between mathematical communications on the one side and discourses in the humanities on the other hand that the former are very far away from everyday communication and that discourses in the humanities are not. Most educated laymen have no principal difficulties to understand topics of the humanities, in decisive contrast to mathematical conversations. It is possible to generalize these observations by assuming that the farther away topics of communication are from those of everyday discourses the more rigidly the according sign systems are structured by syntactical rules and the more rigid are the boundaries between different topics of the same field and between the topical field on the one hand and other topical fields on the other. Observations on topics of empirical natural sciences, which are not as rigidly structured as mathematics and accordingly not as rigidly separated from other topical fields, confirm this; even less structured are the topical fields of the social sciences, which are mostly more related to the humanities than to the natural sciences.

The example of "Paris" of the third chapter may help to illustrate this. The quoted misunderstanding of Lady Edgeware who thought that she listened to a conversation about the capital of High Fashion was of course due to the fact that "Paris" is not an unambiguous concept but has at least two meanings.[33] Although the participants

[33] We omit the fact that the capital of France is not the only town with that name.

in the discussion about "Paris" as a prince of Troy were rather irritated about Lady Edgeware it would be quite possible to change the topic of the party discussion from Homer's epic poem to the capital of France. One can say that "Paris" in this sense functions as a kind of bridge between the two topical fields of classical literature and cities of High Fashion like Paris, London or Milan. The switching of topics in everyday communication is in particular easily possible because of the existence of such "bridge concepts". Even somebody who is in contrast to Lady Edgeware well acquainted with ancient Greek literature may associate "Paris" with "High Fashion" and may be moved to switch the conversation to that topic.

Although in the sciences there are a lot of concepts that are burrowed from everyday language like, e.g. "field" in mathematics and in physics most of the concepts used in these discourses are artificial ones and do not occur in everyday language.[34] This is a significant indicator for the separation of these sign systems from those used in everyday language. The usage of abstract symbols like "$\int dx$" or "$|A_i|$" makes it quite impossible to switch discourses that use these very unambiguously and precisely defined concepts. The more a sign system is characterized by the occurrence and frequent usage of such abstract symbols the more rigidly the according topical field is separated from other topical fields that do not contain such symbols. Therefore, for example the obvious similarity between the sign systems of mathematics and physics lead to the wrong impression that mathematics and physics are sciences with the same research domains. Yet mathematical discourses have *per se* nothing to do with those of physics, although it is of course possible to use physical examples for the illustration of mathematical propositions.

It is certainly not by chance that sign systems with very rigid syntactical rules belong to topical fields that are equally strictly separated from other topical fields and vice versa. Strict syntactical rules are needed if the meaning of the according propositions must be unambiguous with each use and such unequivocal meanings restrict the communication to the initial topic of topical field respectively. The converse, of course, is also true.

When formalizing these considerations about the "rigidity properties" of the sign systems that are characteristic for a certain topical field it is useful to introduce a "rigidity measure" Ri for each particular sign system and by that for the according topical field. We define as usual $0 \leq \text{Ri} \leq 1$; $\text{Ri} = 1$ means that it is practically impossible to change the topical field without common consent of the communicators; accordingly $\text{Ri} = 0$ means that it is practically always possible to switch the conversation from one field to another, in particular via the use of certain "bridge concepts". In the case of mathematics Ri is certainly approximately 1; $\text{Ri} = 0$ or nearly zero is characteristic for most topics of everyday communication. The humanities can be characterized too by rather small Ri-values and so on. The Ri-measure determines, in other words, the degree of the possibility to change the theme of communication. In terms of communicative acts Ri determines the

[34] Unfortunately "field" does not mean the same in mathematics as in physics.

probability according to which the communicators will change the topic or even the topical field.

Because Ri is determined by the syntactical rules of a certain topical field and by those rules that allow or forbid the changing of topics and because these two kind of rules, as was just mentioned, always occur with the same characteristics, we may combine the two kinds and speak of them in general as *semiotic production rules*. It is now clear that these rules characterize communicative processes with respect to their "contents", i.e., insofar communicative processes are determined by their respective topics. It is a truism but nevertheless important to note that Ri is culturally determined in the sense that all communicators are bound by it. In this sense the Ri-measured semiotic production rules are as "objectively" obligatory as the social rules of interaction.

Consider for example a discourse on physical laws or regularities of the universe. In feudal stratified differentiated societies like, e.g. the European Middle Ages, the cultural dominant *Weltanschauung* (world view) is mostly determined by religion, which is the last arbiter in questions about truth. Therefore, in such societies a topic like physics is characterized by a rather low degree of rigidity because it is easy and nearly self-evident to lead the discussion from physics to religion. The question if the sun moves around the earth or conversely the earth around the sun is finally decided in Christian cultures by referring to the Bible, in this case for example to the story of Joshua and the battle of Jericho, when Joshua ordered the sun to stop. Consequently, the sun moves around the earth because such it is written in the Bible. Speaking in terms of cultural differentiation such a society is characterized by a high degree of connectivity between different cultural themes. In particular, religion acts as a common bond between themes that do not belong together according to our cultural understanding.

Now consider the same discourse in a society like the modern Western kind. Since the Enlightenment and since the emerging of functional differentiation, i.e., the emergence of autonomous subsystems, it is a truism that questions of religion and questions of science must be separated. It is not the task of science to prove or disprove the truth of religious assertions and it is neither the task of religion to tell science how to proceed.[35] With respect to each other the themes of physics and of religion are characterized by a high degree of rigidity. But this high degree is due to the fact that such a society is *globally* characterized by a high degree of cultural differentiation: Each functional subsystem is culturally defined by its respective themes and these themes are in the same degree separated from another as are the functionally autonomous subsystems themselves.

Therefore, it is plausible to postulate a cultural "law" of rigidity: Generally cultural important themes are characterized by a high degree of rigidity if the society and in particular its specific culture is differentiated in a significant way, due to

---

[35] This is well illustrated by a famous remark of the astronomer and mathematician Laplace to Napoleon, who asked about the role of god in the model of the universe presented to him by Laplace: "Sire, je n'ai pas besoin de cette hypothèse" (I do not need this hypothesis (of god)).

differentiation processes on the social level, and vice versa. To be sure, in everyday discussions it is possible to jump from physics to religion, to art or to movies. But this just reflects the informal character of such discussions that are not determined by *general* social and cultural rules. In such informal communicative situations also the values of the sd-parameter are not as important as in "official" situations. Informal communications can frequently be characterized by symmetrical relations between the communicators (stratified dimension), a lot of knowledge that is common to both communicators (functional dimension) and common belonging to a certain social segment. That is why also the semiotic production rules in such informal discourses are not primarily determined by the rigidity degree of the themes but more by individual factors like common interest of jumping from theme to theme. But as soon as the communicative situations become more official, both the values of the sd-parameter and the degree of rigidity play an increasing important role for the determination of the course of communication.

CHAPTER 5

THE COGNITIVE DIMENSION OF COMMUNICATION

Because of the frequently mentioned two-dimensional character of communication it is certainly not sufficient to analyze only the social dimension of communication, i.e., the social rules that determine the behavior of the communicators as social actors. In a certain sense social actors are treated as black boxes if only the social context is taken into account: nothing is said by only observing social interactions about the "internal" processes of the communicators. To be sure, sociology often has to concentrate only on the social behavior and interactions and thereby is able to neglect the internal processes. We demonstrated in the last chapter that by modeling only interactions determined by social rules of behavior it is very often possible to gain satisfactory results. The great founding fathers of theoretical sociology frequently stressed this point. For example, Marx once said that theories of society do not deal with humans – and in particular not with their internal processes, one might add – but with the social relations between humans. Yet even Marx had to acknowledge the importance of the human *Bewusstsein* (consciousness) when developing his famous theory of Historical Materialism. Therefore, even theoretical sociology cannot neglect the role that the internal processes of social actors play. Social action theories, of course, always took that into account.

A theory of communication is even more incomplete if it is not also a theory of the internal processes of social actors as communicators. Communication, as we sketched in the last subchapter, is always communication on some particular subject. These subjects or themes respectively are sent and received in forms of messages that contain a certain meaning, a particular degree of information, and a certain degree of relevance for the receiver. Because informational degree and meaning are not simply pressed upon the receiver but are generated by processing the message according to certain cognitive rules, the modeling of cognitive internal processes is as important for our task as the modeling of social contexts by modeling social rules of interaction.

The modeling of cognitive processes by computer based models is even more advanced and established than the modeling of social processes. Indeed, since the invention of the computer in the first half of the last century the metaphor of the computer as a "thinking machine" has accompanied the construction of both hardware and software. The famous – and sometimes infamous – research field of Artificial Intelligence (AI) is a well known indicator for the permanent interest that researchers in the cognitive sciences have taken in the use of computer based models (cf. e.g. Thagard 1996). Because we shall discuss some of the classical AI-approaches and problems in later subchapters, we can leave this topic for the moment. For an exhaustive overview of the state of the art we can refer to Polk and Seifert (2002).

It is perhaps *the* classical methodical problem in the cognitive sciences that the internal processes of human beings cannot directly be observed but must be analyzed in an indirect way. Even recent advances in neurobiology that allow the observation of the human brain when it is performing particular tasks do not tell us *how* the brain operates but only *where* certain neural operations are taking place (cf. Lakoff and Núñez 2000, 26). In other words, the question *how* meaning and informational degrees are generated by the brain as a cognitive system cannot be answered by looking at neurobiology. They must be answered by constructing theoretical and that is mathematical models and by comparing these models with the factual cognitive observable behavior of human communicators.

We wish to emphasize this aspect a bit more. The undeniable correctness of classical behaviorism was certainly its insistence on the postulate that only observable facts, i.e., observable behavior should be taken into account when explaining such complex processes like human thinking and speaking and by refuting traditional speculations on the human mind via the infamous "arm-chair reasoning". But the behaviorists, as not only Chomsky correctly argued in the famous "Skinner-Review" (Chomsky 1959), overlooked the fact that the reduction of science to only *directly* observable facts is a "reductive fallacy", that is it limits the possibilities of science without need. Even physicists often have to deal with processes that are not directly observable – like processes in stars – but that can be studied in an indirect manner, namely by the use of theoretical and in physics of course mathematical models. In the perhaps most famous study on the theoretical proceeding of science Popper (1969) has made it very clear that theoretical science does not follow the restrictions of the behaviorists but on the contrary is characterized by the use of theoretical models that explain the observable and observed fact via an indirect manner. If science would not proceed this way no *theoretical* science would be possible.

The cognitive sciences have learned this lesson quite well. To be sure, sciences always have to be empirically founded (with the exception of mathematics, of course). Therefore, human beings as the objects of cognitive research have to be observed and in particular be asked about their own internal processes. But the explanation of the cognitive behavior of human actors has to be done in terms of theoretical models that hypothetically postulate the logic of the cognitive processes in the human brain or mind respectively.

Before we discuss some general aspects of the logic of cognitive processes, as far as they are important for our subject of communication, we wish to make these methodological general considerations a bit more clear by demonstrating two examples of the modeling of certain cognitive processes. Both examples are "constructive" ones, i.e., in both examples the respective persons have to construct a certain assimilation schema in the sense of Piaget (see above subchapter 3.3) in order to perform certain orientation tasks. That means that the persons have to structure their respective experiences to understand the world they live in and have to act in.

5.1. THE STORY OF TOM

"Tom", whose real name is of course quite another, is an adolescent of about 17 years who lives in a hostel for deviant youths in a large town in the West of Germany. He was interviewed about his biography by one of our students. The interview was a so called semi-structured one, i.e., the interviewer determined the topic of the different questions and the temporal succession of the questions. These were all "open" ones, that is Tom was asked to answer in his own language with the terms he thought appropriate. In the following sections we quote some of his self-descriptions in our translation from the German original.

His social relation to other people may be defined with an infamous term by Spencer, namely "Social Darwinism". There are weak people and strong ones and Tom wants, of course, to belong to the strong ones.

Tom: "You must succeed with respect to the others, you must show that you are stronger, either physically or mentally – either you hit the other if he does not obey or you use psycho-tricks... There are always other guys who want the same thing as you, a job or a woman. Then you have to fight – either with fists or with psycho-tricks."

Tom belongs to a gang of Hooligans where of course this worldview is permanently confirmed.

Tom's world view is in particular very clear with respect to men and women:

"You must always show that you are the boss. Women do not want weak men, they want strong guys."

In the dichotomous world view of Tom "right" men belong to the strong people and "right" women belong to the weak ones. That is given by nature, as Tom emphasizes:

"For example, earlier at the times of the primordial men the men had to hunt and the women have cared for the children and did the cooking. That is a natural order because women are not strong enough to do the work of real men."

In consequence of this natural order women have to obey men and have to do the task that nature wanted women to do. Accordingly men have to do the jobs designed for men by nature and they have to dominate the women. Any other social order is against nature and must be opposed.

Tom learned this dichotomous world view rather early in his socialization process, namely by observing his parents where the father was the dominating person who even sometimes hit the mother while the mother seemed to be the weak one. This interpretation is valid for Tom without question, despite the fact that the father left the family and the mother had alone to care for Tom and his two sisters. Tom had to go into the hostel because the mother was not able to care for all children and because Tom got into conflict with the police. But the hostel he lives in gives Tom a serious orientation problem because the educators in the hostel are mainly women and only few men who all try to practice a rather permissive style of education. This is clearly against the law of nature because on the one hand women should not be allowed to give orders to young men like Tom and on the other hand the male educators in the hostel behave like women – they cook, they even dress similarly like the female educators and they often accept the orders of the women. In particular they are with only one exception physically rather weak – "they have no muscles, they cannot win in a real fight". Consequently Tom tries to dominate not only the other youths in the hostel but also the educators by using his "psycho-tricks".

Obviously Tom's world view operates as a strict binary assimilation schema in particular in a normative sense. "Real" men are those male persons who are dominant and willing to fight with all means. Men who do not have these characteristics are not "real" men but weak ones who are even dominated by women. Accordingly, "real" women are those females who accept the natural order of things, who are subordinate with respect to men, and who restrict their activities to the "womanly" tasks like cooking and caring for children.

For the explanation of the genesis of such a rigid assimilation schema it is useful to apply the well known theory of "model learning" by Bandura (1986) to the case of Tom. Bandura's theory describes the process of socialization and in particular the formation of certain world views by emphasizing the role of persons who act as "models" for the learner. One can compare the "model" in Bandura's theory, by the way, to the role of the "significant other" in the socialization theory of Berger and Luckmann (1966). The term of "model" does not necessarily mean a positive model because it is in this sense neutral. A model can be a person who functions as a positive example, i.e., the learner wishes to be like this model. A model can in contrast also be a person who is a negative example in the sense that the learner wants to avoid becoming like this person by all means.

When looking at Tom's biography it is evident that his father acted as a positive model, although he left his family and in this way showed himself to be a very irresponsible person. Yet Tom still adores his father, even more than seven years after his disappearance, because the father was "strong" in Tom's meaning of the word – "he was always respected by his colleagues in the pub and he never hesitated to hit somebody who tried to insult him". The mother was left alone with the responsibility for the children and tried her best, which Tom admitted: "The mother tried very hard, but I was too much for her, including the care taking for the sisters". Yet Tom nevertheless sees the mother as a weak person who was dominated by the father. As Tom wants to belong to the strong and dominating ones the mother can only be a negative model, which teaches Tom what he must avoid by all means.

The models represented to him by the parents are reinforced by Tom's peer groups, in particular the gang of Hooligans, and by his own experiences with the other youths and the educators in the hostel. Tom is successful in dominating other people and he learns that it is possible even to dominate adults, i.e., the female educators and the male educators who are no "real" men. In this sense Tom has no reason to doubt his dichotomous world view with respect of the distinction between strong ones and weak ones and in particular with respect to his classification of men and women. Therefore, it can be assumed that Tom will orientate also his future social relations via this world view, at least as long as he is successful in doing so.

For our communication theoretical purposes the analysis of world views is rather relevant because factual communication processes are determined by the respective social rules *and* the personalities of the communicators, which are expressed in the manner they assimilate experiences and whole situations. Tom for example does not accept the social situation of the hostel, in which he is clearly in a subordinate position and should accordingly behave. The sd-value in the second dimension is rather high for a communicative situation between Tom and anyone of the educators. As Tom tells himself the other youths in the hostel behave according to this social structure, but Tom does not and in addition he has only contempt for the other youths. In the case of Tom, therefore, the personal world view overrides the social rules of the context. Tom's communicative behavior with respect to the educators and the other youths can in this case not be explained from the social situation but only from the particular world view of Tom. It can safely be assumed that in cases of social/communicative deviance from the respective social rules the particular world view must be taken into account as the decisive factor. If and when Tom perceives the educators and/or the other members of the hostel only via his dichotomous assimilation schema as men and women who are not "right" he will always try to dominate them and to treat them according to his Social Darwinist world view.

To be sure, such strict normative assimilation schemas do not always lead to social deviance. It is quite possible to imagine a person with Tom's world view who nevertheless yields to a social context and behaves according to the particular social rules. In this case the person would distinguish between his personal feelings and emotions on the one hand and his factual behavior on the other. A private soldier may despise his sergeant but follows his orders. It is certainly a question how the person evaluates the situation, that is if he thinks that he can succeed by ignoring the rules or not. In the case of Tom his own experiences taught him – see above – that he is in most cases strong enough to come out as the winner.

Interestingly enough there was one person in the hostel who was respected by Tom and whose orders were carried out by Tom without great trouble. This person was the interviewer who worked as one of the male educators in the hostel and whom Tom knew rather well from common training in the fitness room of the hostel. Despite the fact that this educator also behaved in a "womanly" fashion by doing work in the kitchen and participating in other necessary house work, Tom accepted this educator because of his physical abilities – the educator was stronger than Tom – and because of a comparatively non permissive style of education. Tom obviously saw this educator as a "real" man because the educator had authority and was able to successfully insist on his orders. This is, by the way, the main reason why Tom spoke quite freely and without hesitation about himself in the interview.

The formal model by which we reconstructed the genesis and the actual effects of Tom's world view consists of the combination of two different types of artificial neural networks, namely a so called bi-directional associative memory (BAM) and a Kohonen Feature Map (KFM) or self organizing map (SOM respectively). BAM-networks are called "bi-directional" because they are trained to associate two different vectors X and Y. If after the training the X-vector is given as input the

BAM associates the other vector Y and vice versa – they associate in two directions. This process is performed by generating during the training process a certain weight matrix via algebraic operations; the learned matrix then generates the Y-vector if the X-vector was given as input and vice versa.[1] The KFM we used for the case of Tom is of the Ritter-Kohonen type we described in the preceding chapter. A KFM of this type uses, as we mentioned, not only a weight matrix that is varied during the training processes but also a "semantical matrix", i.e., a matrix that contains relation values between concepts and their characteristics.

In the example of Tom the BAM was used to associate certain characteristics with the two concepts "man" and "woman". As a result of the respective training processes the different BAM-nets (it is always necessary to use more than one BAM for technical reasons) were able to associate X-vectors like X = (strong, is right, successful . . . etc.) with the concept "man" – the according Y-vector – and other X-vectors like X' = (weak, complains, cooks, . . . etc.) with the concept "woman" The training process simulates the learning process, which is orientated to a model, in the sense that the BAM-nets were given the characteristics of "man" and "woman" in the form of the X-vectors and the BAM-nets learned to associate the respective concepts as Y-vectors. Learning in the sense of Bandura's theory, of course, does not take place in the way that the learners are given explicit instructions like "a person who is weak and complains is a woman" but that they learn to associate the characteristics they observe in the persons of their significant others with the generalized concepts of "man" and "woman". After the training, as was mentioned, an input of certain characteristics generates the according concept as was the case with Tom.[2]

The BAM-nets are the base for the formation of the final worldview. This formation is done by the KFM that refers to a semantical matrix generated by the BAM-nets. Such a matrix has, e.g., the following characteristic:

	strong	*hits*	*weak*	*complains*
man_1	1	1	0	0
man_2	1	1	0	0
$woman_1$	0	0	1	1
$woman_2$	0	0	1	1

The matrix we used actually is much greater but for visualization purposes this little figure is enough. The task of the KFM is to cluster different persons on the base of the individual characteristics of the persons. Because the dichotomous assimilation schema of Tom is in particular characterized by a strict distinction between "men" and "women" according to the border line between "strong" and "weak" a valid

[1] Technical details of BAM-nets that differ in some aspects from the neural nets so far discussed can be studied in any textbook on neural nets.

[2] With a well known term from learning theory this form of learning can be called as learning by examples (*exemplarisches Lernen).*

result of the simulation of the world view's genesis must consist of principally strictly separated clusters of male persons and female ones.

Technically each artificial person is represented by a 13-dimensional vector, consisting of zeroes or ones. The first two components determine the sex of the respective person, the next four components represent the characteristics "complains", "weak", "wears certain sandals" (a typical symbol for permissive educators), "cooks and cleans the house", i.e., the characteristics of women, the next four components represent "strong", "is right", "is able to hit others", "is successful", i.e., "male" characteristics, and the last three components represent individual characteristics like "big", "slim", and "fast". To be sure, these last three characteristics are of only secondary importance for Tom's assimilation schema, but they are necessary to take into account the individual differences between the respective persons. Tom's assimilation schema clusters men and women in a homogenous fashion into different groups but of course the individual differences between different men or women do not vanish by this process. A "1" means again that a certain characteristic belongs to the respective person and a "0" that this is not the case.

The following figures show the results of three simulation runs with the KFM. Figure 1 is the result of an input of three women and three men who all have the characteristics that are, according to Tom's world view, typical for "real" men and women. In the case of the men, e.g., that means that the input vectors of the men all are 0 in the components 3, 4, 5, and 6, the next four components have the value of 1, and the last three components are generated by a random distribution of ones and zeroes. Accordingly the vectors of the women consist of components 3 to 6 with values 1, the next four components have the value 0 and the last three components again consist of ones and zeroes distributed at random.

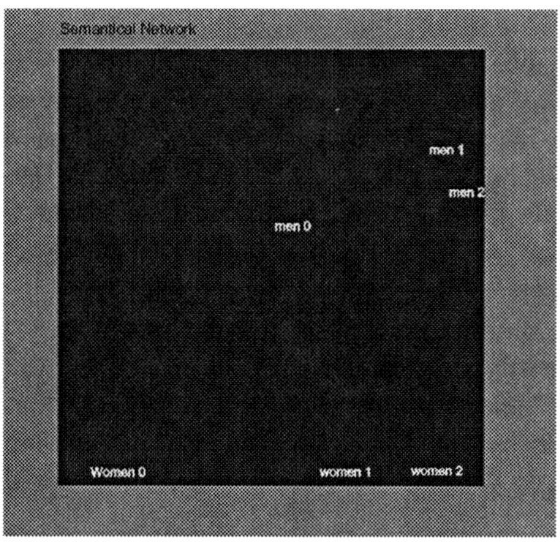

Figure 1. Two distinct clusters of men and women

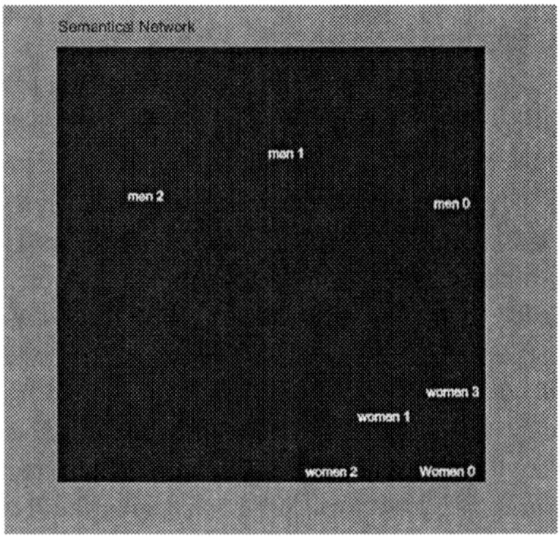

Figure 2. The same clusters with one new person

One immediately sees the strict distinction between men and women by the spatial distance between the two "gender clusters". This spatial distance can in addition be interpreted as the representation of the social distance between the worlds of men and of women, which is in accord with Tom's assimilation schema: Women have nothing to do in the world of men and vice versa.

The next figure is the result of a simulation with the same values of the components of the "gender specific" vectors. After the formation of the clusters that are shown in figure 1 we added another person, that is another woman with the same vector components to the initial group of six persons. As the figure shows the KFM immediately puts the new woman into the female cluster, i.e., each new person that the artificial representation of Tom's assimilation schema "perceives" is assigned to the respective social category.

The simulations shown in figures 1 and 2 represent the childhood of Tom with his own experiences. Tom's social world is characterized by only "real" men and women who all have the characteristics that are typical for the respective sex. That is why newcomers can be assigned to their clusters without any problems because the newcomers, although being different individuals, conform to the prototypes of men and women that the mother and the father of Tom represented.[3] But at the latest when Tom had to go the hostel he learned that there are "not genuine" men and women who are not in accord to the learned prototypes. This experience was also simulated; the result is shown in figure 3.

In this simulation three of the four men in the figure are still characterized by the vector components as in figures 1 and 2. The vector of the fourth additional man

[3] The model learning theory of Bandura apparently is in this aspect rather similar to the theory of "prototypes" by Rosch (cf. e.g. Lakoff 1987; Rosch 1973).

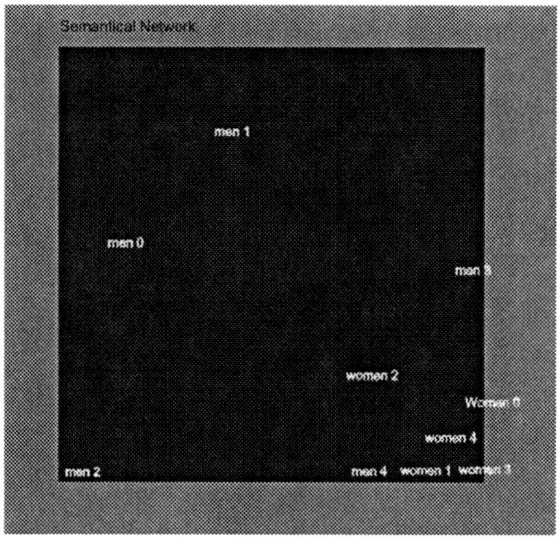

Figure 3. Gender specific clusters with a "not genuine" man

differs insofar as he "cooks and cleans" and "wears the typical sandals". In addition the component "strong" got the value of 0. Accordingly the program appoints this man to the female cluster, that is it identifies this man as a "fake". In this respect the KFM behaves like Tom who does not accept such men as "genuine" but sees them rather as a kind of women in disguise.

The program could be much more differentiated, for example by taking longer vectors with more individual characteristics and/or by substituting the zeroes and ones in the semantical matrix by real numbers, i.e., by coding the characteristics as "more or less strong" etc. Yet these results obtained with the simple binary coding already demonstrate that the genesis of the world view and the view itself can be rather exactly simulated.

This simulation of the genesis and the operation of Tom's assimilation schema illustrates the methodical approach we mentioned in the beginning of this chapter. The basis was the assumption that Tom's socialization process can be explained by using the model learning theory by Bandura and by presuming that Tom's father and his mother were something akin to prototypes in the sense that by observing them Tom was able to construct his schema. This construction process was reinforced by the fact that during Tom's childhood he only got acquainted with men and women who were genuine representatives of the prototypes. The simulation confirmed this theoretical assumption by obtaining results in the manner of Tom's worldview. In particular, the simulations also demonstrated that Tom assimilates men and women not primarily according to their biological sex but with respect to their prototypical characteristics (figure 3). Therefore, Tom's communicative behavior is determined by his assimilation schema, as we mentioned above; the confirmation of the theoretical assumption by the simulations is a strong argument for its empirical validity.

To be sure, the results of the simulations do not prove once and for all that the "Bandura-hypothesis" is in a literal sense "true" because its confirmation is

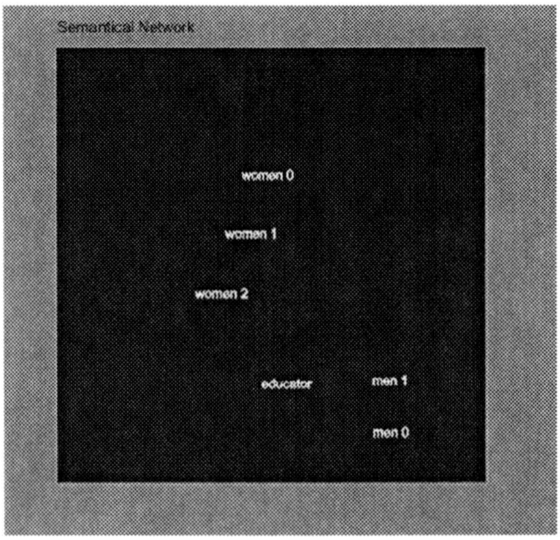

Figure 4. Acceptation of an educator as a "real" man

only an indirect one. Other theoretical explanations, e.g., in terms of Freudian psychoanalysis, are still possible. Yet our theoretical assumption has the advantage of being comparatively simple. By applying Occam's razor we may take this theoretical explanation as the best explanation we have so far obtained.

We mentioned above that Tom respects at least one person in the hostel, namely the male educator who acted as interviewer. Apparently Tom sees this educator as a genuine man, despite the fact that the educator takes over duties in the household, which is a womanly task that genuine men should not take over. In order to test the assumption that this educator is accepted as a genuine man we introduced a representation of him into the KFM by giving his vector all male characteristics but additionally the characteristic "cooks and cleans the house". The result of the simulation is shown in figure 4.

Apparently the educator is appointed to the male cluster which means in Tom's assimilation schema the acceptation as a genuine man. From an educational point of view it can be speculated that only such male educators have a chance to correct Tom's socialization process because Tom certainly will only listen to people he respects as genuine men. Therefore, the results of such simulation may give rise to very practical considerations about the possibilities of re-socialization in the case of deviant and aggressive youths. But such considerations are not the subject of this study.

5.2. WAS IT MURDER? THE FORMATION OF ANALOGIES

Verbal communication, as is well known, is frequently characterized by the usage of special rhetorical forms of speech, for example the use of metaphors and analogies. In particular the formation of analogies is not only an important rhetorical figure of speech but also a very useful method for heuristic thinking processes and heuristic proofs. To be sure, deduction by analogies – *deductio per analogiam*, as the scholastic logicians called this form of proof – is not an exact proof method. But it is frequently useful for heuristic purposes, and arguments by using analogies are important and often successful rhetorical strategies. In order to understand the internal cognitive processes when constructing analogies we developed a mathematical or computational model respectively by applying it to a concrete case.[4]

In contrast to the story of Tom this case is not a real one but taken out of fiction, that is from a detective novel by the Dutch author Janwillem van de Wetering "The Mind Murder". We constructed the respective model during a course on the parallels between the intelligence concepts of Artificial Intelligence and the logical reasoning of literary detectives (Klüver and Stoice 2004). Besides other forms of logical reasoning like logical deduction and proof by contradiction we analyzed and modeled in this course the formation of analogies. "Formation of analogy" is here defined in a rather pragmatic way as the perception of *structural* similarities or even structural equalities in two or more cases that are different in content. We are quite aware of the fact the concept of "analogy" is used with a lot of different meanings but as the characterization of a certain form of methodical and logical reasoning our pragmatic definition includes most of the other ones.

The story of the novel of van de Wetering is quickly told. At Amsterdam the officers of the murder department learn about the case of a man to whom happened a lot of on a first sight impossible incidents. For example, one evening he came back from office and not only his wife was gone but also his apartment was totally empty – no more furniture, carpets and so on. The man continually lost his nerves and believed himself to be insane. The officers suspected a murder case because the wife could not be found. But finally the wife appeared on the scene and it became clear that the incidents were performed by the wife who wanted to punish her husband. Therefore, a case that looked like a murder case was no murder at all.

The officers then learned about another case that happened immediately after the first one. A foreign tourist was found dead in the back of a car that had been stolen. The investigation of his death demonstrated that the man died because of *ulcus viciosus* – disease of stomach. Thus it seemed that there was no murder but just a "natural death". But the officers also learned that to this man happened a lot of impossible incidents too. For example, the tourist had bought a new car, a Porsche, and as usual the Porsche had the steering wheel on the left side. One day the man discovered that his new car suddenly had the steering wheel on the right side. When he asked the manager of his hotel to have a look at the car the wheel

[4] The difference between the terms "mathematical model" and "computational model" is not always clearly defined. Mostly "mathematical models" mean models that use the traditional tools of mathematics, in particular difference and/or differential equations like the Lotka-Volterra equations we described in chapter 2. The term "computational model" on the other hand is mostly used to characterize computer based models like artificial neural nets. We believe this distinction to be quite superfluous because mathematics is not reducible to classical calculus and computer based models use, of course, mathematical equations and algorithms too. Therefore, we shall use these two terms in a synonymous manner.

was again on the left side. Thus everybody believed that the man was becoming insane. The man himself obtained from these incidents a nervous breakdown and in the end he died from his stomach disease.[5]

The officers suspected that in this second case the chain of seemingly impossible incidents also was the result of intentional actions, i.e., that as in the first case somebody had tried to destroy first the mental and then the physical health of the victim of these incidents. They came to that conclusion because they saw the analogy, i.e., structural similarity of these cases: Both were characterized by a chain of impossible events that simply could not happen by chance. Because in the first case the events were caused by an intentional actor, by a formation of analogy the second chain of events must – or at least could – also be the effects of intentional planning and actions. This was indeed the case because the culprit behind the second case knew of the disease of stomach of his victim and the culprit wanted to punish the tourist for some deeds in his past. One can say that the culprit used the disease of his victim as a murder weapon by knowing that the disease could become the death of the sick man if he was driven to nervous breakdowns.[6] After knowing that the second case was indeed murder it was rather easy for the officers to learn about the identity of the culprit.

One can compare, by the way, the procedures of the two culprits in both cases with the well known method of "crisis experiments" that was introduced into ethnomethodology by Harold Garfinkel (1967). As in the two cases of the novel by van de Wetering in crisis experiments the test persons are deliberately put into impossible situations and tested for their reactions to it. For example, a test person is requested to go into a restaurant and order a meal. The waiter is instructed not to ask the test person for his wishes but to discuss with him the miserable conditions of the profession of a waiter, to ask the test person about the meaning of his own life, to criticize the participation of the guest at an act of exploitation of the waiter and so on. The goal of such crisis experiments is always to destroy the confidence of the test persons in the stability of their everyday life and the according certainty what to expect in well known every day situations. Van de Wetering, of whom we do not know if he was perhaps inspired by ethnomethodology when writing his novel, formulated that very well when the police commissioner in the novel told about an impossible experience he had himself and said that he "felt suddenly something like a gap in reality".

The police officers were able to solve this case, i.e., to perceive that it was a murder case because they, as all human beings, are trained in the formation of analogies from their everyday experience. We all immediately see the similarity of different cases if, for example, we perceive the conflict between two children in a kindergarten about some unimportant issue – unimportant of curse only for

---

[5] The solution of the puzzle of the Porsche was, of course, that somebody had interchanged the car of the tourist with another Porsche that was very similar to the first car but had the wheel, unusual in Europe, on the right side. This second car was then again interchanged with the first car.

[6] That is of course the reason for the title of the novel.

observers – and if we watch the permanent emotional strife between neighbors about an apple tree whose braches touch the wall of one neighbor. In both cases the causes for the strife are ridiculous from an observer's point of view and in both cases the reasons for the strife are just the causing effects for a process that quickly renders itself independent and feeds, so to speak, on its own dynamics. The difficulty in the murder case at Amsterdam was just that on the first sight the second case could not have been a murder. Therefore, the officers had to consciously remember the first case and to construct the according analogy.

In order to model such formations of analogies we used a so called hetero-associative network (HS) that operates in a basically similar fashion like the BAM-nets we described in the preceding subchapter. Our HS is a feed forward network, consisting of four layers, that is an input layer, two hidden layers and an output layer (see above chapter 2). It belongs to the type of supervised learning networks. The following figure 5 illustrates the architecture of our HS.

The line at the top is the input layer, the next two lines represent the two hidden layers and the line at the bottom the output layer. "Feed forward" means that the activation flow between the units starts at the input layer, then the neurons of next line are activated, then those on the third line and finally the units of the output layer. The output units either give their activation values to those of the input layer and the process starts again with the new activation values until a point attractor has been reached or the activation flow is stopped at the output layer after one or several runs. Then the respective output is compared with a certain target vector and the difference between the target vector and the output vector determines the magnitude of changing the weight matrix of our network. For this HS we used the so called Back Propagation rule, one of the most effective learning rules in the field of neuroinformatics:

$$(5.2.1) \quad \delta_j = \left\{ \begin{array}{l} f_j'(\text{net}_j)\,(t_j - o_j) \text{ if } j = \text{ output neuron} \\ f_j'(\text{net}_j) \sum\limits_k (\delta_k w_{ik}) \text{ if } j = \text{ hidden neuron} \end{array} \right\}$$

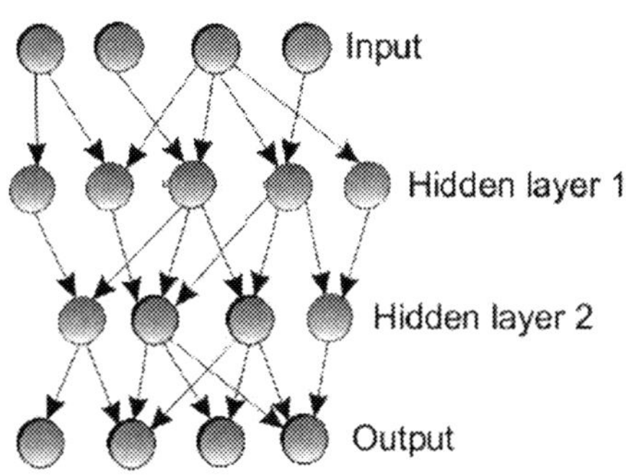

Figure 5. Hetero-associative network

The task of a HS is as in the case of BAM-networks the association of pairs of different vectors.[7] If a pair of vectors X and Y is learned then the network generates Y as output if X is inserted as input vector. We used, by the way, such a modeling technique for the problem of typifying that was described in the preceding chapter. The training process accordingly consists of inserting one vector of the pair that shall be learned as input and the other vector as target vector with the goal that at the end of the training process the target vector is identical with the output vector. The larger the network is the more pairs of vectors can be learned by one HS. Such networks are used, for example, for the task of prognosticating the quotations of shares: The network is successively trained with the quotation of shares of Monday and Tuesday, of Tuesday and Wednesday, of Wednesday and Thursday, and of Thursday and Friday. By assuming that the logic behind this time series remains the same, the network is given the quotation of shares of Friday and the HS has to generate a vector that represents the quotation of shares on Monday. For short range predictions this procedure can be quite successful, but only under *ceteris paribus* conditions. Because the stock market is influenced by many external factors that the network of course cannot prognosticate the predicting validity of such prognostications is rather limited.

In our example of the murder case at Amsterdam the network should learn to associate chains of events with a certain structural similarity – in our case the seemingly impossibility of certain incidents – and to associate these chains with another vector that represents "intentionally planned action". In addition the HS had to learn to distinguish between these chains of events and such chains that represent events that happened by chance. "By chance" means of course from the point of view of the officers in the detective novel. We accordingly represented the chains of events from the first type with vectors consisting of 10 real numbers between 0 and 1, ordered as series according to their size; the target vector was a four-dimensional vector with real numbers of the same interval (the four dimensions are arbitrarily chosen). The components of the target vector are again ordered as a series according to the size of the components. Chains of the second type were represented as vectors with real components out of the same interval but chosen at random. The target vector for the second type of vectors is again a four-dimensional one but the components are also chosen at random. The HS then was trained with four pairs of the first type, i.e., it had to associate vectors like (0.1, 0.2, 0.3, 0.35, ...) or (0.1, 0.15, 0.2, 0.35, ...) always with the target vector (0.1, 0.2, 0.3, 0.4). The vectors of the second type had to be associated with the target vector (0.5, 0.3, 0.8, 0.1).

The task of the HS was that after the training process in particular with respect to the first type of vectors a new ordered vector was given as input that represents the second chain of events in the detective story. Indeed, after the training process with the first four vectors of the first type the HS was able to correctly generate the first target vector, representing "intentionally planned action". In other words, the HS is able to perform a formation of analogy by "perceiving" the structural similarity

[7] That explains their name from Greek *heteros* = other.

between the new chain of events and those that it had been trained with before. When the same HS got another vector as input of the second type it accordingly associated the second target vector, i.e., it perceived random events as such.

In one aspect the HS had a certain advantage in comparison to the Amsterdam detectives. The HS received its one type of learning examples in an explicit order and could compare them with examples that did not exhibit any order. In contrast to the inputs of the HS the detectives had first to discover the order of their experiences, it was not explicitly given to them. Yet one must bear in mind that human beings like the officers from the Amsterdam police learned for several decades to think in analogies and to apply that kind of thinking to certain problems. We could have make the training problem for our HS more difficult and accordingly give more training examples but for our subject it is sufficient to see how such a problem can be modeled via the usage of certain neural networks. It can be safely assumed that the human brain operates in a similar fashion when constructing formations of analogies. To be sure, there must not be biological neural nets in the brain exactly like our HS-model that perform the formation of analogies. But such biological nets have to be *functionally equivalent* to our model in the sense that they are able to learn from singular examples and to apply their trained topology to new problems and situations that are structurally similar to those the network already knows.

As in the problem of the emergence of social order (see above 4.3) the training task of the network is, speaking in terms of complex systems theory, to develop such a topology via the learning rules that determines certain basins of attraction. These basins consist of all the different vectors that as input cause the network to generate the associated target vector. This basin must not be too small because then only few analogies between different vectors, that is the representation of different perceptions, can be constructed. The human brain is capable to construct analogies of a wide range. Mathematically this means just basins of attraction with a size sufficiently large to make this possible.

Yet the basin of attraction must not be too large because in that case very different perceptions that have literally nothing in common would be associated with the same target vector. In extreme cases like those mentioned in chapter 3.3. the basin of attraction can be so large that all perceptions would be associated with the same meaning like in the case of the young man who associated every perception with "sex". We have again a typical optimization problem of the sort of two opposing parameters: As large as necessary but as small as possible. Our own social experience and in particular our experience as university teachers tells us how difficult for many people it is to solve this optimization problem in a satisfactory manner.

5.3. COGNITIVE FUNCTIONS, MEANING PROCESSING CAPACITIES, AND LOCAL ATTRACTORS

In chapter 2 we referred to the fact that the different rules of interaction of a complex dynamical system and its topology can be understood as a general function f of transition that generates a subsequent state S′ from a preceding one $S - f(S) = S'$. This transition function f determines the dynamics of the system as long as neither the rules of interaction nor the topology of the system are changed. By characterizing certain states as attractors and the set of states that lead to the same attractor as the respective basin of attraction we showed that the knowledge about certain characteristics of the interaction rules and the topology, i.e., the knowledge about the values of the particular ordering parameters makes it possible to predict the *principal* behavior of these systems. Thus complex dynamical systems can be described in a general manner, for example by placing them into the different Wolfram classes of complexity.

The considerations at the end of the last subchapter also give some insights into an important characteristic of cognitive systems that can be described as their "meaning processing capacities". This term can be defined the following way:

Consider a simple neural net consisting of four units with feed forward activation flow. The activation function is the – in the meantime – well known linear function

(5.3.1) $A_j = \Sigma_i w_{ij} * A_i,$

if A_j is the activation value of the receiving unit j, w_{ij} are the weight values of the connections between the sending units i and the receiving unit j and A_j are the activation values of the sending units i. For the sake of simplicity we assume that no other functions and no thresholds determine the dynamics of our network. The weight matrix of the network is

	x_1	x_2	y_1	y_2
x_1	0	0	1	0
x_2	0	0	0	1
y_1	0	0	0	0
y_2	0	0	0	0

Obviously x_1 and x_2 are the components of the input layer and y_1 and y_2 those of the output layer; there are only connections with weight values $w \neq 0$ between the units x_i and y_i.

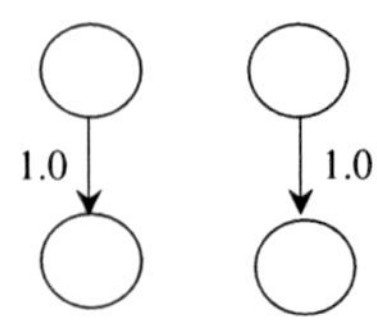

Figure 6. The network as a graph

An input to this network means the external activation of the components of the input layer. It is easily verified that in all cases the output, i.e., the activation values of the y-components, is exactly the same as the input, i.e.,

(5.3.2) $A(x_1) = A(y_1)$ and $A(x_2) = A(y_2)$.

Now consider an equally simple Boolean network, consisting of three units a, b, and c. The adjacency matrix is

	a	b	c
a	0	1	1
b	1	0	1
c	1	1	0

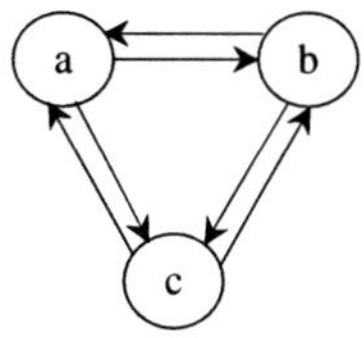

Figure 7. The graph of the Boolean network

The network contains only one Boolean function, namely $f(a, b) = c = f(b, c) = a = f(a, c) = b = 1$. In other words, the only function in this network is the so called tautology function that attaches the value 1 to all receiving units regardless which values the sending units have. For example, $f(1, 0) = f(1, 1) = 1$.

The dynamics of the network is, of course, very simple. All initial states immediately generate the only point attractor $a = b = c = 1$. As there are $2^3 = 8$ possible initial states the point attractor (1, 1, 1) obviously has a basin of attraction of size 8.

This is very different in the case of the feed forward neural net of figure 1. When we define an initial state of this network as the respective input to the x-components while the activation values of the y-components are zero, then each input vector $(A(x_1), A(x_2))$ generates exactly the same vector as output, and, because the net is a feed forward one, the final state is a point attractor, consisting of the activation values of the four components. The dynamics is again very simple, but the respective basins of attraction of the point attractors are very small, namely they are all of size 1. Each final state unambiguously determines one and only one initial state that generates the according attractor.

This difference between the two networks can be described as the difference in meaning processing capacity. In the case of the Boolean network the differences between the respective initial states simply vanish when the network unfolds its dynamics. When we consider, in analogy to the neural net, an initial state of the net as a signal that is received by the net, then always the same meaning is attached to each signal. This is, by the way, an extreme example of meaning processing systems that we considered in chapter 3.3.: The semantical net, consisting of different concepts from the programming language "Java" always generated "Java" as the central meaning, regardless of the different messages. Our Boolean network is even more extreme because it can generate only one particular attractor as the meaning of different signals. It can be compared with certain pathological cases of human one-sidedness where each perception is interpreted from the same point of view, i.e., it is given the same meaning. We already mentioned the case of the distorted man who understood each perception as a sexual signal. We may, therefore, characterize this network as one with a very small meaning processing capacity, measured in the size of the basins of attraction (in this case of the only basin of attraction).

Apparently our neural net has a much larger meaning processing capacity. Because it is very sensitive with respect to different signals the basins of attraction are extremely small and in particular there are a lot of different attractors and different basins of attraction likewise. Indeed, there are as many attractors as there are different initial states, that is as many as the coding of the units allow. The relation between the set of initial states and that of final attractor states can hence be characterized as a bijective function.

These two examples allow us to define the concept of meaning processing capacity. We demonstrated that the proportion between final attractor states and initial states is in the case of the Boolean network 1 : 8, in the case of the neural network 1 : 1. *Then the meaning processing capacity MC of a complex system is the proportion between the possible final attractor states and the possible initial states.* Apparently $0 \leq MC \leq 1$, with $MC = 0$ only in the case that the system does not generate any attractor state. In more informal terms, the characteristic of meaning processing capacity defines the capability of a complex system to attach different meanings to different signals, measured as the proportion of the sizes of the sets of initial states and final attractor states.

It is important to note that *per se* a large meaning processing capacity is not necessarily an advantage for a complex system. In the last subchapter we referred to the fact that the MC must neither be too large nor too small, that is, the respective basins of attraction must be on the one hand large enough to enable the system to perceive similarities. The example of the formation of analogies is possible only with networks whose basins of attractions are large enough to associate different vectors with the same target vector. A system that has to form analogies, therefore, must not have a too small MC-value. In the third chapter we gave the example of the aunt who had changed her hair-style and whom we recognize nevertheless, which means a basin of attraction large enough to perform this recognizing. On the other hand, the aunt was recognized including the difference in her personalities. That could be done only with another network that has a large MC-value, i.e., that has only small basins of attraction at its disposal. A whole system that has to perform both tasks, i.e., perceiving similarities *and* perceiving even small differences has, therefore, to consist of at least two different subnets with respective different MC-values.

In the two little examples both networks generated only very simple dynamics, i.e., dynamics that places these networks into Wolfram class 1 or at most 2. In other words, despite the very different MC-values of the two systems both belong to the same or nearly the same complexity class. Hence, it seems that the meaning processing capacity of a complex system is independent from the complexity by which the dynamics of the system is characterized.

Yet things are not so easy. The meaning processing capacity has a striking similarity to another ordering parameter, discovered by Wuensche and Lesser (1992). This parameter Z is defined by the probability to compute a preceding state *S(t – 1)* from an actual state *S(t)*. To compute the Z-value for a whole system one has to consider all possible states and compute their respective singular Z_S-values, i.e., the probability to determine the preceding states. The arithmetical mean of these singular values is the Z-value for the system, i.e.,

(5.3.3) $Z = \Sigma_i Z_i / n,$

if there are n possible states.

For example, the neural net in our example above is characterized by $Z = 1$ because for each possible state its preceding state can be unambiguously computed, i.e., with a probability $p = 1$. In this case is $Z = MC$. It is evident that the values of Z are in a large degree dependent on the size of the basins of attraction: The larger the basins are the smaller is the probability to determine a preceding state of an attractor and vice versa. That is why MC and Z are the same in the case of the small neural net. In this important aspect MC and Z describe the same characteristic of a complex systems, namely the size or average size respectively of the basins of attraction.[8]

But MC and Z are not always the same measure, which can be shown for the case of the Boolean network above. It is characterized by $MC = {}^1\!/_8\ 0 = 0.125$. For the computation of the Z-value one has to take into account the fact that there are 8 possible states. One state, namely (1,1,1) is the only attractor and could be generated from 8 possible preceding states. This yields the probability $p = 0.125$. In the case of the 7 other states one has to consider that these states are all initial states because there are no preceding states that could generate one of these states. Therefore, for 7 of 8 possible states the Z-value is $Z = 1$. The whole Z-value is then $(7 + 0.125)/8 = 0.891$. Yet if one takes into account only those states that factually have a preceding state then obviously Z becomes equivalent with MC.

It is known from the research done by Wuensche and Lesser (loc. cit.) that Z functions as an ordering parameter in a way rather similar to that of the P-parameter and of the λ-parameter mentioned in the second chapter. Like MC, C (the number of canalyzing functions) and λ $0 \leq Z \leq 1$ (remember that Z measures probabilities) and in a general sense low values of Z, that is $0 \leq Z \leq 0.5$ generate only simple dynamics of Wolfram classes 1 or 2. Only higher regions of the Z-values obtain more complex forms of dynamics. To be sure, there are always exceptions, as we showed in the case of the Boolean network, but Z like the other ordering parameters just give statistical regularities that always allow for exceptions. That is in particular the case with very small systems like our BN which

---

[8] Wuensche and Lesser originally introduced the Z-parameter in order to measure the basins of attraction fields.

is characterized by proportionally many, namely 7 of 8, so called Garden of Eden states, i.e., states that are possible only as purely initial states. These particular states are responsible for the rather high Z-value in contrast to the low MC-value. Larger systems with comparatively few Garden of Eden states allow a more immediate comparison between MC and Z and fit better in the predictions of the Z-parameter.[9]

The mentioned similarities between Z and MC suggest, with all necessary caution, the hypothesis that the meaning processing capacity also determines, if only in a rough sense, the dynamics of complex systems: The smaller the MC-values, the simpler the dynamics and vice versa. In fact, Wolfram (2002, 250 pp.) even redefines his complexity classes by the degree of "information processing capacity" which, although not defined in an exact manner, is rather similar to the concept of meaning processing capacity that we just introduced. The dynamics of a complex system, according to Wolfram, is directly depending on its information processing capacity: the larger it is the more complex is the dynamics and vice versa again.

In an intuitive way these results make sense because we would always assume that the complexity of a system depends on its processing capacities and vice versa. But by themselves these insights are not detailed enough.

When we consider systems of classes 3 and 4 the meaning processing capacity increases. Systems of classes 1 and 2, even if they are significantly larger than our two examples, only generate few attractors and in particular either only one attractor state for the whole system or few local attractors that remain isolated, i.e., have no effects on the whole system. In classes 3 and 4 local attractors occur rather frequently and they can *principally* spread out over the whole system. Systems of class 4 differ from those of class 3 in the respect that the former generate local attractors, yet their effects usually do not affect the whole system but only some regions. In systems of class 3 on the other hand the effects of local attractors usually spread out over the whole system, i.e., each part of the system becomes affected by local attractors in different regions.

These considerations are important for the following reasons. If we remind again of the example of the aunt with the new hair-style it is clear that the recognition of the aunt despite her changed appearance *and* the understanding in what way she has changed is only possible by a whole network that generates not only one attractor but two, namely one for the recognition of the aunt and one for the perception of her changes in hair-style. In addition, these two local attractors must be connected because we easily see "in our mind" the aunt as she appeared earlier and as she is now. Therefore, perception networks that are capable of remembering the aunt as in our example must be systems of class 3 or 4 – systems of lower classes are not able to perform such remembrance abilities.

On the other side such perception networks cannot be of class 3 because these systems are literally unable to generate local attractors that remain fixed for the time

[9] For Garden of Eden states cf. Wolfram 2002.

of the perception process. Each local attractor that is generated at some time t will be affected by other regions of the system at some time $t+n$ and will usually be changed by this disturbance. The result of such a dynamics is that the system is not able to generate fixed, that is unambiguous forms of meaning that remain constant during the perception process. In a somewhat metaphorical way of speaking such systems are unable to decide which particular meaning must be attached to some external signal because they always change an earlier meaning via the processing of the signal through the whole system. These systems are occupied only with themselves and are not able to transfer the result of meaning processing into action. They are like the mentioned donkey of Buridan that starved to death because it could not decide which one of two identical hay-stacks it should start eating. Systems of class 3 that are often termed as "chaotic" systems are the extreme opposite to systems that generate always the same attractor regardless of the particular signals: these systems generate too few different kinds of meaning, whereas systems of class 3 generate too many.[10]

Only systems of class 4 have the meaning processing capacity to generate different local attractors that are partially connected on the one hand and that do not affect the whole system on the other hand. This characteristic that is realized by suited system's topologies guarantees that the local attractors remain fixed and therefore attach constant meanings to external signals. In addition, only such systems have in contrast to systems of class 3 a "memory", that is they recognize a signal again after a certain time. We remember our aunt because the topology of the system has not changed in the meantime – at least not with respect to the aunt; that is why the same attractor "aunt as we knew her" will be generated even if some years have passed since we saw her for the last time.

It is well known for a long time that our brain is a parallel processing system in contrast to the serial way the most computers, the so called von Neumann computers, are operating. To understand this characteristic we have to assume that our brain just operates in the way we described with the aunt example. An external signal is decomposed, e.g., in "principally known elderly female" and "changes in her appearance". Then both components of the signal generate a local attractor and these are recombined again by particular connections between them. In the end of this parallel processing process the whole personality of the aunt will be stored by the topology of the whole network, that is the aunt will be remembered again if we meet her some months later. Parallel processing, therefore, is the simultaneous generation of two or more local attractors and their recombination via respective connections.

We mentioned the fact that quasi-chaotic systems of class 3 are not only unable to generate constant meanings but that they are accordingly unable to act, like the unlucky donkey. Therefore, systems with sufficient meaning processing capacity

[10] We wish to remind that finite systems, if they are not stochastic, always generate attractors because they are periodic. That was discovered by Poincaré in his "Theorem of Eternal Return" and means that the concept of "chaos" must be applied very carefully to finite systems.

must connect not only the different local attractors that together attach the meaning to the whole signal or message respectively but also those attractors that belong to the action part of the whole system (see above chapter 3.4.). The attachment of unambiguous and constant meaning to different signals is necessary but not sufficient for a system to exist in a difficult environment. To be sure, each system has to learn what kind of connections it must construct between "meaning attractors" and "action attractors" during its developmental processes. We shall deal with the process of learning in the next subchapter. But after a successful learning process these connections have to be kept constant and neither the meaning attractors nor the action attractors must be changed by other regions of the system. We have again an example of the frequently applicable truism: As many connections between different local attractors as necessary and as few as possible.[11]

The generation of constant local attractors is obviously necessary for memory and in that aspect essential for maintaining the identity of a complex system. This is immediately understandable in the case of cognitive systems where the loss of memory is equivalent with the loss of the personal identity. Yet meaning processing capacities and the generation of local attractors is essential for social systems too, although not in these terms. In chapters 2 and 4.2 we already mentioned the fact that local attractors are rather common in social systems. The Amish in Pennsylvania are a famous example of such social local attractors. Yet if such local subcultures remain isolated from the rest of the society then the society risks to become decomposed, i.e., to lose its identity as a whole culture. Therefore, societies must be more complex than systems of class 1 or 2. On the other hand, societies too need local attractors for the reason that people do not live in a whole "society" which is an abstract concept but in subcultures like those of certain religions and in particular regions, towns and so on. In addition, local attractors that represent certain subcultures and traditions, must remain fixed over a longer period in order to make life understandable for the members of the society. That places successful societies in class 4 because class 3 would render these societies unable to act as a whole.

The term of "meaning processing capacity" can be taken quite literally even in the case of social systems. Such systems must be able as a whole to understand external signals in the way we just described, i.e., they must be able to understand similarities as similarities and differences as differences. In Klüver 2002 we discussed this problem with respect to the culture of a society, that is not only the accepted knowledge of the society but also the accepted methods of problem solving. Therefore, the culture of a society determines the *social* meaning processing capacity. Societies that are too simple in this aspect not only tend to stagnate but also risk to perish in difficult and changing environments. The local cultural attractors that generate the respective local social attractors are then the established methods

[11] Presumably the ability to concentrate on one problem at a time is dependent on the capability to "switch off" certain connections that combine the problem with other association fields but that hinder the process of problem solving.

and world-views of the culture that either are or are not sufficient for the task of surviving. History is full of examples where this capacity was not sufficient. The "handling of meaning", to vary Wolfram a bit (Wolfram 2002, 252) "is in some respects fundamental" for all complex systems that have to maintain their existence in difficult environments and in particular for those of communicative processes.

In chapter 4.4. we introduced the sd-parameter as the measure of the social dimension of a communicative process and postulated that the sd-value of a communicative situation determines in a large way the cognitive processes of the communicators and the communicative process as a whole. When considering the reflections on meaning processing capacity we have to vary this postulate a bit: A rather small MC-value probably makes possible only an equally simple cognitive dynamics, even if the sd-value of the situation is characteristic for complex cognitive dynamics. In other words, the MC-values of the respective cognitive systems determine if complex communication processes are possible, i.e., if the communicators are both able to fill out the space of freedom that the sd-values of the situation permit. It is evident that communicators with low MC-values, i.e., with a capability of only simple cognitive dynamics, are not able to use the freedom in a situation with comparatively low sd-values, that is, situations that are characterized by social and cultural equality between the communicators. In that case the MC-values are obviously more determinant than the social sd-values.

On the other hand, high MC-values make complex cognitive dynamics only possible if the social situation permits it, i.e., if the sd-values are sufficiently low. It seems that the relation between the sd-parameter and the MC-parameter is not a symmetrical one: Given sufficiently high MC-values then the sd-values of the situation will determine the complexity of the cognitive dynamics and this way the complexity of the whole communicative process; low MC-values on the other hand will practically always generate just rather simple cognitive and communicative dynamics, regardless of the sd-values.

5.4. THE MEANING OF LEARNING

In the preceding chapters we have frequently used the term "learning" in different contexts. That is of course not by chance: Learning, at least human learning, is mostly performed via communicative processes and communication very often consists of learning and results of certain learning achievements. To be sure, there are learning processes that do not occur in the medium of communication. Robinson on his island had to learn how to build a blockhouse without any communicative assistance by other more experienced house-builders. Yet practically all learning processes that are socially organized are communicative processes. Accordingly, although communicative processes must not necessarily contain components of learning even such informal discourses like the discussion between friends on the chances of a certain football team will end with some learning results, in particular by the exchange of information about the health of some players, the strategy of the trainer and so on. It is hardly possible to analyze communication without taking into regard the importance of learning. But what is learning?

We do not intend, of course, to discuss all the innumerable learning theories that have been formulated and frequently are very valuable for psychological and teaching purposes. Because we are interested in a *general* framework that allows to reformulate both social and cognitive processes in terms of complex systems theory our interest is to give a precise definition of learning that can be integrated into the conceptual framework we have developed so far.

Since the famous hypothesis of Hebb (1949) learning in neurobiological terms is considered as the systematic variation of the synaptic connections between neural clusters. Speaking in more general terms learning can be defined as the systematic variation of the "structure" of a cognitive system and the fixation of the successful variations. In particular the structure changed by learning must at the end of the learning process be capable to generate attractors (meaning) and to "remember", that is to generate the same attractors after a certain time. In addition, the cognitive system must be able to compute via its structure the information degree of the respective message. Therefore, we have to clarify the concepts of structure and structure changing.

Consider once again two of the examples we have given so far, namely the "Java network" from chapter 3.3. and the semantical network of Tom, described in chapter 5.1.

Both networks are the result of learning processes. In the first example the student constructed his Java network by receiving messages like "Java is a programming language", "Java is very well suited for constructing libraries" and so on. Each time the student received a message with concepts new for him he integrated them into his network, that is, he inserted the new concepts into his network and generated new connections between the new concepts and the initial ones. Because the general subject of these learning processes was "Java" the result is a network with the concept "Java" at its center.

Accordingly Tom's network is the result of learning processes consisting of – verbal or non verbal – messages like "real men are strong", "women are weak and

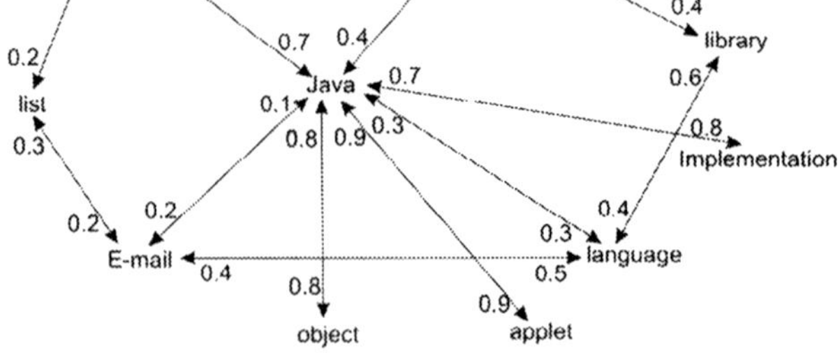

Figure 8. The Java network

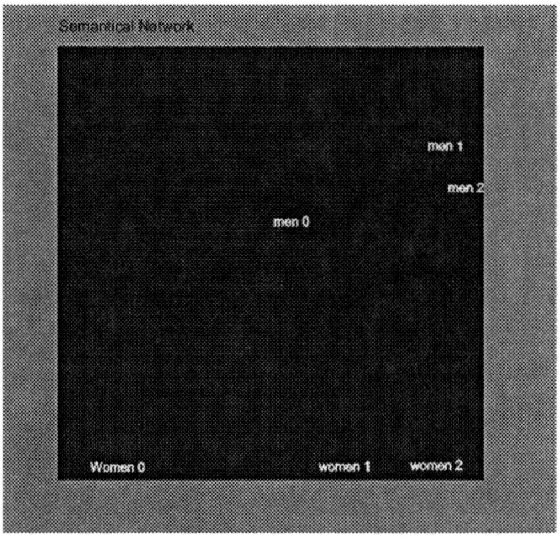

Figure 9. The semantical network of Tom (example with only "right" men and women)

submissive", "men are dominant" and so on. The result is a semantical network that consists of two different and separated clusters, i.e., a female cluster and a male one. There is no strict center as in the Java network but a dichotomous structure that divides the social world in "real" men and "real" women.

In both cases the result of the respective learning processes is something akin to an ordering algorithm that places each new message or perception respectively into the structure of the semantical network. We already referred to the developmental theory of Piaget: the two semantical networks are nothing else than the well known assimilation schemas of Piaget's theory, i.e., ordering schemas for the interpretation of new messages and perceptions. These schemas are always the result of according learning processes which are in particular performed by the operation of accommodation, i.e., the revising and enlarging of assimilation schemas. Therefore, we may assume that learning is the construction of certain assimilation schemas by the accommodative variation of initial schemas. For example, a child who has generated an assimilation schema of "dog" tends to integrate all animals it sees into this schema and accordingly calls the neighbor's cat also "dog". When the father of the child corrects it by pointing out that this animal is a "cat" the child has to enlarge its schema by adding the concepts "smaller than most dogs", "making meow", and "cat" with the according connections between "cat" and the other new concepts.

It is now important to remember the distinction between so called general rules of interaction and topological rules that we introduced in chapter 2. If learning consists of the accommodation process of changing a cognitive structure – a schema in the terms of Piaget –, then either general rules can be changed or topological ones or both. This can be illustrated by the example of the learning of logical disjunction and logical conjunction. A Boolean net that is able to perform the operation of logical disjunction is the following:

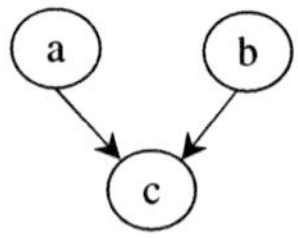

with the adjacency matrix

	a	*b*	*c*
a	0	0	1
b	0	0	1
c	0	0	0

and the connecting function $f(a, b) = c$ as the logical disjunction. If the learning process demands that the disjunction should be replaced by the logical conjunction then the adjacency matrix, i.e., the topology of the system, remains the same but the Boolean function f must be changed. In this case learning consist of the changing of a general rule.

Learning as the changing or addition of general rules is frequently the case in social systems. For example, the permanent members of the security council of the UN have, as is well known, the so called veto right. Logically this means that, besides the votes of the non permanent members, the voting process is organized according to the logical conjunction: only if permanent member A *and* member B *and* member C *and* member D *and* member E agree, then the council can pass a motion. This right has often been criticized by nations that are not permanent members. If the UN is willing to "learn" in this respect, that is to give all members the same rights without any veto right, then the logical conjunction must be changed into a certain disjunction, e.g., if (A is willing and B and C) *or* (B is willing and C and D) *or* (C is willing and D and E)..., then the motion can be passed. Other examples of the changing of general rules in social systems can be easily given.

But of course social systems also change topological rules, e.g., if a firm decides to make communication processes less hierarchically than they actually are. If originally an employee could only speak with his immediate superior and if after some reforms the same employee is allowed to speak with practically all members of the firm then obviously some topological rules have been changed.[12] A lot of political reforms are nothing else than the changing of topological rules, in particular those reforms that intend to increase degrees of democracy.

[12] We defined in chapter 2 topological rules as those that determine which elements of a system interacts with which others and to what degree these interaction will and can occur.

As far as we know the brain does not learn by changing general *rules* like the activation rules of artificial neural nets, but it learns by the variation of its topology in another manner. A neural net that is able to perform the operation of logical disjunction is the following feed forward network, operating with the linear activation rule

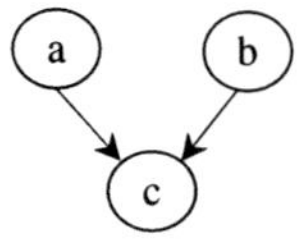

with the weight matrix

	a	b	c
a	0	0	0.5
b	0	0	0.5
c	0	0	0

and a "threshold value" θ at the input of c with $\theta > 0$. Threshold value means roughly speaking that in this case c only gets activated if the input is larger than 0. A threshold value is the mathematical representation of a switch that only opens if the input is larger than a certain value – or smaller, which is also possible. The threshold is connected with the units via a threshold function that is defined in this example as

$$\text{(5.4.1)} \quad \begin{array}{l} c = 1, \text{ if input } i > 0, \\ c = 0 \text{ else.} \end{array}$$

In another formulation we get the more general threshold function for this case as

$$\text{(5.4.2)} \quad \begin{array}{l} c = 1, \text{ if } i > \theta, \\ c = 0 \text{ else, with} \theta = 0.4. \end{array}$$

By defining the threshold as a switch the threshold apparently belongs to the topology of the network in the sense that it decides if some units are activated at all (cf. chapter 2). One easily verifies that the value of c, depending on the initial values of a and b is computed according to the logical disjunction, i.e., $c = 0$ if $a = b = 0$ and $c = 1$ else.

If the network has to learn the logical conjunction instead of the disjunction the simplest way is to change the threshold value θ from 0.4 to 0.6. Again it is easily verified by using the second version of the threshold function that the neural network now processes as a Boolean net representing the logical conjunction.

In other words, neural nets like our brain learn by changing their topology – either thresholds values or weights or both. General rules like activation rules are usually not changed although this is in principle possible too.

The changing of a structure in order to generate new and more suited schemas of assimilation then means the changing of rules – topological ones or general ones. It depends on the kind of systems, which of these possibilities are applied. The reason that in contrast to the brain and artificial neural nets social systems frequently learn by changing explicit rules is probably due to the fact that social actors as the carriers of the interactions and learning processes of social systems usually think in general rules as the structure of social systems. Changing social structures as the learning processes of social systems in form of the changing of general rules is the kind of variation, which is to be expected in this case. The changing of certain topological values on the other hand, which is typical for certain cognitive systems like the brain and neural nets, is appropriate for these systems for the simple reason that there are no explicit cognitive rules in the brain but only the interaction of neurons according to very general rules of interaction. Its artificial counterparts, the artificial neural nets, follow the same logic. The relation between rules and topologies like those of brain and neural nets will be discussed in later paragraphs, as will be the question how it is possible to learn by changing explicitly formulated rules.[13]

According to this general logic of learning in cognitive systems learning processes of these systems are mostly determined by rules that direct the changing of topological values like weight values or threshold ones. Typical for these learning rules are the so called Hebbian learning rules (named after Donald Hebb), i.e., rules that change the weights of the connections between artificial neurons. One well known example is the "delta rule" that we explained in chapter 2. For a remembrance we show it here once more:

$$w_{ij}(t+1) = w_{ij}(t) \pm \eta(t_i - a_j)o_i = \eta o_i \delta j$$

Approximately speaking the delta rule is an algorithm that changes the weight wij between the sending neuron i and the receiving neuron j at time t into the weight $w_{ij}(t+1)$ at time $t+1$. The degree of the changing is dependent on the size of the error δthat is why it is called delta rule, of course). Although the delta-rule contains only the procedure of weight changing it is easily possible to enlarge this rule with respect to the changing of thresholds by substituting $w_{ij}(t)$ with $\theta j(t)$, if j is the receiving unit. In the example given above of the learning of the logical conjunction the iterated application of the delta rule would have increased the initial value of $\theta_j(t) = 0.1$ to $\theta_j(t+n) = 0.6$. It is of course a practical question if only the weight values shall be subject to the application of such learning rules or the threshold values or both.

Hebbian learning like the delta-rule or the back propagation rule that we mentioned in the preceding chapters are applied in the case of so called *supervised* learning, i.e., learning processes where the correct solution is at least in principle known and where the cognitive system has to adjust its structure in the way just

[13] The learning of so called rule based systems or expert systems respectively will be used as a clarification of the learning process by the conscious changing of rules.

described. In particular, frequently in a process of supervised learning the size of the error the learner has made is known to him. Learning in this case means that the system is able after the learning process to generate the correct answer if the problem or a similar one is given once or several times more. If the correct solution and then of course the size of the error are not known but if the system gets immediate feed back whether some solution A is better or worse than a solution B one speaks of *reinforced* learning. This kind of learning, which is the logic of evolutionary processes too, is very common in practical contexts. Because the usual learning rules are not directly applicable – the size of the error is not known but only if the system is on the right track –, the variation of the structure must use some kind of evaluation function (cf. chapter 2) that determines if a new solution is better than the older ones. Such evaluation functions are well known from, e.g., the field of evolutionary theories and algorithms (cf. Klüver 2002). Yet also in these cases of reinforced learning the process consists of the variation of certain topologies, i.e., mainly the variation of weight values and threshold values via the feedback by the evaluation function. In a mathematical sense, of course, the mentioned learning rules are evaluation functions too because they valuate the learning success in direct dependence of the size of the error.

The third learning type is the so called non supervised learning where the learning system has to construct some "internal order" of the perceptions or messages respectively the system has received. Non supervised learning occurs without *immediate* feed back from the environment with respect to the success of the learning processes. Consider for example a child who has constructed a semantical network about animals that contains the concepts "fish", "fins", "swimming in water" and so on. Now consider this child in a zoo where the child is watching a show with dolphins. Without doubt the child will integrate these fascinating animals into his semantical sub network that contains the concepts belonging to fish. Without feed back from, e.g., his parents the child will interpret the perceptions of dolphins as the perceptions of fishes – the child has performed a process of non supervised learning by constructing an increased semantical network. Note that this is a simple case of accommodation that was done without feed back or assistance from his social environment, namely the inserting of perceptions "fishes that jump out of the water and play with balls" into his net. To be sure, if the child demands the next time at the zoo to go to the show with the funny fishes many parents will try to explain that and why the categorizing of dolphins into the concept "fish" is wrong. In that case the learner gets correcting feed back and has to correct his internal constructions.

In a strict sense the distinction between non supervised learning and supervised one is misleading in the sense that learning always consists of the processes of varying certain structures on the one hand and taking into regard the corrections by the environment on the other. The example with the dolphins shows that the difference is mostly whether the feed back immediately occurs or not. But feed back has sooner or later always to occur, either from a natural environment or a social one. Robinson, who had to learn how to build a blockhouse of course got his feed back from the material he worked with as is the case with all such processes of working. The child gets his corrections from its social environment and that is one extremely important condition for communication at all: if the internal constructions of, e.g., semantical networks are not permanently corrected by the social environment then in a long run the different learners as communicators would have no chance of mutual understanding in the sense defined in the third chapter. Learning as the basis for communication is dependent on the permanent feed back from the social environment. Of course, semantical networks do not become identical for different persons, but socialization, understood here as a permanent process of feed back with respect to the learning processes of children and youths, guarantees that the assimilation schemas are sufficiently similar in order to make communication possible.[14]

The Kohonen Feature Maps (KFM) we described in several examples, e.g., in the story of Tom, is one of the best known mathematical models of non supervised learning: it organizes its weight matrix only according to internal criteria, namely the size of the respective activation values of its units. Via the rule "the winner takes all" the neurons with the greatest activation values form the centers of clusters and each other neuron is attached to one cluster or at the common border of different clusters. This process is non supervised because there are no external target vectors and no evaluation function that valuates different solutions. Yet we demonstrated in the example of Tom that for the simulation of non supervised learning processes via the application of a KFM one has to take into account the fact that, e.g., Tom could construct his world view only because he was in certain aspects quite successful, i.e., he obtained permanent (positive) feed back from his social environment.

When we now consider the relation between learning by changing certain topologies and learning by changing explicitly formulated rules in more detail we seem to be in a slight puzzle: On the one hand humans consciously think according to certain cognitive rules and learn by changing or enlarging respectively these rules; on the other hand the human brain as all brains learns by the variation of the according topologies. The question, therefore, is how the variation of some topological values can result in the construction of the according rules or the according cognitive schemata respectively.[15]

The example of the two logical functions of disjunction and conjunction above already gives some hints how this process must be understood. We demonstrated that a very simple neural net that performed like a Boolean net consisting only of the logical disjunction was able to perform the logical conjunction by increasing

[14] Several theorists of communication stress the point that the success of communication, i.e., mutual understanding is quite improbable because each communicator constructs his internal structures by autonomous processes, i.e., in a non supervised way (cf. e.g. Luhmann 1984). Such scholars practically always neglect the effects of socialization that operates as an assimilating factor with respect to the non supervised constructions of the internal (assimilating) cognitive schemata.

[15] To be sure, the classical conception of intelligence as the performing of rule based cognitive operations is too narrow as, e.g., the history of the early AI very clearly demonstrated. Nobody seriously believes today that "real" Artificial Intelligence, whatever that will be, can alone be achieved by the construction of rule based systems.

the threshold value. The result of this learning process is again a net that functions exactly like the according Boolean net, that is like a rule based system. Although the Boolean net and the neural net significantly differ with respect to their internal structure, their operations are in that sense identical that both give the same output in dependency of the same input. In this sense the two networks are functionally equivalent and for an external observer practically identical.

A very different second example can serve to make this aspect even clearer. In chapter 5.2. we demonstrated the possibility of solving certain detective cases by the application of a hetero-associative neural net. In this context, namely the mentioned course on Artificial Intelligence and Detective Stories, we developed other programs in order to solve the murder case of a detective story of Agatha Christie, that is the story of "The Spanish Chest". It is not necessary to tell this particular story whose logical structure is very similar to other stories of Christie.[16] For this story we used two different programs, i.e., a rule based system or expert system respectively and an interactive neural net. The expert system contained different general rules like "*if* a person X has an alibi, *then* X is not the murderer", "*if* X has a motive *then* X is a suspect", "*if* X had access to the murder weapon *then* X is a suspect" and so on. Besides these general rules that are necessary for each murder case the program also contained rules that are specific for the particular case of the Spanish Chest like for example "*if* X loves the wife of the victim *then* X has a motive" and "*if* X is knew where the victim was at the time of the murder *then* X is a suspect" and so on. In particular the program contained an "identification rule", that is "*if* X has a motive *and* no alibi *and* access to the weapon *and* knowledge about the whereabouts of the victim at his death *then* X is the murderer (or one of them)".

We used this expert system in the mentioned course on "Artificial Intelligence and the logic of literary detectives". The task of the participants of this course, students of communicative science, was to insert the facts of Christie's story into the program, according to the succession in which the facts were given to the reader in the story.[17] We omit the technical details how the students should operate with the program; the interesting question for the students was if they could identify the murderer before Poirot as the detective in this story would explicitly tell the identity of the murderer and his reasons for naming just this person, and/or if they could do it before the program named the murderer. To cut a long story short, the students of this group were not able to identify the murderer and in particular they were not able to insert all the necessary facts into the program. That is why the program could also not identify the culprit. By demonstrating that the program had not all the facts that were told in the story and by adding these facts omitted by the students we showed that the program was indeed capable of solving this particular murder case.

---

[16] Readers who are able to read German can learn more about the story and the details of the programs in Klüver and Stoice 2004.

[17] The students got only some pages of the story at a time; therefore, they could not cheat, i.e., look at the end of the story how the detective Hercule Poirot solved the case.

The program that we named "HERCULE 1" in honor to the literary detective "learned" only in the way that it got explicitly formulated rules like those we mentioned and that it also got the facts of the story in the order that the detective, Poirot, presented them to the readers. To be sure, humans very often learn the same way, i.e., they take over some explicitly formulated rules and are instructed how to apply them to certain examples or facts respectively. The learning of arithmetic, for example, is frequently done by learning rules like "2 + 3" means "adding 1 to 2, then another 1 and then another 1" (cf. e.g. Dehaene 1997). Accordingly a reader of detective stories first has to learn that a motive means that the respective person is at least a suspect, that is he has to learn a rule like those we mentioned. Therefore, the development of the expert systems by us and the inserting of the facts by the students can rightly be interpreted as the model and example of certain learning processes. Yet how are these rules implemented in the brain or, asked from another point of view, how can the brain learn such rules if the brain consists only of nets with certain topologies?

We answered this question by applying an interactive net (IN) to the same problem of the Spanish chest. The task of constructing a suited IN was again performed by other students of this course who were instructed by us how to do this. The results of one IN-example that was able to solve the case is shown in figure 10.

The net consists of 11 neurons, one for each suspected person whose names form the first group of neurons, and four "category neurons" like "motive", "access (to the weapon)", "no alibi", and "knowledge (about the whereabouts of the victim)". The 11th neuron is "murder X" that was externally activated when the weight matrix had been constructed. The weight matrix was constructed with three values, namely $w_{PC} = 1$ if a certain person P must be attached to one category C, e.g., P has a motive; $w_{PC} = -1$, if the person P cannot be attached to a certain category C, e.g., P has an alibi, and $w_{PQ} = 0$ for all relation values between two persons P and Q. The task of the students who worked with the IN was a) to decide how many units their IN must have and b) how the facts of the story were to be translated into the according weight values of the IN. (The students received the story in the same

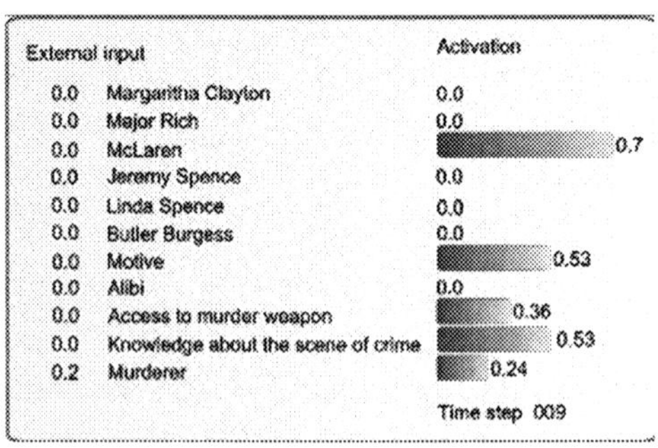

Figure 10. An IN for the case of the Spanish chest

way as those of the first group.) Figure 10 shows the final result: After the external activation of the neuron "murder X", i.e., after putting the question to the IN "who dunnit?", the IN generates a point attractor after ca. 9 runs. This final state shows that only the person "McLaren" is significantly activated which means that only McLaren could have killed the victim.

The success of the second group of students, by the way, was better than that of the first group. Although several students only constructed networks that did not generate a point attractor all the resulting networks at least identified the factual murderer McLaren with some probability. Some students constructed an IN with results like those shown in figure 10.[18] To put it into a nutshell, these students apparently were better than the others, but for the sake of fairness we have to point out that the second group got more instructions from us than the first.

The IN "HERCULE 2" is a very suited example for the question how the brain is able to construct rules. Although the IN was not trained the way of, e.g., the hetero-associative net for the story of van de Wetering but manually completed by the students, the final topology of the IN is in a logical sense equivalent to the rules of the expert system that we described above. The rule "*if* a person X has no alibi *and* a motive *and* access to the weapon *and* knowledge about the whereabouts of the victim *then* X is the murderer or at least one of the murderers" is represented in the IN by weighted connections between X and the respective categories with $w_{XC} = 1$. Accordingly, a rule "*if* a person Y has no motive *then* Y is not the murderer" is represented in the IN as $w_{YM} = 0$. The solution of the case by the expert system is done by checking all possibilities "is Major Rich the murderer", "is Ms. Clayton the murderer" and so on. In all cases the answer of the program is "no" with the exception of McLaren. The IN operates in another way but one that is logically equivalent: the constructed topology allows only the final activation of the neuron "McLaren", that is the IN excludes all other possibilities. To put it into a nutshell, the manual training of the IN results in a topology that *for an external observer* looks as if the system has rules at its disposal that are applied to a certain case.

It seems rather plausible to assume that this is the way the brain learns rules and how to apply them. When we remind of the perception network (PN) described in chapter 4.3, then the PN learned how to behave with respect to different persons that belong to the same type by its training with the examples of people of certain types. The PN first learned to remember how to deal with the *person* A and stored the rule "*if* you meet person A *then* act with the respective action vector". In addition, it learned how to behave if another person B was perceived who is different to person A but belongs to the same type. In this case the PN applied the rule "*if* you meet a person B that belongs to the same type as A *then* act in the same way with respect to B as you do with respect to A". To be sure, neither the "detective IN" nor

[18] "Probability" means in this context that not only "McLaren" was finally activated but also other persons, in particular the person that was initially suspected by the police (Major Rich). In some cases the respective networks "oscillated" with attractors of period 2 between the possibilities of McLaren and Major Rich.

the PN of the ordering model consist of explicitly formulated rules but of certain topologies that enable them to operate in the equivalent fashion like a rule based system. In both cases the networks learned by the variation and completion of their respective topologies and in both cases the final systems acted like rule based systems. Therefore, from the point of view of learning networks like our brain a rule is nothing else than the result of the construction of a suited topology; the correct application of a rule then is a certain input to the network combined with the respective correct output as, e.g., in the case of the Spanish chest.[19]

Not only symbolic AI but also many branches of the cognitive sciences have assumed that the learning of rules and their correct applications is at the core of learning and intelligence in general. But if the brain contains no rules but "only" suited topologies the question arises how the concept of rules has obtained such prominence. We shall deal with this question in the next subchapter and shall before this consider some other questions of learning processes.

The examples we demonstrated so far of different learning processes all were orientated to the famous definitions of Piaget, i.e., learning is understood as a process of the construction of assimilation schemata by accommodation. The respective results then could be interpreted as the formation of, e.g., semantical networks or also as the formation of certain rules and the capability of rule application. In this sense learning always changes and increases a certain capability of the processing of external signals or messages respectively.[20]

In the preceding subchapter we defined the meaning processing capability MC as the proportion of the final attractor states and the possible initial states of a cognitive system. If successful learning processes mean an increased capability of signal processing then of course learning processes may frequently change the MC-values of the system too. If, for example, certain situations demand that the respective cognitive system should be able to distinguish different signals more exactly than before then obviously the system has to orientate its learning processes to the task of increasing its MC-values. If on the other hand the system should learn to perceive similarities or analogies respectively then the system must learn to decrease its MC-values. In that way it is possible to define learning tasks in a mathematical fashion. But note again that it depends on the problems the system has to solve if the learning process has to decrease or increase the MC-values. *Per se* neither the increasing nor decreasing of the MC-values is good or bad for the system. In the case of the Amsterdam murder the officers had to decrease their MC- values in order to perceive the analogy between the two different cases, if the officers were initially not able to perceive it without learning.

---

[19] Several researchers in the field of neuroinformatics analyze this relation between rules and topologies under the heading of "rule extraction by neural networks" (cf. e.g. Sestito and Dillon 1994). They frequently use different approaches than that just described. In this book we can just mention the fact that our approach is apparently a new one (see below next subchapter).

[20] "External" refers to the environment of the respective cognitive system that is occupied with certain cognitive processes. If this cognitive system is a subsystem of a larger cognitive system then "external" can also mean another cognitive subsystem of the whole system – a part of the brain for example may receive signals from other parts of the same brain.

In the story of Tom with his dichotomous world view Tom should learn to increase his MC-values because his simple world view contains too few different attractors; a resocialization of Tom, therefore, should concentrate on the task to teach him to use more subtle distinctions between different persons.

Learning may not only result in the construction of cognitive schemata in the sense defined above and by this way in the successful solving of certain problems but it may also consist of the acquisition of certain learning strategies. This is known in learning theories as the "learning of learning" and unfortunately frequently only used in an informal and rather metaphorical manner. Yet for some aspects of this difficult concept a more exact clarification is possible. Communication, after all, can also consist of teaching the other better ways of learning and thus understanding each other better.

The learning rules we so far gave as examples for the formal representation of learning processes are deterministic algorithms in the sense that they are recursively applied and lead to a result, i.e., an attractor in a solution space. Learning rules like all deterministic transition functions, therefore, depend on the initial states of the learning systems and lead either only to suboptimal results or need a lot of time to obtain the favorable results. Such algorithms can be understood as the formal representations of, e.g., human learners who know only certain learning techniques and apply them to the problems they have to deal with. But even the comparably simple two detective cases we considered demonstrate that it is often necessary to switch learning strategies and in particular to vary the learning strategy that seems to be best suited for the problem at hand. When such problems arise the learning system has at least two possibilities:

On the one hand it may be useful to enlarge a deterministic learning algorithm by the addition of a stochastic component. Deterministic algorithms that are used for optimizing processes – learning is basically just that, namely an optimizing process – tend to reach a result that must be characterized as a "local optimum", that is as a result that could and should be improved but not by further application of the deterministic algorithm alone. One can compare this situation with a mountain climber who has reached a small peak by climbing steadily higher and higher *and* by avoiding to go deeper in the process of climbing. Such a climber will never reach the highest summit because to do this he had to go down and try another trail, which he will not do. But if this is the only solution to reach the summit the climber would do better if he inserts a stochastic component by going down again and trying by chance another trail. In other words, if a purely deterministic algorithm only reaches suboptimal results then the factual state should be changed by chance and with a recommenced application of the learning algorithm another way could be explored.[21] We may call such algorithms "semi- stochastic" ones because they

[21] The so-called evolutionary algorithms like the genetic algorithm are constructed according to that principle – like the biological evolution itself: They contain deterministic principles and stochastic components like mutation and the random selection of cross over parts (see above chapter 2). This may be a mathematical explanation for the success of the biological evolution.

differ from purely stochastic processes by their deterministic components and use random procedures only if they get stacked fast in a local suboptimum. To learn the introduction of stochastic components into established learning procedures can be looked at as an important type of the learning of learning.

A less radical option to vary learning strategies is to change – increase or decrease – some parameters of the strategy. Consider for example the delta rule that we mentioned in several contexts; it contained a certain "learning rate" η. One may understand this learning rate as the formal representation of the individual quickness – or slowness respectively –, in which human learners differ. If the learning process of an artificial network is too slow then it may be favorable to increase the learning rate. But as in the case of the MC-values it is not always favorable to increase η: If the learning rate is too large then the network often "overshoots its mark", i.e., it transgresses the optimal result and will not stabilize. A comparison with human learners demonstrates that this is not seldom the case with learners who are too quick with finding a solution. Therefore, the important aspect is to keep the learning rate and other factors that determine the learning process as variable as necessary. Learning how to vary such factors is another type of the learning of learning.

Consciously performed learning processes of human learners frequently demand the changing of established rules of thinking or of action. We mentioned in chapter 2 that the changing of rules demand the introduction and application of meta rules that determine the variation of the first rules. Such meta rules can be applied, of course, to learning strategies too, either in the ways just described or by determining if and when to switch from one learning strategy to another one. To illustrate a process by which a cognitive system changes its rules via the application of meta rules we quote an example by John Holland (1992), the inventor of the genetic algorithm (GA).

Consider a frog that has to learn how to catch flies and to flee from an approaching stork (in reality, of course, frogs do not have to learn this but know it by instinct). In the beginning of the learning process the frog has some rules like "*if* a small object is near, *then* open your mouth" or "*if* a large object approaches *then* do nothing". It is rather obvious that our frog has to learn fast because if it does not it either will starve because no fly will voluntarily go into the frog's mouth, or the frog will be eaten by the stork. Now let us assume that the rules of the frog's cognitive and action systems are formally represented as vectors of the kind R = (1, 0, 1, 1, #, 0, 1). The vector is divided in a perception part, let us say the first four components, and an action part, in this case the last three components. In the perception part a 1 means that a certain characteristic of an object is perceived, for example "big"; accordingly a 0 in this component means that the object is not big but small. A 1 in the action part means that a certain action should be executed, for example "jump away"; accordingly a 0 means "stay at the place". The # means that the situation is not clear: A # in the perception part means that a certain characteristic cannot be identified as, e.g., either "small" or "big"; a # in the action part means that the frog does not know how to act. The example above can then be understood as a rule R_1: "*if* an object moves *and if* it is small *and if* it is grey *and if* it buzzes *then* be undecided (or act at random) with respect to moving *and* open your mouth". Factually R is not one single rule but the combination of several individual rules. The reason for this form of representation will immediately become clear.

We can understand this vector as the formal representation of the frog as a cognitive system. This single frog apparently is not very suited for surviving in an environment full of flies and storks. Therefore, let us consider other frogs that are characterized by other rule vectors, for example by $R_2 = (0, \#, 1, 0, 1, \#)$ with the meaning "*if* an object does not move *and if* it is neither small or big *and if* it is not grey *and if* it buzzes, *then* jump to it *and* open your mouth or keep it shut at random". We can add more frogs until we obtain a population of 10 frogs with different vectors as their formal representation.

We have used the terminology of "different frogs". We can of course also consider these different vectors as the representations of one frog only that tries different rule systems at random. But for the sake of simplicity we refer to a population of several frogs that are all considered as rule based cognitive systems. These frogs are more or less "fit", i.e., they are more or less suited for surviving in a certain environment of flies and storks. Now we apply the "genetic operators" of the GA to the vectors of the different frogs by taking those that are best suited for survival and "marry" them. For example, a frog consisting of a vector $R_3 = (0, 1, 1, \#, 1, \#)$ is certainly better suited for survival than the frog with the vector R_1. The genetic operators are "crossover", which means a recombination of two vectors, e.g., taking one part of a first vector, replacing a part of a second vector by the part of the first and putting the surplus part of the second vector into the first. For example, a crossover of R_2 and R_3 can obtain $R_4 = (0, \#, 1, \#, 1, \#)$ and $R_5 = (0, 1, 1, 0, 1, \#)$, by changing the components 3 and 4 in both vectors. In addition one can apply the second genetic operator of mutation by changing at random one component in the resulting vectors, in our example R_4 and R_5. By the mutation of the first component we obtain the vectors $R_6 = (1, \#, 1, \#, 1, \#)$ and $R_7 = (1, 1, 1, 0, 1, \#)$. The mutation of 1 transforms it into 0 and vice versa; the mutation of a # transform it at random either to a 1 or to a 0. Each application of the genetic operators, therefore, transforms two vectors – the "parents" – into two new ones – the "children".[22]

This operation is iterated, i.e., in each generation only the best ones are taken for "marriage" and by that for "reproduction", i.e., the transformation of initial ones into new vectors. Note that in this case we have an example of reinforced learning, that is the goal or target vector respectively is not known but an evaluation function or fitness function respectively decides if the "children" are better than the parents and which of the parents and children are the best ones of their generation. The whole process stops either if a certain optimum is reached, i.e., if the fitness values of the vectors do not improve any more – a meta attractor has been generated – or

---

[22] It is also possible to take more than two vectors at a time for the application of the genetic operators. But usually it is sufficient to take just two – like in the prototype of biological heterosexual reproduction.

if another criterion has been fulfilled. Despite the fact that there is no explicit goal the GA very often successfully is "muddling through" to an optimum, as Holland once described the way of processing of the GA.[23]

The GA operates *on* the cognitive and action rules of the individual frog or the population of frogs respectively. In the sense defined in chapter 2 the rules of the GA are an example of meta rules that change the rules of a system and sometimes even increase or decrease their number. The transformations of the cognitive systems of the frogs, therefore, is a classical example for learning as the systematic variation of cognitive rules in contrast to the changing of a topology like in the case of artificial neural nets. To be sure, the frog or frogs respectively do not change their rules in a conscious way. But it is easy to imagine cognitive or social systems that change their rules of cognition in a conscious way similar to the example of the GA-application. If we take just one frog then we can understand the whole process of GA-applications as a system that undertakes some *Gedankenexperimente* (thought experiments), that is, it imagines other rules and analyzes their positive or negative consequences for its own future. By the systematic variation of these rules, similar or equivalent to GA-application, this system may reach at last some sufficiently suited rules which it takes over. Scientific simulations of possible futures of a society can be understood just this way, i.e., as the thought experiments of a social system with its own rules of interaction and cultural world views.

The example of the frog demonstrated the possibility of the conscious changing of certain cognitive rules, in this case by recombination and mutation. It is easy to imagine the same procedures applied to learning rules and not only cognitive rules of perception and problem solving. Learning of learning, therefore, may also be understood as the systematic variation of certain learning rules or strategies respectively by the way of a variation similar to GA-procedures. If, as Bateson once remarked, all new ideas are basically nothing else than the recombination of old ones, which is certainly a bit exaggerated, then new learning strategies can be frequently interpreted as the result of the recombination of old and established ones. After all, a lot of heuristic procedures like the famous brain storming are basically just recombination techniques.

We emphasized at the beginning of this subchapter that learning is an integral part of many, if not the most communicative processes. As we will demonstrate in the later chapters very often a factual process of communication can be understood, modeled in a formal manner and in some ways even predicted, if the process is understood as one of mutual learning. To be sure, our considerations on learning do not contain all the many different aspects learning consists of. But apparently it is possible to define several main aspects of learning in a precise manner and to

[23] Against some classical arguments for biological evolution as a goal orientated process the operations of the GA demonstrate in a mathematical exact way that no goal is necessary for evolutionary processes, neither in biological nature nor in socio-cultural evolution. There just has to be an unambiguous evaluation function that allows distinguishing between "better" or "worse".

demonstrate in what way learning components can be integrated into formal models of communication. This will be continued in more detail in the following chapters

5.5. SUB SYMBOLIC AND SYMBOLIC COGNITIVE PROCESSES

George Herbert Mead was one of the first theorists of communication, or symbolically mediated interaction as he called it, who emphasized the distinction between non symbolic and symbolic interaction (Mead, 1934), although he did not designate it with these terms.[24] In a similar manner Watzlawick et al. (1967) analyzed such distinctions with their concepts of analogous and digital communication. To be sure, neither Mead nor Watzlawick, Beavin and Jackson gave precise definitions how these distinctions could be integrated into formal, mathematical models of communication. In order to solve this problem we introduce the distinction between sub symbolic and symbolic cognitive processes, a distinction that was termed by researchers in Artificial Intelligence. Certainly this distinction is not exactly the same which Mead and/or Watzlawick et al. meant with their specific concepts. Yet we will try to demonstrate, after having clarified our concepts, that the terms of symbolic versus sub symbolic is very well suited to capture those characteristics of communicative processes that were meant by Mead and Watzlawick et al.

Because we start with a clarification of the term "sub symbolic" we wish to remind once more of Vladimir, the dog of Pavlov that served as an illustration in chapter 3. Vladimir generated at the beginning of its training or conditioning processes respectively reactions that were exclusively determined by its biological instincts. Therefore, at the beginning of the conditioning process Vladimir reacted to the signal "food" and did not react to the signal "bell". By naming "food" as signal "a", "bell" as signal "b", and the reaction "producing saliva" as "c", and if we define "$a = 1$" as the occurrence of the signal a, "$b = 1$" as the occurrence of the signal b, and "$c = 1$" as the factual reaction, then we obviously obtain a formal representation in form of a Boolean function $f(a, b) = c$ ($a = 0$ of course means that a does not occur and accordingly with b and c):

$f\ (1, 0) = 1$
$f\ (0, 1) = 0$
$f\ (1, 1) = 1$
$f\ (0, 0) = 0.$

In other words, the reaction c depends only on the occurrence of a; according to the definition of Kauffman (1995) f is a canalyzing function because only the variable a determines the factual result, i.e., the value of c (see above chapter 2). This function is not one of the classical logical operators that have special names like conjunction or disjunction. The training process of Vladimir finally results in the changing of f to another function g with

[24] We are quite aware of the fact that the term "Symbolic Interactionism" was not created by Mead but by his pupil Blumer.

$g(1,0) = 1$
$g(0,1) = 1$
$g(1,1) = 1$
$g(0,0) = 0$

Apparently g is nothing else than the logical disjunction because c = 1 always occurs if either a = 1 occurs or b = 1 or both. We can easily imagine the training process of Vladimir as the construction of a) a neural network that operates like a Boolean net in the fashion of the function f and b) the transformation of this first network into a second one that operates like another Boolean network, characterized by the function g. We leave it to interested readers to construct such neural networks with appropriate weight and threshold values (cf. the examples in the preceding subchapter).

In a similar way one can demonstrate the learning of a logical conjunction. Imagine a young man who is interested in making the acquaintance of attractive young women. This young man reacts, as Vladimir "by instinct" to the perception of young females who are attractive to him. Yet he has to learn that he may only address such females if the situation is suited, for example the common being in a disco, and that he may not address the females in order to explain his wishes if he meets them in an official situation like an examination. Therefore, if "a = 1" denotes the perception of an attractive specimen of the other sex, "b = 1" denotes a suited situation, and "c = 1" denotes the young man's move to address this particular female, the result of his learning process is a net characterized by a function $h(a, b) = c$:

$h(1,0) = 0$
$h(0,1) = 0$
$h(1,1) = 1$
$h(0,0) = 0.$

The according neural network was shown in the preceding subchapter.[25]

In the usual way to describe such learning processes in a formal manner one would of course use terms of logical rules, for example "*if* an attractive female is perceived *and if* the situation is suited *then* address her and tell her abut your interests". But, as we emphasized several times, there are no such rules in the brain and that is why a learning process must be described with concepts of the generation of networks.

In Vladimir's case it is evident that Vladimir constructed a logical net or the neural equivalent of it, but certainly on a subconscious level. Vladimir does not "think" about his experiences with bell and food but simply reacts to the permanent

[25] To be sure, adult persons who are familiar with such problems of making desired acquaintances know that situations are not simply suited or not suited, but are that "more or less", as well as the perceived specimens of the other sex are "more or less" attractive. Accordingly the own reactions may be more or less direct. Such differentiations can also be modeled by the use of the so-called "fuzzy logic", but that is beyond the purposes of this study. In particular, beginners in the difficult process of making desired acquaintances will mainly behave in a fashion according to a simple logical function.

coupling of the two signals by changing the weight values and thresholds until it becomes the equivalent of a BN determined by the logical disjunction. Because these processes occur on such a subconscious level we call them "sub symbolic", meaning with this term that neither the learning processes nor the results are symbolically coded – in the respective cognitive system, of course. The symbolic description of the resulting network of Vladimir as equivalent to a Boolean function and hence to a logical disjunction is just the formal interpretation of external observers but not a part of the brain of Vladimir. Of course, the logical equivalence between certain Boolean networks and the according neural networks is still valid.

The case of the young man is a bit more complicated because the young man may have learned the specific logical conjunction – although of course not in terms of mathematical logic – by symbolically coded instruction processes, e.g., by his parents or by friends who are more experienced in such matters. Yet any observation of young men and women who have to solve the difficult problem of looking for suited partners shows that most of them go on by trial and error and that means again an unconscious learning process. Without denying the importance of social symbolically coded learning for such problems we may assume in the case of our young man that his learning processes, like those of Vladimir, occur on a sub symbolic level in the sense just described.

Because Boolean and neural networks are basically dynamical systems both Vladimir and the young man not only learn the logical functions of conjunction and disjunction this sub symbolic way but also the combination of events or their perceptions respectively with other events and/or one's own actions. A repeated experience of "*after* event a *then* event b" generates a sub symbolic connection that can be formally interpreted as the knowledge "*because* event a *hence* event b" and that means in terms of logical functions "*if* a *then* b", i.e., the implication. The same is valid for the deduction rule of the *modus ponens*, i.e.,"*if* event a *then* event b, *and* event a, *hence* event b". In other words, the generated connections allow the perception of causal relations between events; the causal relations between one's own actions and the according results are learned the same way.

We demonstrated the meaning of sub symbolic learning processes and their respective sub symbolic results with the learning of logical relations. It is of course not difficult to imagine how other learning processes are performed in the same subconscious manner and lead to according sub symbolic results. Consider, for example the generation of sub symbolic semantical networks that consist of different sub networks with the according attractors as the meaning attachments for different perceptions. Children do this before they are able to speak and experiments with subhuman primates indicate that they perceive their environment as an ordered structure, comparable to symbolically coded networks.[26] The conclusion seems

---

[26] Dehaene, for example, (loc.cit.) refers to experiments done with children in an age well under one year and with subhuman primates, which demonstrate that these cognitive systems are even able to understand simple arithmetical structures without being able to express these structures in a symbolic code.

obvious that such phylogenetical and ontogenetical developmental processes result in the construction of sub symbolically networks that are in a functional sense equivalent to those we know from the symbolic levels. We may, therefore, define the sub symbolic level of the brain or of any other cognitive system as the level where by learning processes the according networks are constructed and where neither the learning processes nor the resulting networks are expressed in a symbolic code by the cognitive learning system. Such sub symbolic levels of learning and network generation are certainly primary and fundamental in both phylogenetical and ontogenetical senses: All living organisms learn in a sub symbolic way and only our own species is known to have also symbolic levels at its disposal. Hence sub symbolic processes are the primary ones in a phylogenetic sense. Yet they are also primary in an ontogenetic sense because children certainly start their developmental process on a sub symbolic level that is presupposed by the later symbolic ones.

The networks of the sub symbolic level are mainly constructed by the ordering of environmental perceptions: for example, the ordering of animal perception is generated via the perception of different animals plus their similarities and differences. The frog in the example of Holland "knows" in a sub symbolic fashion the similarities between flies and gnats; hence the frog is able to behave in the same fashion with respect to gnats as to flies. On the other hand the frog also perceives the differences to large animals like storks or big predator fishes; therefore, it is able to behave in another way to storks than to flies. This sub symbolic knowledge structure is in the case of frogs without doubt phylogenetically achieved during the evolution of the frog species. But as each phylogenetically acquired trait is the result of successful individual learning processes – in particular by the acquisition via favorable mutations and recombination – the cognitive capabilities of frogs are achieved by an interplay between environment and the learning organism(s).[27] The learning process of Vladimir is another illustrative example for the construction of sub symbolic structures as an interplay between the brain of Vladimir and the training environment, i.e., the laboratory of Pavlov.

Human beings, and perhaps in a very limited sense some representatives of subhuman primates (Hill 1974; Marquardt 1984; Pinker 1994), are able to translate their perceptions into acquired symbolic codes, in the case of humans of course most important language. The classical theories of meaning we referred to in the third

[27] Although it may seem a bit paradoxically to include processes of mutation and recombination with learning we have to remind of the general definition of learning in the last subchapter. Mutation of an individual organism is in this sense just a variation of a certain structure, done by trial and error, which is a particular learning rule too (although not frequently a successful one). To be sure, we certainly do not want to assume a Lamarckian view of biological evolution in the sense that learned capabilities in the usual sense of the word are passed on to the next generation, although recent results in evolutionary biology hint that in some cases Lamarck was not so wrong as Darwinists usually believe (cf. Falk and Jablonka 1997). The classical Lamarckian transmission of individually acquired traits is certainly a characteristic of socio-cultural evolution and not of the biological one (cf. Klüver 2002).

chapter are very frequently centered around the meaning of symbols, i.e., symbolically coded perceptions. The evolutionary advantages of having symbolic codes at one's disposal have been frequently described and we need not enumerate them again. For our purposes it is sufficient to point out that symbolic codes and in particular language usually are characterized by two different functions that may be called the "representative function " and the "communicative function". "Communicative" means of course that such codes are a very suitable medium for complex communicative processes: In contrast to sign systems that are used by animals symbolic codes allow a communication that is independent of the particular situation – it is possible to communicate about events and objects that are not in sight, that exist only in the past or will exist in the future or have never existed and will never do so. In particular it is possible to lie, that is to assert propositions that are not true.

These possibilities of symbolic codes are a consequence of the particular representation function of symbolic codes. The German linguist Weisgerber expressed this aspect with the illustrative remark, that "language is a key to the world".[28] The meaning of this beautiful metaphor is that we "unlock" the world, i.e., make it accessible for us by representing the perceived world in symbolic signs. In this sense we create a second world in our mind by constructing a symbolic order – e.g., by constructing semantical networks. To be sure, this is a constructive process and not merely a mirroring of the world in symbolic structures. The "acquisition" of the world by language, as Weisgerber called this process in the same context, is on the one hand dependent on the cultural context of the language, on the other hand of individual characteristics of the language user and – perhaps – on certain aspects of the used single language itself. Inhabitants of a big town like New York City construct other representations of the world than farmers on an island in the South Sea. Hence "construction" always means a process that is determined by active kinds of structuring and must not be confused with passive mirroring.[29]

Although sometimes the thought was postulated that world perception by humans is always a linguistically mediated one, which is at the core of the so called Sapir-Whorf Hypothesis, there can be no doubt that the acquisition of symbolic codes like language does not mean that sub symbolic perception and the according sub symbolic order, acquired in phases of early development, vanish in this acquisition process. We all know of our everyday experience that world can be perceived without transferring the perceptions into linguistic or other symbolical codes. We observe a dog but being busy with other thought processes we do not take much notice to it and do not consciously think "dog". In particular, recent results from neurobiology suggest that many perceptions and resulting actions occur on a sub symbolic level (cf. e.g., Roth 1996): In many experiments the test persons had

[28] In the German original *"Sprache ist der Schlüssel zur Welt"* (Weisgerber 1962)

[29] The hypothesis that world is differently represented in different languages was most famously expressed in the so-called "Sapir-Whorf hypothesis". It is beyond the goals of this study to discuss this problematic assumption – for a very critical review cf. Pinker 1994.

certain parts of their brain activated when they were ordered to act in some ways, but not the parts where conscious thought processes occur, and the test persons even began the action before they consciously decided to act. In other words, the test persons were stimulated on some sub symbolical level that operated independently of and earlier than the "conscious" part of the brain where symbolic coding is performed. The conscious reflection in form of symbolically coded signs occurred significantly later and was apparently not the cause for the respective actions. If that is a proof that there is no free will, as some philosophers concluded (cf. Roth loc. cit.), is an open question and we shall come back to it.

Because sub symbolic structures do not vanish the emergence of symbolic ones must be understood as the emergence of a second level that is constructed on the foundations of the sub symbolic structure. To be sure, "level" is just a shortening metaphor: there are no levels in the brain or in artificial cognitive systems in the usual meaning of the word. Instead there are loops and other connections that connect different cognitive networks. Therefore, the emergence of a symbolic level means the emergence of particular networks that are connected with the sub symbolic ones. Consider for example the sub symbolical network of a child that performs the logical operation of disjunction as in the example of Vladimir. In contrast to Vladimir whose cognitive processes remain on the sub symbolic level, i.e., are *only* performed via a sub symbolical network, each physiologically normal child is able to reflect its sub symbolic operations in a conscious way by using certain, usually linguistic symbols. The child, therefore, is able to think in concepts like "*if* I see and smell food *or* hear a certain bell (e.g., at school), *then* it is time to eat and my mouth becomes wet". We have to imagine this capability as the result of a construction process like this:

sub symbolic network

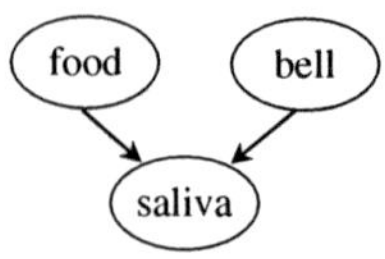

with the weight matrix for a logical disjunction

	a	b	c
a	0	0	0.5
b	0	0	0.5
c	0	0	0

and a threshold $\theta = 0.4$.

If the child perceives either food or a bell then the network becomes activated, i.e., it obtains an input for the neuron "food" or "bell" respectively; the neuron "saliva" then becomes activated and transfers the activation to an action net that produces saliva. The conscious consideration means that another network is constructed with the same structure, i.e., weight matrix and threshold:

"food" means that the according neuron now represents the concept of food, i.e., the symbolically coded perception and accordingly "bell" and "saliva" denote the respective concepts. Now the child's perception of, e.g. food, activates at first the sub symbolical network with the resulting activation of the action net. The sub symbolical network in addition also activates the symbolic net, in this case with the activation of the neuron "food". The whole process then can be understood as a) the sub symbolic perception of the signal of food, b) the production of a certain action via the activation of the action net, and c) as the conscious reflection "I see food and my mouth becomes wet" by the activation of the symbolical network. If we call the sub symbolical network SSN, the action network AN and the symbolical network SN we obtain the process shown in figure 11.

The neurobiological results we mentioned above may be understood that way: the process of the activations of AN and SSN does not simultaneously occur but at first the AN becomes activated and then the SN. Yet these results can also be interpreted that the activation processes of AN and SN are simultaneously performed, that is action = production of saliva and conscious reflection on it occur at the same time. It is sufficient to assume that the processing of the signal of food is performed at first by the sub symbolic net and *then* by the AN and the SN.

We mentioned before the fact known from our everyday experience that it is quite possible to perceive and process certain signals without adding a conscious reflection. The child in our example may be used in such a way to the process of producing saliva when seeing or smelling food or when hearing a certain bell that the SN will not be activated. Only if the child is asked "why is your mouth wet?" then the child will be stimulated by this additional environmental signal to activate the SN too and by this to activate another action AN_2 that produces the answer "because my mouth always gets wet, if I perceive food (or the bell)". This is demonstrated in figure 12.

In the well known developmental theory of Piaget, whose mechanisms of assimilation and accommodation were mentioned by us several times, the cognitive development of children occurs in several different phases or levels respectively.

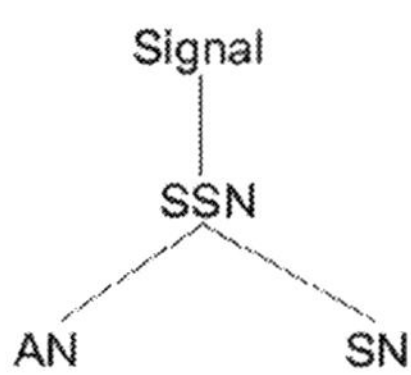

Figure 11. sub symbolic and symbolic nets

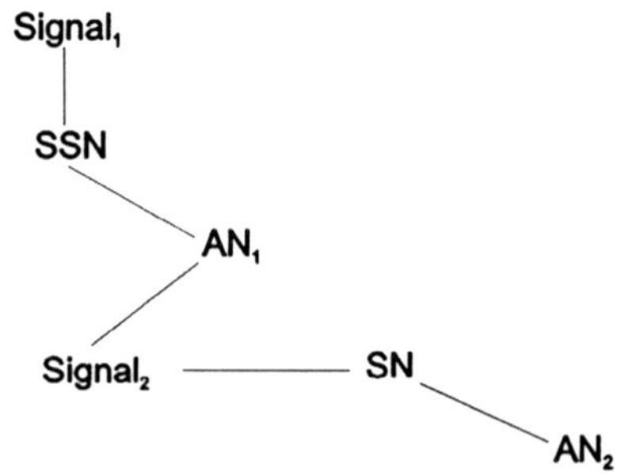

Figure 12. Adding of another action by a symbolic network.

In the first two cognitive levels, the pre-operational one and the concrete operational phase, the child is only able to perform cognitive operations if it perceives, i.e., sees and touches, the objects of the cognitive processes. For example, operations of adding numbers or comparing the size of different objects presuppose that certain objects like pearls or balls can be perceived in order to solve the problem "$2+3=5$". In other words, these cognitive processes rely on a sensual perception and thus are dependent on a concrete situation. In particular, the child is only able to generalize in a limited way: the fact that it is possible to infer from "2 apples + 3 apples = 5 apples" to beans, balls and to abstract numbers is not in the cognitive range of the child.

Our distinction between sub symbolic and symbolic levels, i.e. networks, allows to explain this stage of development by assuming that the child always must construct at first its respective sub symbolic networks and then the symbolic one. We may further presume that the child in this stage is an example of the mentioned neurobiological results: Sub symbolic networks that were trained with concrete examples of the adding of objects or the measuring of geometrical size solve the problem at hand, before a symbolic network is able to formulate the right answer – in our example "5". In this sense each cognitive development is dependent on the initial generation of sub symbolic networks that *immediately* process the signals given to them by the environment, while the symbolic networks only indirectly process the signals by the intermediating activation effects of the SSN. Apparently not only the mentioned neurobiological findings can be explained by our model, but also the experimental results of Piaget and his theoretical interpretations by the theory of developmental stages.[30]

Piaget, as is well known, also postulates a third stage, i.e., the formal operational phase. In this stage of development the children or youths respectively are

[30] We omit the temporal assertions of Piaget when exactly a child in the average enters a certain phase and when it makes the transfer to the next. These assertions have often been in doubt and in particular it is to be assumed that the changing of cultural environments since the times of Piaget's experiments have accelerated the processes of stage development.

able to manipulate symbols, for example mathematical and logical ones, without having to refer to concrete objects within the range of their sensual perception. In particular they have become able to think in a "hypothetical-deductive" manner, i.e., they can imagine purely hypothetical conditions and situations and draw conclusions from these hypothetical assumptions. In terms of our distinction between the symbolic and the sub symbolical level this indicates that cognitive operations no longer are as dependent on concrete sensual perceptions as they were in the earlier phases. A problem "what is $5+3$?" can be solved by the symbolic manipulation of numbers, which are very abstract concepts, and the child does not need any longer to refer to apples or other concrete objects. One may say that in this developmental phase the symbolic level has achieved a certain form of independence with respect to the sub symbolic level. To be sure, the capability to perform such operations on the symbolic level like adding or multiplying are the results of the emergence of according net structures on the sub symbolic level. But having achieved the ability to construct similar or even isomorphic structures on the symbolic level, the sub symbolic level is not needed any longer or at least not permanently.The independence of the symbolic level explains a lot of intellectual achievements that cannot be explained by direct relations between physical or social environment and the sub symbolic level. Consider for example word combinations in poetry like a verse from the German poet Rilke: "...and dreams open their eyes like little children under cherry trees...". Nobody ever has seen dreams which opened their eyes and in particular the attributing of sensual organs like eyes to internal brain processes like dreams would be pure nonsense in everyday language. Yet we are used to such word combinations in poetry and not only admirers of Rilke will believe that here is a particular fine example of literary art.[31]

For another example consider the Lotka-volterra equations we mentioned in the second chapter that model the behavior of a predator-prey system:

$$\text{(5.5.1)} \quad \begin{aligned} \partial x/\partial t &= ax - bx^2 - cxy \\ \partial y/\partial t &= -ey + cxy, \end{aligned}$$

if x is the population of prey, y designates the population of predators and a, b, c, and e are some systems parameter like the rate of reproduction. Lotka and Volterra formulated these equations on the basis of data from the Hudson Bay Company: this company whose main interest at the beginning of the 20th century was the trade with furs had observed the variations of the populations of hares and lynxes on an isolated island in the Northwest Pacific. Yet it is not imaginable that Lotka and Volterra formulated their equations by just observing lynxes and hares or just

[31] In the German original the verse is "...und Träume schlagen so die Augen auf wie kleine Kinder unter Kirschenbäumen..." We wish to excuse our poor translation but we do not know if there exists an English translation that better captures the music of Rilke's language.

looking at the according data of the trading company.[32] The perception of animals alone hardly leads to the formulation of specific differential equations.

Of course, it is quite possible that for example Rilke once observed little children sleeping under cherry trees and got inspired by this sight to write his poem. It is equally possible that Lotka once saw a hare family with many young hares and watched how some predator caught one of the hares. But there is no direct way to form such symbol "clusters" like a poem or differential equations from sub symbolic network structures that represent some external signals. Writing beautiful poems or in their way also beautiful equations is only possible if we assume that the symbolic level may develop a dynamics of its own, i.e., symbolic structures are generated according to a logic that is not necessarily represented on the sub symbolic level when the symbolic structure is constructed. The combining of words like "dreams", "eyes", "children", and "cherry trees" is only possible if the according parts of the brain, i.e., those responsible for symbolical operations, "emancipate" themselves from the basic logic of the sub symbolic structure.

It is even possible that such symbolic structures, when they have been constructed, generate a feed back loop to the sub symbolic level and change it. In cognitive psychology the term "gestalt switch" is known for a long time, which means that a particular kind of perception is changed. In a very simple sense even Vladimir undertook a gestalt switch when he learned to perceive the bell as a signal for food. Such gestalt switches may frequently be the result of the generation of symbolic structures that cause new sub symbolic structures. After hearing or reading the poem of Rilke it is easily imaginable that the next sight of children and cherry trees will lead to the association "dream that open their eyes" and the figure of the trees and children will be perceived as a combination of these physical objects and abstract entities like dreams. In the same way it is possible that after becoming acquainted with the equations of Lotka and Volterra the next time hares and predators will be seen as dynamical processes that follow the logic of the equations. Perceptive restrictions like the man who only sees attractive naked women in the figures of a Rorschach test may hence often be generated by a feed back loop between symbolic level and sub symbolical one (although probably not in the case of this man). An according graph looks like this:

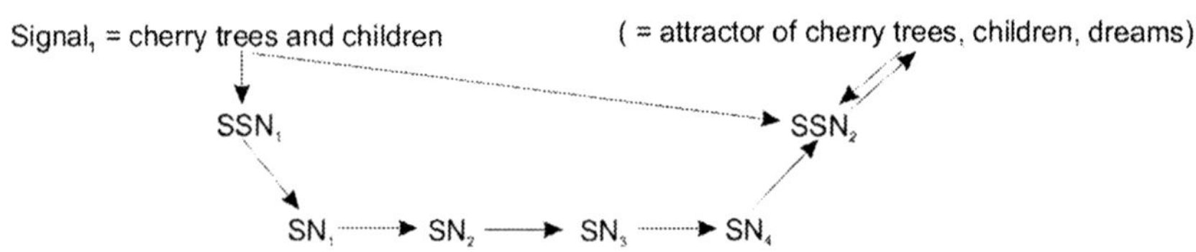

Figure 13. The influence of symbolic structures on the sub symbolic one

[32] Lotka and Volterra were of course trained in the mathematical analysis of dynamical developments via the use of calculus, i.e. differential equations. From their biography it is easily understandable how they got the idea for these equations.

The connection between SSN_2 and the verbal explanation (= attractor...) means that the perception of $signal_1$ has changed in the way that the perceiver "sees" the former figure in a new way because of his symbolically formed gestalt switch.

A little conceptual clarification is here necessary. In the preceding paragraphs we sometimes suggested that "symbolic" and "conscious" are equivalent concepts. That is of course not always true as the example of the poem demonstrates. Creative symbolic achievements like poems or scientific theories are often constructed without permanent conscious reflections. Conscious thought processes are, as far as we know, always symbolically coded ones but the converse must not be the case.

Human communication is not only performed by symbolic media, as in particular the fact of non verbal communication demonstrates. Yet of course symbolically coded communication and in particular linguistically coded one is at the core of all social interactions. Each spoken or written message, therefore, operates as a signal that may be received directly by a symbolic network. An answer to this signal in form of an equally coded message then is the result of the coupling of other symbolic networks that generate in the end an action, i.e., the spoken or written answer:

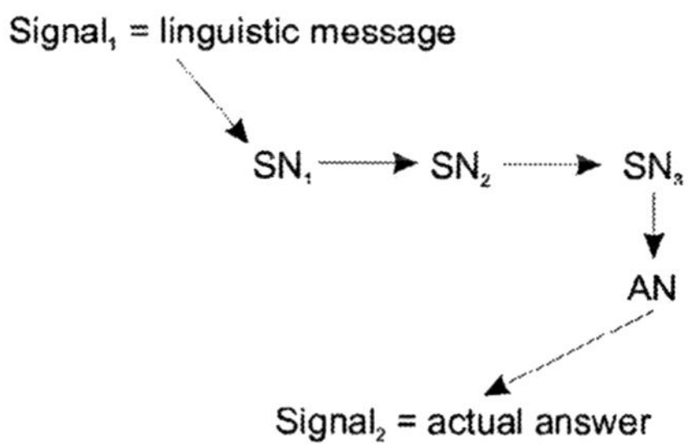

Figure 14. Coupling of symbolic networks.

The consideration that cognitive processes, stimulated by external signals, may frequently pass over the sub symbolic level and are directly processed by the symbolic one does not diminish the importance of the sub symbolic level in general. Many of our daily actions are based on the fact that we have such sub symbolic levels at our disposal, which enable us to act literally without thinking – even to perform logical operations and other cognitive processes. Yet the phylogenetical invention of symbolic codes like language or the symbol systems of mathematics and logic not only lead to the emergence of additional symbolic levels but also to the possibility to pass over the sub symbolic level in several cases – verbal communication and creative achievements are two of the most important examples.

At the end of this subchapter we once more return to the question of free will, although this is not strictly a question of a communication theory. The mentioned neurobiological results seem to indicate that free will is just an illusion of the conscious mind that "believes" to be the main cause of conscious actions. But this argument is valid only if we assume that the relation between signals and actions is always so simple as in figures 11 and 12. The considerations, visualized in figures 13 and 14, on the frequent independence of the symbolical level demonstrate that things are not so simple. It can be easily imagined that frequently a SSN starts to activate an AN and thus initiates an action but that at the same time on the symbolical level some conscious considerations lead to another decision and that the started action will be changed or not undertaken at all respectively:

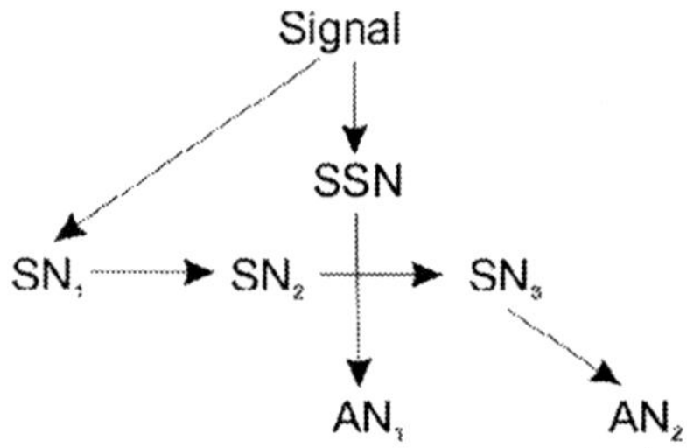

Figure 15. Correction of a first intended action by symbolic operations.

In this case the activation of AN_1 by the SSN is hindered by the different SNs as a result of conscious reflections on possible actions.

To be sure, such considerations do not prove that there is in fact something like a free will and that it is possible to demonstrate it by scientific methods. Even experiments done by the neurobiologist Libet (Libet 2004) that are consistent with our model and that are interpreted by Libet himself as a strong indicator for the existence of a free will do not "prove" our principal freedom to act in a conscious manner. Personally we doubt that such fundamental philosophical questions can be decided at all by scientific reasoning. We just wanted to show that the converse is not necessarily true, namely the assertion of the non existence of a free will. Caution is always recommendable and in particular with respect to such questions.

There is certainly a lot more to say on the topic of the cognitive dimension of communication. But before this study deals only with cognitive aspects of communication we wish to summarize the considerations of the preceding chapters by demonstrating a general formalism for the modeling and understanding of communicative processes.

CHAPTER 6

THE GENERAL EQUATIONS OF COMMUNICATIVE PROCESSES

We frequently accentuated the aspect of the two-dimensionality of communicative processes, i.e., the determination of communication by social rules and cognitive ones. In other words, a factual communication is embedded in a social situation that can be mathematically characterized by the sd-parameter and contains certain cognitive processes that depend on the meaning processing capacity of the system, the themes of the communication and the initial cognitive processes that are started by the beginning of the communication. Therefore, communication consists of the socio-cognitive interactions of two or more cognitive systems. In particular, the social rules that characterize the communicative situation can be understood as a "mapping" of the cognitive subsystem of the sender into another cognitive subsystem, i.e., that of the receiver.

In chapter 2 we described the set of all rules of interaction and the topology of a complex system as a "transition function" f: this function generates a subsequent state from a preceding one and it is mathematically describable as a function that maps one system state on another. Hence if S_1 is an initial state of a system and S_2 the next one then $f(S_1) = S_2$. It is important to remember that such a transition function usually consists of rules of interaction on the one hand and a certain topology on the other hand. The latter determines what interactions are possible in the system at all.

For example, the social topology of an examination situation is characterized by a strict asymmetry between examiner and candidate, i.e., the candidate is only allowed to speak after the examiner has put a question or gives other signals that the candidate may speak. The according rules of interaction are that only the examiner determines the concrete topic of the communication, that the examiner has the right to put questions and to evaluate the answers of the candidate. The candidate only has to answer and to ask for another formulation of a question if he did not understand it (severe examiners do not even allow this right). The social topology of the situation consisting of the two lovers sitting on a park bench on the other hand is characterized by a strong symmetry: each communicator has factually the right to choose a subject of the conversation, to speak or to be silent and to change from symbolically coded communication to non verbal forms. In both cases the transition function f determines quite different forms of state successions, i.e. trajectories.

"State successions" in this case of communicative processes refers to the cognitive systems of the communicators although it is also possible to define social states of the situation. Yet for our purposes we define communicative processes as a socially determined mapping of one cognitive state of the first communicator onto another cognitive state of the second one. But as communicative dynamics consists of the interdependency of a social dynamics and a cognitive one the cognitive state of the second communicator is not only generated by the application of the respective social rules by sender and receiver but also by an according application of the cognitive rules of the receiver, including the respective cognitive topology. Therefore, the receiving of a message within a certain social situation starts a certain cognitive process within the receiver and generates that way the meaning of a message, computes the information degree and the relevance degree, and generates an according answer via the action net.

Consider for example a conversation between two students of computer science about "programming in the language Java" and remember the example of an according semantical net in chapter 3.3. The cognitive topology of one student consists of the weighted connections between the different concepts with the concept of "Java" at the center of the network. We shall define the term "center of a semantical net" more precisely in the next chapter. If we accept the interactive network from chapter 3.3. as an adequate representation of the cognitive subsystem of this student, then in addition to the cognitive topology the rules of interaction (for the cognitive units) are defined by the linear activation function typical for this kind of artificial neural nets. A received message of the kind "(Java, library, memory)" then starts a cognitive transition function, consisting of the activation function and the particular connection weights of the semantical net. The described attractors of the messages are the result, i.e., the next cognitive state, of the application of these cognitive transition functions. Hence, a "mapping" of the sender's cognitive net into the receiver's apparently means the socially determined start of some cognitive processes within the receiver, additionally dependent on the content of the message, of course.

It is useful for several purposes to describe these considerations in a more precise formal manner. We designate the set of social rules that determine the communicative process in a certain situation as f, the set of cognitive rules of the sender, i.e. the first communicator, as g_1, the set of cognitive rules of the receiver as g_2, the cognitive system of the sender as A, and the cognitive system of the receiver as B. By taking into account that the cognitive systems of sender and receiver will change after one communicative step, we designate the state of the cognitive system of the receiver as B_t, i.e., the state of this cognitive system at time t and accordingly A_t for the sender. Note that "sender" and "receiver" are only meaningful for the beginning of the communicative process because in the next communicative steps, of course, the sender will become a receiver and the receiver a sender. The first step of the communicative process then can be written as

$$(1) \qquad f(A_t) = g_2(B_t) = B_{t+1}.$$

In more informal terms, the application of the social rules on the cognitive system of a sender (= sending a message) causes the application of the cognitive rules of the receiver on his cognitive system at time t, which in turn produces the (new) state of the receiver's cognitive system at time t + 1. For the sake of brevity and clarity we designate both social rules that are characteristic for the sender and the receiver respectively as f; although the example of the examination demonstrated that in many cases different social rules are valid for the two communicators.

Now the receiver becomes by answering the sender and by the same formalism we obtain

$$f(B_{t+1}) = f(g_2(B_t)) = f(f(A_t)) = g_1(A_t) = A_{t+1} \quad (2)$$
$$\text{hence } A_{t+1} = f(f(A_t))$$

Accordingly the next message by the first sender with the cognitive system A will generate the next cognitive state B_{t+2} of the first receiver by

$$B_{t+2} = f(f(B_{t+1}) \quad (3)$$

The general case of n communicative steps can, therefore, be characterized as

$$A_{t+n} = f^{n+1}(A_t) \text{ and } B_{t+n} = f^n(B_t) \quad (4)$$

if f^n designates the iterated application of f for n times. In a certain sense these equations can be understood as a recursive process that generates a succession of cognitive states in both communicators by the recursively iterated application of social rules on an initial cognitive state. It is evident why the two cases of equation (4) differ in the number of the applications of f.[1]

Equations (2), (3), and (4) can be understood as a formal description of a communication by only taking into account the social dimension and the according communicative behavior that can be observed by an external observer. Such a description, however, is only something like a "behaviorist" description of the process. When considering that new cognitive states of the communicators are also generated by the application of the respective cognitive rules then we can write the equations (2) and (4), i.e., the equation for A as

$$A_{t+1} = g_1\,(f(A_t)) \quad (5)$$

and

$$A_{t+n} = (g_1 \circ f)^n(A_t)), \quad (6)$$

if $(g_1 \circ f)$ designates the application of first f and then g_1.

The respective general equation for B becomes

$$B_{t+n} = g_2(f \circ g_2)^{n-1}(B_t). \quad (7)$$

[1] Such recursive processes are quite common in complex systems as we described in chapter 2. In Klüver 2000 we called such processes the "Münchhausen Principle" as a reminder of the famous story of the lying Baron who claimed that he drew himself and his horse out of a swamp by pulling at his hairs. In this sense a communicator generates his own cognitive states by himself.

In other words, the new states of both cognitive systems are the result a) of sending a message with respect to the "old" cognitive state, i.e. by applying f, and b) after having received a message of applying the respective own cognitive rules to the old cognitive states. Apparently this is still a recursive process but one, which is generated by the successive applications of social and cognitive rules likewise. The equations obviously are founded on the assumption that the process is symmetric in the sense that each communicator sends and receives as frequently as the other one. It is additionally assumed that the social and cognitive rules do not change during the communicative process. We frequently mentioned the fact that this assumption is often not valid. For example, in didactic communications the teacher usually expects that the cognitive rules of the pupil will and should change as the result of the teaching process. Accordingly the social rules may change if, e.g., a student finishes his studies by the supervising of a professor and then the social rules of communication between the student and the professor will become more symmetric. Therefore, the general equations (6) and (7) describe the most simple case and, therefore, not seldom are for empirical communicative processes just an idealization. Yet despite this *caveat* there can be no doubt that many communications, in particular those that last only for a short time, are performed with constant rules f and g. Hence equations (5) and (7) are not only idealizations but also valid for many empirical cases. We shall deal with the problem of changing rules f and g in the following paragraphs.

When considering some particular cases of communication we obtain some general insights:(6.1.) Let us assume that for a particular subject of communication A = B, i.e., the respective association fields or in the case of verbal communication the respective semantical networks are practically identical. In this – extreme – case that may occur only if the communicators are very well acquainted and share a lot of common experience it can be assumed that the applications of $(f \circ g_1)$ and $(f \circ g_2)$ nearly always generate point attractors in the cognitive networks. In addition, all messages will carry only a low degree of information because the messages are expected by the respective receiver(s); the messages functions as a confirmation of the expectation. The communicative process itself remains constant. Such simple processes may in particular be occur in the case of old couples married for a long time.

(6.2.) In subchapter 5.3. we defined the meaning processing capacity of a cognitive system as the proportion of the possible attractor states and the possible initial states of the system. "Possible" means those states that can principally be realized by the system, regardless of the factual states that of course here depend on the communicative situation. For our purposes it is useful to define in addition the *functional capacity* of a cognitive function:

Consider a cognitive system represented as a semantical network like, e.g., in the examples of Tom or in subchapter 3.3. The units of this networks, usually representing different concepts are connected by weighted relations. We saw in the examples that sometimes two concepts are "directly" connected and sometimes only via connections with intermediating concepts. The number of the concepts of this networks is n. Now we assume that there are k_n direct connections, i.e., there are k_n pairs of different concepts with direct connections. Obviously the maximum number of such connections is $n^2 - n$, because we count only pairs of different concepts.

When this network is "activated", that is, it is caused to process a certain message, then the message will activate some concepts and these concepts will activate other concepts via their links. By remembering that a cognitive function g consists of certain rules of interaction *and* the specific topology of the system, in our case represented by the set of connections, the processing of a message will result in the activation of principally all concepts in dependency of the topology, i.e., the set of direct connections. Now we have to take into regard the fact that such a cognitive topology is not arbitrary but that there are cultural norms, which determine the "rightness" or "wrongness" of particular cognitive topologies. For example, a semantical network about the Trojan war may contain the correct direct links between "Hector", "son", and "Priamos", that is the ordered pairs of concepts (Hector, son) and (Hector, Priamos) but not the pair (Priamos, son) because nowhere in the Homeric epic the father of Priamos is mentioned. Accordingly, in a semantic network about European capitals and their famous monuments the pairs (London, Tower) and (Paris, Arc de Triomphe) are correct constructions but not the pairs (London, Eiffel Tower) and (Paris, Tower Bridge). In other words, for each conceptual field represented in the according semantic networks the correct number k_n of direct connections is fixed by cultural norms. In addition to this "objective" number of direct links, i.e., the objectively determined cognitive topology we have to take into account the fact that of course the factual number of direct connections in a certain cognitive network is a "subjective" one, i.e., the subjective number k_{sn} of direct links is dependent on the learning biography of this cognitive system. Therefore, k_{sn} will usually be different for different cognitive systems (with the possible exception of the extreme case A = B mentioned above. Note that k_{sn} must be computed by only counting the culturally accepted pairs of concepts.

Now we can define the functional capacity fC(g) of a cognitive function g as $n + k_{sn}$. Expressed in more informal terms, the functional capacity of a cognitive function is measured by the size of the according semantical network plus the number of correct direct links between the concepts. The cognitive function operating on a small semantic network will obviously have only small functional capacity, even if nearly all concepts are – correctly – linked in a direct way.

Now consider two communicators A and B in a situation where $fC(g_A) > fC(g_B)$ and where B is a learner. Then "learning" may be defined as the cognitive process of B where B tries to minimize the difference between $fC(g_A)$ and $fC(g_B)$ with respect to a certain topic. In the time available for the learning process there are, e.g., $m \geq 1$ steps possible for B to apply *and change* his cognitive function. Let us designate by g_{B1} the cognitive function of B at the start of the communicative learning process, g_{B2} the changed cognitive function after the first learning step and so forth, i.e., g_{Bm+1} designates the final cognitive function after m learning steps. Note that $g_{Bk} = g_{k+1}$ is quite possible if B did not learn anything during the kth learning step. We further assume that $fC(g_A) = \delta + fC(g_B)$ and that $\delta_i + fC(g_{Bi}) = fC(g_{i+1})$. In other words, the functional capacity of g_B differs from that of g_A by the difference δ and δ_i is the measure for each learning step by which the cognitive function of B changes.

If $\delta = \sum_1^m \delta i$ then n learning steps are necessary for B to obtain $fC(g_B) = fC(g_A)$.

If the situation, i.e., the social function f only allows n learning steps and if $n > m$ then obviously B will not reach the cognitive level of A, even if all learning steps are such that B's cognitive function is changed by all of them. By writing $\Pi_i g_{BI}$ for the iterative application of the different cognitive functions of B we obtain for the "successful" case

(8) $$fC(\Pi_i g_{BI}) = fC(g_A)$$

and for the case that B did not reach the level of A

(9) $$fC(\Pi_i g_{BI}) = fC(g_A) - \delta_r,$$

that is the difference resulting from the r missing learning steps.

(6.3.) In the preceding two examples the social function f remained constant, i.e., it did not change. The assumption that in many if not most cases of communication the social rules remain the same as in the beginning of the communication is certainly valid, as we mentioned above, and as the social knowledge about usual communicative processes confirms. Yet there are also cases where not only the cognitive function of one or several communicators varies as, e.g., in the case of pedagogical communications but also the social function. Because we defined the social framework of a communicative situation by the sd-parameter, changing of the f-functions means a variation of it. Such a sd-variation may occur in all three dimensions:

(a) The sd-value in the first, i.e., segmentary dimension may decrease if the two communicators communicate for a rather long time or if they frequently repeat their communications respectively. If one of them was in the beginning a newcomer with respect to the common social segment then he will be more and more accepted as a "true" member of the segment; accordingly lower becomes the specific sd-value.

(b) In a case of increasing familiarity between several communicators whose social status is different it may happen that the communication becomes more like one between social equals. For example, a trusted secretary may criticize in some cases her boss and he will accept it because of the familiarity and of course because of her proved trustworthiness. Because the chef would not have accepted such a communicative behavior in the beginning of his professional relationship with the secretary the according sd-value had changed during their professional cooperation.

(c) Pedagogical communications have in general the goal of decreasing the knowledge difference between teacher and learners. If that is the case, which each teacher always hopes to realize, then the according sd-value will change as a consequence: the communication between teacher and learner(s) will become more symmetric because of a variation of the sd-value in that "functional" dimension.

(d) To be sure, there also are situations where the sd-parameter is varied in two or all three dimensions together, for instance between a graduate student and a professor: with the increasing learning success of the student and his equally increasing capability to do research on his own the sd-values of their common communications will decrease in both the functional and the stratified dimensions.

By the way, these variations of the sd-parameter all presume that the ta-value is rather high, i.e., that either there is much time for the single communications or that the communicative processes will be continuously repeated. In addition, the sd-values of communicative situations may certainly not only decrease as the examples above demonstrate but also rise. For example, a rather symmetric communication between a superior and his subordinate (case (b)) may become asymmetric again if in a conflict between the two communicators the superior reminds the other of his superiority and in this sense re-introduces the original sd-value.

A formal representation of these considerations obtains slightly altered equations; as a reminder we repeat the general equations for the case of constant f- and g-functions:

$$(10) \qquad A_{t+n} = (g_1 \circ f)^n (A_t),$$

if $(g_1 \circ f)$ designates the application of first f and then g_1 and

$$(11) \qquad B_{t+n} = g_2(f \circ g_2)^{n-1}(B_t).$$

Let A_t and B_t again designate the state of the cognitive systems of the two communicators at time t, and let f_t and g_t designate the particular social and cognitive function respectively at the same time t. Note again that in some cases $A_t = A_{t+1}$, $B_t = B_{t+1}$, $f_t = f_{t+1}$ and $g_t = g_{t+1}$, i.e., neither the cognitive systems of the communicators nor the social and cognitive functions change during the communication or at least during some steps of the communication. If we designate the iterated application of the social and cognitive functions respectively, by which they change, as

$$(12) \qquad \prod_t^{t+n} f_i \text{ and } \prod_t^{t+n} g_i,$$

then the general equations for the case that both the f- and the g-function are continuously changing become

$$(13) \qquad A_{t+1} = \prod_t^{t+n} (g_{1t+i} \circ f_{t+i}) \, (A_{1t})$$

and

(14) $$B_{t+n} = g_2 \circ \prod_{t}^{t+n-1} (f_{t+i} \circ g_{2t+i})\,(B_t)$$

Again it is assumed that both communicators are sending and receiving n times.

For the frequently occurring case that the g-functions of one or both communicators are changing but that the f-function remains constant the equation must accordingly be written. We just demonstrate this for the case of A:

(15) $$A_{t+n} = \prod_{t}^{t+n} (g_{1t+i} \circ f)(A_t)$$

In more mathematical terms one can say that these equations describe a communicative process as a three-dimensional Markov Chain, that is a recursive process with the recursion operating on A and B respectively, and also on the socio-cognitive functions f and g.

For the sake of completeness we note that in contrast to this recursive chain description we may symbolize the communicative process as an interdependent interaction of A and B via the socio-cognitive functions. For the "simple" case of constant functions f and g we obtain

(16) $$\mathrm{B}_{t+n} = \mathrm{f}^{\mathrm{n}}(\mathrm{g}_1^{\mathrm{n}-1}(\mathrm{A}_t),\ \mathrm{g}_2^{\mathrm{n}}(\mathrm{B}_t))$$

and

(17) $$\mathrm{A}_{t+n} = \mathrm{f}^{\mathrm{n}}\,(\mathrm{g}_2^{\mathrm{n}}\,(\mathrm{B}_t),\ \mathrm{g}_1^{\mathrm{n}}\,(\mathrm{A}_t))$$

The general case with variable f and g can be written as

(18) $$A_{t+n} = \prod_i f_i(\prod_i g_{2i}(B_{t+i}), \prod_i g_{1i}(A_{t+i}))$$

and accordingly in the case of B. (Note that we have written the "function product" just with the variable i to make the reading of the formulas a bit easier.)

As a preliminary remark we remind of the semiotic production rules introduced in chapter 3. The equations just developed describe the communicative process insofar as it is determined by social and cognitive rules or functions respectively. Yet they are still incomplete because the semiotic rules are not included. This will be done after some general reflections on several characteristics of the equations and the resulting states of the communicative systems in particular cases. The interesting question is under what conditions a communicative system will reach attractors and additionally meta attractors.

6.4.1. The most simple case has been dealt with in 6.1., i.e., the case where for the topic of communication we may assume that roughly A = B. The most probable consequence is that the system (A, B, f, g_1, and g_2) will generate point attractors, i.e., steady states where neither the cognitive systems nor the resulting communicative behavior will change. To be sure, in this case conversations may last some time, but they will always end in some point attractor "if all is said", and because of the extreme similarity of the cognitive systems all meanings of the respective messages will be unequivocal und nearly the same for both communicators.

We may also say that this communicative system is in a meta attractor. A meta attractor was defined in the second chapter as an attractor in the rule space of a system: a system is in a meta attractor if some meta rules operate on the rules of interaction but these are not changed any more.[2] This communication system is in such meta attractor: the communicators follow established rules of speaking and thinking and even if one of the communicators tries to change the respective rules the old ones will soon determine the communication again. Such a case can be called a "trivial meta attractor".

6.4.2. Now let us assume that both cognitive systems A and B are in an attractor state. That means that the communicative exchanges of messages do not change the systems anymore although the systems are different. In that case the combined function $F = f \circ g$ is in a meta attractor because the g-functions of both systems do not change and hence the f-function will not be changed either.

The converse is also true, although only with a certain temporal delay. If $F = f \circ g$ is in a meta attractor state then f and the cognitive functions g remain constant. Then both cognitive systems A and B will also reach an attractor state because after a certain time no *new* messages will be received. That will always be the case if only after some time. Therefore, if the ta-factor is sufficiently large the attractor states of the cognitive systems and the meta attractor states of F are necessary and sufficient for one another. It is important to note that A and B must not be equal in contrast to case 6.4.1. If, e.g., a pupil's answers are *in the eyes of the teacher* sufficient for the respective pedagogical situation then the whole communication system will not change any more, i.e., attractor and meta attractor states are generated although the teacher and the pupil still have different cognitive systems at their disposal. The same is the case with the frequently mentioned two lovers on a summer evening in a park: in this situation they will be together in a *communicative attractor*, i.e. attractor + meta attractor, although their cognitive systems will still be different with respect to many subjects, e.g., with respect to the exact meaning of "love".

The derived equivalence between attractors and meta attractors can be of importance with respect to empirical investigations, namely observations of communicative processes. It is always difficult to understand cognitive systems as they can not be observed in a direct manner. Only the verbal behavior of the communicators allows indirect conclusions about the state of the cognitive systems. Yet the communicative behavior as a whole makes it possible to understand if (a) the

---

[2] Political systems where reforms (= changing of the rules of interaction like laws) are performed but the systems do not change their trajectories can be said to be in a meta attractor, which may explain the uselessness of some reforms.

social f-function is constant and (b) the cognitive functions are constant too. This can be concluded by observing the particular answers the communicators produce after the reception of a message: if the answers are constantly produced in the same way then obviously the g-functions also are in a meta attractor, hence $F = f \circ g$ and therefore A and B are both in an attractor state.

6.4.3. Let f be constant but one or both cognitive functions vary. This is for example the case in all pedagogical situations, i.e., situations where one of the communicators has to vary his cognitive function and the other not. If both cognitive functions are variable with constant f we have a situation where both communicators are willing to learn from one another. Attractor and meta attractor states will be reached if and only if the cognitive systems "stabilize", i.e., they do not accept more changing and remain in an attractor state. According to the equivalence between attractor and meta attractor of course a meta attractor will be generated too.

6.4.4. Now let f be variable and both cognitive functions constant. In such a case a form of communication is necessary that Watzlawick et al. (1967) call "meta communication". In other words, a variable f-function is possible in this case only if the communicators talk about their manner of communication and mutually or only partially decide to change the social communicative rules. Then either the new social rules f' will determine the communication and the communicative system will reach a meta attractor and hence an attractor. Or the new rules will not hold good. In most of such cases the communicators will return to the original rules and another meta attractor state will be reached.

Generally these considerations demonstrate that the generation of attractors and meta attractors is something that can be expected in the usual cases of communication. In other words, a "normal" characteristic of communicative processes in a statistical sense of the word is the frequent emergence of some kind of "communicative order", i.e., the production of attractor and meta attractor states. The generation of attractor states is of course not always sufficient for a "true" mutual understanding of the communicators but it is certainly a necessary condition. Hence there seem to be mathematically describable reasons for the fact that communications mostly do not end in permanent disorder and misunderstanding.

6.4.5. For the sake of completeness we finally consider the case that all functions are variable. According to the considerations with respect to the sd-parameter this can only occur if the sd-values are comparatively low, i.e., the communication is rather symmetric. Only then the communicators are able to vary in particular the f-function by mutual agreement – consciously or unconsciously. If we assume that such variations of the initial sd-values either monotonously increase or decrease the values then we can describe such function variations as a monotonous sequence of sd-values with either $sd_1 \leq sd_2 \leq sd_3 \ldots \leq cd_{n-1} \leq sd_n$ or an according sequence with $sd_1 \geq sd_2 \ldots \geq sd_n$. The second case of course means that the communicators agree that their communication may become less and less formal; the first case means that for certain reasons the communication must become more rigidly. For example, if a student misunderstands an informal behavior of a professor and wrongly believes that he (the student) has become a social equal then the professor will often be forced to increase the sd-value in the stratified dimension. He thus reminds the student that their communicative situation is still characterized by a high degree of social inequality.

The interesting question in such cases is if and under what conditions the respective sequence of sd-values will converge, that is the communicators interact with new and fixed sd-values. This is certainly not a question that can be solved by formal considerations and/or according computer simulations. Yet the formalism so far described makes it possible to undertake empirical experiments and thus analyzing variable communication processes in order to solve the problems of probable convergence. To be sure, usually the variation of all functions, in particular those of the f-function, will be ended by the factual end of the communication and that means by the influence of the ta-factor.

6.5. To complete the communicative formalism we have finally to take into account the semiotic production rules which we introduced in chapter four. These rules determine the "rigidity" of a communicative topic or, in other words, they determine how easily the communicators can change a subject without disturbing the communication. For example, a discourse on number theory in mathematics is characterized by a high rigidity degree because it is hardly possible to talk about other themes without an explicit consent of all communicators. In contrast to this example a communication on theatre is determined by a rather low rigidity degree: one can easily switch from theatre themes to literature in general, from there to movies, television and so on. To be sure, the respective semiotic production rules are often not as important as the socio-cognitive rules f and g. But if all other things are equal, i.e., the socio-cognitive rules, then two communication processes can still differ a lot if they are determined by semiotic production rules with significantly different rigidity degrees. Let h designate the set of all semiotic production rules valid for a certain communicative situation. Then the order in which the first sender with the cognitive system A will apply the respective rules is

$$(19) \qquad f \circ h(A),$$

i.e., the sender first applies the h-function according to his topic and then the f-function according to the social characteristics of the situation. Note that the h-function like the f-function is relevant only for a sender and the g-function only for a receiver. Then the "basis" case with all functions remaining constant (including the h-function) becomes

$$(20) \qquad A_{t+n} = (g_1 \circ f \circ h)^n(A_t)),$$

and

$$(21) \qquad B_{t+n} = g_2\,(f \circ h \circ g_2)^{n-1}(B_t).$$

Accordingly the general case with all functions variable becomes

$$(22) \qquad A_{t+n} = \prod_{t}^{t+n} (g_{1t+i} \circ f_{t+i} \circ h_{t+i})(A_t)$$

and

$$(23)\qquad B_{t+n} = g_2 \circ \prod_{t}^{t+n-1} (f_{t+i} \circ h_{t+i} \circ g_{2t+i})\ (B_t)$$

For the case of constant f and h which is certainly the normal case we obtain

$$(24)\qquad \mathrm{A}_{t+n} = \prod_{t}^{t+n} (g_{1t+i} \circ f \circ h)\ (A_t)$$

and accordingly for B.

Strictly speaking the equations (1) to (24) are equation schemas because they do not contain the respective rules for concrete communication systems but just give a general framework. To apply these equations to artificial or empirically real communications one has, of course, to insert the specific rules that determine particular communicative processes. Yet such general frameworks are not unusual in the mathematical sciences as the general field equations in theoretical physics demonstrate. The Maxwell equations in electrodynamics, for example, have to be solved for particular cases in order to obtain the specific time functions for, e.g., light propagation. The case is similar with the even more famous Einstein field equations. Therefore our general equation schemas demonstrate the logic of communicative processes. The analysis of particular communications has in addition to be done by discovering the specific socio-cultural and semiotic production rules.

Here again one sees how useful it is to use the equally general formal tools of Soft Computing. In a similar sense as the equations are a general *theoretical* framework for the analysis of communication the formal models we described in the preceding chapters are general *modeling* frames for the same task. Therefore, the mathematical formalism can be considered as a heuristic device for the construction of empirical research: Each communicative process can be understood as a specific case described by one of the equations above. Then the respective equation can be translated into the algorithms of one of the formal models, for example a cellular automaton if the functions remain constant or a neural net if the cognitive rules are variable. As we saw in chapters 4. and 5. it is possible not only to simulate and explain processes in the history of the specific system but also to prognosticate certain processes that way. The whole process then can be summarized as

empirical investigation → selecting the appropriate equation → choosing a suited model → inserting empirical data and rules → comparing the simulation results with reality → correcting the inputs of the model and eventually the selection of the equations → new comparison with real processes and so on.

In this sense the equations and the models put something like a *theoretical and methodical algorithm* at one's disposal.

The equations demonstrate that communication apparently must be considered as a recursive process where each new step is generated out of the preceding steps. That means just the generation of new states in dynamical systems. Yet the equations also demonstrate that communication can be a lot more complicated than the rather simple recursive processes one usually associates with this term. For example the famous Fibonacci sequence $x_n = x_{n-1} + x_{n-2}$ is generated by always applying the same rule of generation to each new step. The general equations (22) and (23) demonstrate that the recursive process of the generation of new communicative steps does not necessarily follow always the same logic but that this can be altered. Hence an empirical communicative process is often composed of several sub-processes, all following a certain individual logic that was generated during the whole process and that was also changed during the communication. The whole process is still a recursive one but of a higher order: the interdependency of the three types of functions that we described as a three-dimensional Markov chain determines a higher dimensional form of recursive processes.

The examples given in the next chapter will clarify these rather abstract remarks a bit, or so we hope. In particular we shall see that these abstract equations also put at our disposal a systematic classification schema for these examples.

CHAPTER 7

EXAMPLES: COMPUTER MODELS AS OPERATIONALIZATION

At the end of the preceding chapter we referred to the methodical place of computer models in theoretical *and* empirical research. General theoretical considerations and concepts are "translated" into the respective algorithms of computer models that allow to test the theoretical hypotheses. In this sense computer models serve as a methodical tool for the necessary operationalization of theoretical propositions: they form a bond between general theory and empirical reality. In the traditional natural sciences this bond is mainly constructed by the specific solutions of general mathematical equations. This is usually not possible in the social and cognitive sciences because the processes that are investigated in these fields are much more complex. Yet even in the natural sciences the tool of computer models is used more and more, in particular where empirical processes of an overwhelming complexity have to be analyzed. One of the most famous cases, e.g., is meteorology because no equations exist that allow unique and applicable solutions to predict the weather.

As far as we see, the usage of computer models is the only way to realize a science of communication that is formally exact, i.e., a mathematical science on the one hand and empirically testable on the other hand. To be sure, the construction of computer models *per se* tells not much about the validity of the theoretical assumptions and the specific algorithms used in the computer models. The decision about the validity of theoretical assumptions and their operationalization by the translation into a computer model is first and last given by empirical examinations. Yet in the preceding chapters we already showed that it is indeed possible to construct such computer models that allow empirical confirmation. Although not all of the computer models shown below have been empirically tested so far the first results give hopeful hints that our computer models describe and explain the complex processes of human communication in an adequate manner.

The computer models all are constructed by following the methodical way of the natural sciences: Instead of trying to model the whole complexity of communication in one single model we selected certain aspects of this process and constructed according models, i.e., by taking only into account the particular aspects. It is one of the methodical difficulties of the humanities that frequently informal theories are constructed with the aim to capture once and for all each aspect of the respective fields. By doing this one mostly obtains theories that explain everything and that is equivalent with nothing. The methodical way we chose instead is the construction of models that are relatively simple in comparison to the complexity of empirical reality. But on the one hand it is always possible by using *ceteris paribus* conditions to gain important insights into our subject with simple models. On the other hand it is also always possible to enlarge the models, i.e., to insert additional aspects of communication and to approximate the complexity of the models more and more to that of the real process. We shall give examples for both ways in the following subchapters.

7.1. THE DETERMINATION OF COMMUNICATION BY MEANING, DEGREES OF INFORMATION, AND RELEVANCE

Cognitive functions, as we called them in the last chapter, determine in particular the generation of a specific meaning of a message and in addition the degree of information – for the receiver. They also determine the degree of relevance, that is the importance a message has for the receiver. Accordingly we constructed a communicative model by concentrating on the role of meaning, information and relevance for the communicative dynamics. In other words, the model is constructed for the analysis of communicative processes where social differences between the communicators play no decisive role and where the communicators are free to continue a certain communication, to finish it, and/or to open new communicative processes with other communicators.

The model consists of different artificial communicators who communicate in the way that they are sending and receiving certain messages. Each communicator is represented by several semantical networks and each semantical network represents a particular semantical field, i.e. a theme complex like "eating", "programming language" and so forth. These semantical networks are modeled by the use of interactive neural networks, which we used in several examples in the preceding chapters. Therefore, each communicator consists of several, usually five interactive neural networks that form his world knowledge and which are the base of the communication. The messages consist of triples of concepts like, e.g., (Paris, capital, France). For illustration purposes we show such a network with the theme "France".

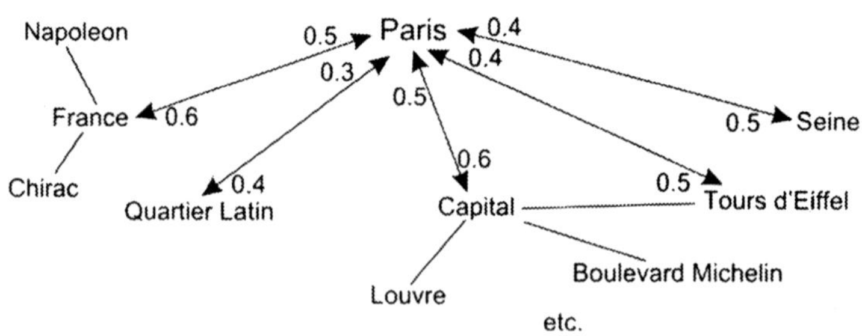

France network

The weight values of the connections between the concepts are all in the interval between 0 and 1. Note that these values represent the order of succession, in which the communicator associates and uses the different concepts. If for example the communicator starts with "Paris", i.e., wants to say something about France's capital then the network searches for the two concepts X and Y that are directly connected with "Paris" and whose connections have the strongest weight values from "Paris" to X and Y. In our network the concepts "capital" and "France" fulfill that condition. Hence the communicator forms the message (Paris, capital, France). Speaking more formally, if a communicator starts with concept Z then the network selects the two concepts X and Y with

$$w(Z, X) \geq w(Z, Y) \geq w(Z, C)$$

for all other concepts C in the network and then the communicator sends the message (Z, X, Y) in that order.

By looking at our network "France" one sees that the concept "Paris" has a certain center function, which we visualized by putting "Paris" in the center of the network. The weight values w(X, Paris) of all concepts X of the network have the characteristic that

$$w(\text{Paris}, X) \leq w(X, \text{Paris}).$$

Our network is apparently structured in such a way that by starting with a concept X the probability is very high that one of the next concepts in the message will be "Paris". We call such a concept a "center concept" and a communicator will always start a communication by using the center concept as first unit of his message. If a communicator has no such center concepts in his respective theme complex then he will start with a concept chosen at random. The whole model contains about 15 communicators, each consisting of ca. five different interactive neural nets. Both the number of the communicators and of the networks can be increased or diminished but for experimental purposes the model is mostly run with this size. Because social structure plays no role in this model one communicator A is chosen at random who acts as the first sender of a message. A selects that theme complex that has the highest relevance value of his themes (see below) and generates a message (X, Y, Z). The receiver B of this message is also chosen at random.

We remind that the start of the network dynamics of an interactive neural net is done by "externally activating" one or several units of the network, i.e., one or several units get a certain positive numerical value and then these activation values are spread over the network according to the linear activation function we mentioned some times above. Other functions are not important here. Before such an external activation all units have the activation value $A = 0$. The receiving of a message by the according network of the receiver hence means that the receiver looks at his network with respect to the theme of the message and if this network contains all the concepts of the message. If these concepts are in the network then these concepts will be externally activated with a medium value $A = 0.5$. If the network contains only two or one of the message concepts then only these concepts will be externally activated. If the receiver's network contains none of the sent concepts then no communication will take place, i.e., the receiver will look for another communicator and will send a new message to him.

The meaning of a message is, as we frequently pointed out, the attractor that is generated in the cognitive system of the receiver of that message. We also emphasized the importance of the generation of point attractors because only in that case the receiver will be able to attach a unique meaning to the message and will accordingly be able to act – to answer in the form of a new message, to follow an order, to go away and so on. Therefore, in our model the first step is to check if the network of the respective theme has generated a point attractor, which is not necessarily always the case with interactive neural networks.

Now several cases are possible:

(a) The network has generated a point attractor. In this case the message is "understood", i.e., the receiver has constructed a unique meaning and is able to answer, i.e., to become a sender. In addition, the receiver B knows all concepts of the message. B then keeps the theme that A had chosen, looks for a center concept or selects one concept at random, and constructs a message the same way as in the case of A. The first sender then acts as a receiver and so on. In order to avoid endless communications between the first two communicators A and B their communication stops after maximal five steps, that is five messages sent by A and by B likewise. After these five steps B selects a new communicative partner.

(b) After receiving the message (X, Y, Z) the semantical network of B generates a point attractor, but at least one concept of the message is not known to B, i.e., it is not contained in B's network. In this case B "asks" for an explanation of the unknown concepts, e.g. Y, that is B sends them back to A. A "explains" the concepts by sending back a message (Y, U, V) if U and V are the concepts with the strongest connections from Y in A's network. The concepts of the original message Z and X are not taken into account in the explanation.

    If this message (Y, U, V) generates a point attractor, and if B knows U and V, B integrates Y into his network by connecting Y with U and V by the weight value of 0.5 in both directions. If B does not know U or V or if the explanation does not generate a point attractor in the respective sub-network of B then B terminates the communication with A and selects a new theme and a new partner.

(c) The network of B generates not a point attractor but an attractor of period 2. Now B is "uncertain" about the meaning of the message as he has two different options at his disposal. Therefore, he "asks" A about his meaning of the message, i.e., B asks for the meaning of all concepts X, Y, and Z. A explains these concepts as in case (b). If B knows all concepts and if the explanations all lead to point attractors, then B increases the weight values by 0.1 between the concepts of the first messages and those concepts by which these first concepts are explained. If B does not know one concept of the explanations then B inserts this concept into his network as in case (b). If B does not know more than one concept of the explanations and/or if the explanations do not generate a point attractor then B again terminates the communication and selects a new theme and a new partner.

(d) The first message (X, Y, Z) generates an attractor with a period larger than 2. In this case B terminates the communication and carries on as in the cases (b) and (c).

These are the communicative rules that depend on the uniqueness of meaning. In addition, we need rules that determine the communicative processes in dependency of the informational degree and the degree of relevance of each message. The informational degree is computed as in the model of subchapter 3.3.; the degree of relevance as a value in the interval between 0 and 1 is distributed at random, i.e., each message has a certain degree of relevance for a particular communicator, but usually a different value for different communicators. The according rules for the communicative processes are now that (1) a receiver B of a message from a sender A will first check the meaning of the message according to the cases (a) – (d) just described. If B has understood the message then he will first determine the degree of relevance dr of the message *for him*. If $0 \leq \text{dr} \leq 0.4$, then B will terminate the communication with A and will select new partners. If $0.4 < \text{dr} \leq 0.6$, then B decides at random, if he wants to continue or to terminate the communication with A. If B continues the communication he carries on as in the next case. If $0.6 < \text{dr} \leq 1$, then B computes the informational degree I (2). Now the same procedure is repeated with respect to I, that is, B decides if he terminates or continues the communication according to the same values of I as was the case with dr. Only in the cases where both dr and I are sufficient high, the communication will be carried on and only then learning will take place.

The reasons for these rules are of course that a communicator will only be willing to talk about some themes if these themes are of sufficient interest for him, i.e., if the message contains enough information and is of a certain relevance for him.

The main purpose of this model is to simulate empirical communicative processes as was already done with another model (see below next subchapter). Because the according social experiments are still work in progress we can here just mention this aim. Yet another question is how different values of the sd-parameter determine such communicative processes. In order to analyze this we first have to define the impact of the values of the sd-parameter on the semantical networks of the communicators. This is done the same way as in the model described above in connection with the sd-parameter (see above 4.5): The value of the sd-parameter determines the proportion of neurons that are "blocked", i.e., that get no activation flows from the other units. If, e.g., sd = 0.2, then 20% of the units are blocked this way. This is of course only the case if the receiver is lower in the "sd-hierarchy" than the sender. If the receiver is the higher placed one than no units will be blocked.

The sd-parameter also determines the probability of learning. It seems quite reasonable that in most communicative processes with different status of the communicators learning will take place with higher probability in the case of the lower placed person than in the case of the higher placed one.[1] In accordance to this consideration we define the probability p_A for learning of a person A and the probability pB of a person B in the same communicative situation.

$$(7.1.1)\quad \text{If } sd_A > sd_B, \text{ then } p_A = 0.5 - (|sd_A - sd_B|)/2;$$
$$\text{If } sd_A \leq sd_B, \text{ then } p_A = 0.5 + (|sd_A - sd_B|)/2.$$

sd_A means the total sd-value of A that is combined by the sd-values of A in the three dimensions. In this sense the learning probability immediately depends on the sd-values of the communicative situation.

Despite the mentioned fact that this model was mainly constructed for empirical purposes we report some general results of different test series.[2] The first series was performed with variations of the threshold values of the degree of relevance and that of information. The research question was if and how the values of these control parameters would determine the behavior of the communicative systems with respect to the degree of semantical correspondence of the groups. The groups varied in size between five and fifteen artificial communicators. The experiments demonstrated that the size of the group is of no decisive importance for the generation of semantical correspondence.

It is not surprising that these experiments showed a significant dependency of the behavior of the system: the higher the threshold values for the degree of relevance and the informational degree were the lower became the final values of semantical correspondence and vice versa. These results are due to the fact that, of course, learning will only take place if the communicators agree to communicate at all. In this sense the results of the tests were not much more than a confirmation: the program behaved as it should because the rules with respect to the two threshold values were constructed to generate such a behavior.

More interesting are the results of the second test series with respect to the impact of the sd-parameter on the group behavior. In this series only the functional dimension of the sd-parameter was taken into account, i.e., the difference of knowledge between two communicators. The values of the other dimension were constantly kept zero. The question was how different sd-values in this third dimension would affect the degree of semantical correspondence of the respective groups. We remind that learning of new concepts is only possible if the learner has

[1] Note the "high" and "low" refer not only and not necessarily to the stratified dimension as the usual meaning of these terms is, but to the total value of the sd-parameter. A person A may be "higher" with respect to its total sd-value than a person B although A is placed lower in the stratified dimension.

[2] The implementation of the program and the performing of the tests were done by Eric Schmieders.

at least one or two concepts of a message already at his disposal, presumed that the communicators are nearly equal in the other dimensions of the sd-parameter. In addition, learning may change the initial sd-value because learning means in this model a decreasing of the knowledge difference of the communicators.

To cut a long story short, the computer experiments demonstrated a significant impact of the sd-values on the processes of the generation of semantical correspondence. The higher the initial sd-values are the less these values are decreased and the lower is the final degree of semantical correspondence, and vice versa. Initial large knowledge differences apparently are unfavorable for a cognitive homogenization of a group.

These results quite correspond to our social experience as teachers and communicators. With respect to the model the results are due to the fact that high sd-values in the third dimension mean that there is a subgroup of members who know a lot about the specific subject and another subgroup whose members know only little about the theme(s). If we call the first group the "experts" and the second group the "amateurs" then it is evident that mutual learning is rather improbable. The amateurs permanently receive messages with only unknown concepts. Being socially equal to the experts and the other amateurs the amateurs will terminate the communication and try a new one with frequently the same result. The experts on the other hand will permanently receive messages – both from other experts and from amateurs – with concepts that are all known to the receivers. Only low sd-values will significantly increase the degree of semantical correspondence of a group. We suppose that these results mirror the situation of empirical groups. But, as we mentioned above, this assumption must be validated by social experiments.[3]

7.2. THE IMPACT OF SOCIAL STRUCTURE ON SEMANTICAL CORRESPONDENCE

In the preceding subchapter the main focus of analysis was laid on the messages, i.e., on the determination of communication by the meaning, informational degree and relevance of the messages in addition with the impact of the sd-parameter on the cognitive processes and hence on the dynamics of communicative processes. In this sense we concentrated on the outcome of particular communicative processes in dependency of their content and the characteristics of the communicative situation.

According to the often stressed importance of social structure we also developed a simplified model in order to analyze the impact of different social structures,

[3] At present this model becomes enlarged by adding a so-called mental image: Each communicator has besides his own semantical networks another one that is a hypothetical network of the respective other communicator. In some cases the first communicator will select his messages by taking into account the mental image of the other. This enlargement will be performed by Jochen Burkart for his doctoral thesis and implemented into a computer program by Christian Odenhausen and Christian Pfeiffer.

measured only with respect to the stratified dimension, on the emergence of semantical correspondence as the necessary condition for mutual understanding of the group members. In other words, in what degree is a social group capable to generate a common culture, consisting of mutually shared concepts as common knowledge about the world. It is a truism that only a common culture can serve as a basis for understanding. We shall see in an expanded version of this model that even if different communicators share a set of common concepts understanding is by no means guaranteed. "Simplified" means that by experimenting with this model the meaning, informational degree and relevance of the messages are not taken into account but only the importance of the social structure of the respective group. Yet we shall demonstrate in the subsequent subchapters that it is possible to enlarge this simplified model in a very complex manner.

We use this simplified model for experimental purposes. Although the characteristics of the messages are not taken into account, it is interesting to see that it is possible to predict some processes of empirical groups by this model with an astonishing degree of accuracy.[4]

(A) The model

The computer system "COMMUNICATOR" consists of about ten communicating actors; to be sure, this number can be changed *ad libitum*, in particular if one wants to analyze empirical groups via the use of the model. Each actor is represented by his semantic network; i.e., a graph consisting of concepts (knots) and edges; i.e., the connections between the concepts.

The connections are weighted. That is, the strength of the logical or semantic relations between the concepts is represented by a real number between 0 and 1. The weights represent, as usual, the associative strength between the concepts. Usually these weights are different for different actors. "Associative strength" is again defined as the order or probability by which the cognitive system of a communicator combines different concepts when "speaking" to another communicator. For example, when a communicator wants to speak about concept A and this concept has, e.g., connection weights $cw(A, B) = 0.5$, $cw(A, C) = 0.9$ and $cw(A, D) = 0.1$ then he will utter the sentence (A, B, C) first and subsequently more frequently than the sentence (A, D). Technically speaking, in each communicative act the probability for choosing (A, B, C) is higher than the probability of (A,D).

The simplification of this model in comparison to that shown in the preceding subchapter is, of course, that the semantic networks of the communicators are only defined via their "static" structure and not by their structure as the determining factor for a resulting dynamics. Yet this simplification is enough for the purpose mentioned above.

[4] The model was implemented into a computer program by two of our students, Simon Cohnitz and Christian Dinnus, who also proposed valuable improvements.

The social structure for this communication group is also represented as a graph with weighted connections. For two communicators, A and B, $w(A, B) > w(B, A)$ means that A is higher in the social hierarchy than B. For normalization purposes we define $w(A, B) = 1 - w(B, A)$. Then it is possible to define a deviance parameter, dev, as a structural characteristic of the group:

(7.2.1) $$\text{dev} = (\sum i \sum j (w(i, j) - w(j, i))/n$$

for all group members i and j ($i \neq j$) and n the number of group members. "Deviance" means the measurement of the difference between a group with total equality – $w(i, j) = w(j, i)$ for all pairs (i,j) – and the factual particular group. In remembrance of the sd-parameter defined in chapter 4. obviously dev is a measure of the stratified dimension with respect to the group. One can easily verify that the definition of the dev-parameter is basically equivalent to the more general definition of the stratified dimension of the sd-parameter, namely a translation of the sd-definition into the terms of the structure of a weighted (and directed) graph. Note that the other two dimensions of the sd-parameter are not taken into account in this model.

It is possible with a simple algorithm to generate a social structure according to a particular dev-value. Note that the mapping between a group structure, defined as a certain graph, and its dev-value is not bijective because different group structures may have the same dev-value. The basic purpose of this model is to analyze the influence of particular social structures on the understanding processes of the communicators, i.e., on the degree of understanding they obtain from the communication. The "degree of understanding" is defined in the model, as in the model of the preceding subchapter, as the degree of correspondence among the concepts of the different communicators. The concepts are distributed at random at the beginning of a run; each communicator gets a set of thirty concepts out of a total set of hundred concepts. Each concept is connected with the other concepts according to a particular strength of connection, namely cw = cognitive weight. In the case of $cw(A, B) = 0$ there is no connection between the concepts A and B. The cw-values are also distributed at random for each communicator; i.e., the cw-values are mostly different for the same concepts in the semantical network of different communicators.

"Communication" again means that one communicator A utters one "sentence", i.e., a sequence of three concepts. Communicator A chooses at random one concept and generates the "sentence" by adding those two concepts that are the most strongly associated with the first one (see above). The receiving communicator B then "answers", that is, he also generates a sentence. If his semantic network contains all the concepts A has produced, then B takes over the first concept of A's message and adds those two concepts that are most strongly connected in *his* network. If

B's network contains only one or two of the concepts A has produced, then B will insert those new concepts into his own semantic network and connects them with the concepts in his network of the message of A that are part of B's network. If B has none of A's concepts, B terminates the communication with A, selects another topic, i.e., a concept with the strongest associating concepts, and selects another partner for communication. A simulation run starts with the communicator whose position is the highest in the group structure. This communicator selects at random his first partner.

"Learning" in this model consists of taking over concepts from a speaker and vice versa. The new concepts are added into the respective networks with connection strengths *according to the social relations between the communicators*. In other words, if $w(A, B) = k > w(B, A)$, if A utters a sentence (X, Y, Z), and if Z is unknown to B, then B enlarges its semantic network by adding Z with $cw(Y, Z) = k$. The reason for this rule is the well known fact that most people are more willing to learn from a person with higher authority and will generate new cognitive connections according to the social authority of the other.

Learning depends mainly on the social positions of the communicators. We assume that a person A, who is socially higher than B, will not immediately learn from someone significantly lower. Only if a highly ranking person A obtains a new concept several times from persons who are ranking more lowly in the social hierarchy then A will take over the new concept. If the more highly ranking person, A, has learned from a more lowly ranking person, B, then the w-value between A and B will be lessened in favor of B; i.e., B will obtain a position more nearly equal to that of A. In other words, if learning takes place then the social differences between two persons will change to greater equality. The reason for this is the often observed fact that people who are regarded as experts in some fields will more likely be treated as equals in factual communication even though their *official* position may be low.[5] If a highly ranking person A takes over a new concept from a lowly ranking person B, and if the social relation between A and B $w(A, B) = k$, then A will integrate the new concept with a connection weight $cw = 1 - k$, i.e., with the social weight value of $w(B, A)$. The reason for this rule should be obvious.

Lower placed persons always learn from the higher placed communicators. In this case the social difference between these persons will be increased; i.e., the higher placed person gets even more authority.

Because the main question being addressed with this model is the dependency of the degree of understanding on the social structure, we show the result of three

[5] One may argue about the empirical validity of this rule. Do more lowly ranked persons *always* learn from their social superiors? In any case, a lowly ranking person must be interested to listen to a higher authority and to implement the information obtained into his memory, i.e. his semantic network, because his superior will expect it. The converse is not the case because the more highly placed person has not to fear negative consequences if he does not remember the information obtained by the more lowly ranking person.

runs with different social structures – different with respect to the dev-parameter. C is the degree of semantic correspondence.

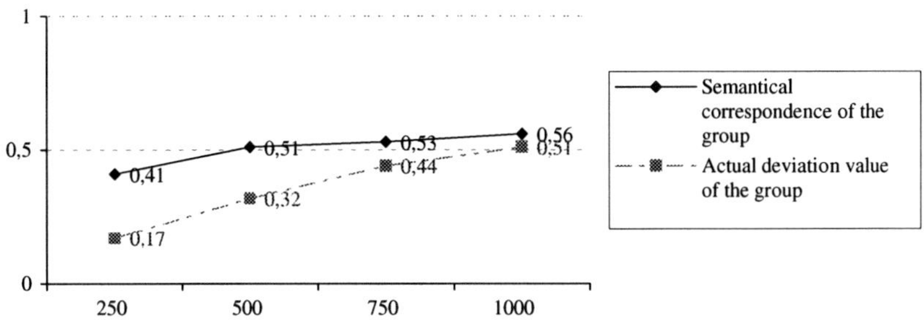

Figure 1. Initial values: semantic correspondence C = 0.19, dev. = 0.0 (a radical democratic structure)

One sees that the effects of the learning processes change the democratic structure (figure 1). After 250 time steps C = 0.41, dev = 0.17; after 500 time steps C = 0.51, dev = 0.32; after 750 time steps C = 0.53, dev = 0.44 and after 1000 time steps C = 0.56, dev = 0.51. Runs with additional time steps showed that these values do not change further – the whole system has reached an attractor state. "Time step" means an exchange of messages between two communicators, i.e. during one time step only one pair of communicators is sending and receiving messages. After such an exchange either A or B as the first two communicators (selected at random) choose another communication partner again at random and the next time step begins.

The figures show the changes of the initial values of deviance and correspondence dependent on the specific initial values. One sees that not only the degree of correspondence is changing, that is increasing, but also the social structure. Even the implementation of a radical democratic structure in figure 3 generates social hierarchies.

As a general result, we found that the rules of COMMUNICATOR apparently favor hierarchical group structures, which one may understand as another version of the famous principle of Matthew. In other words, the learning processes lead to social differentiation along the dimension high-low. Even in the case of a totally hierarchical initial structure (figure 2), the dev-values are only decreased by a small amount. In most cases the C- values never transcended the threshold of 0.6 (except, of course, where we deliberately generated initial values of C > 0.6). Total correspondence or understanding, respectively, is apparently very difficult to obtain in communicative groups where the social structure has effects on the mutual learning process and where the initial understanding is not high. It is up to empirical investigations of communicative group processes to see if these results are valid for factual groups (see below). Our everyday experience confirms most of these results, that is the difficulty to reach high degrees of common knowledge and culture in social groups of communicators.

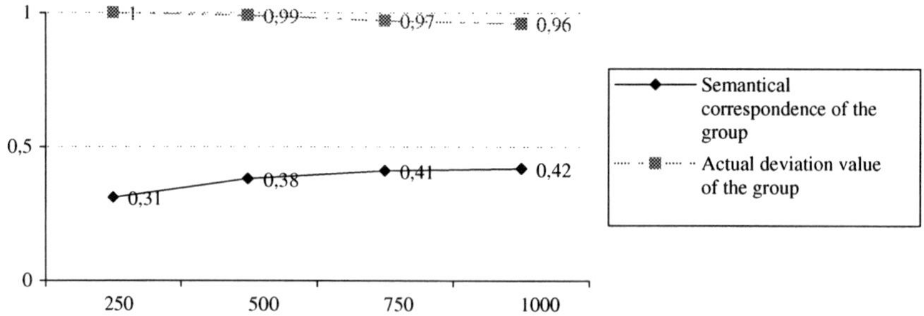

Figure 2. Initial values C = 0.19 (the same semantic correspondence as in figure 1), dev = 1.0 (a strictly hierarchical structure). The state (C = 0.42, dev = 0.96) is again an attractor state (in both dimensions)

One crucial factor in this model is apparently the asymmetric character of learning. While more lowly ranking persons always learn, i.e. take over new concepts, more highly ranking persons learn only when the new concepts are several times repeated. That is why the dev-values nearly always increase, i.e., the group becomes less democratic than it was at the beginning. Even a radical democratic structure at the start, i.e. dev = 0, changes. The explanation for this process is that if only one person learns, e.g., A learns from B and A and B are social equals, then B increases his social position with respect to A. We mentioned in chapter 2 the importance of even small initial differences of complex systems: small initial differences may lead to very different trajectories and accordingly different final states. This effect is exhibited in these experiments: a small advantage in initial learning for some of the communicators result in significantly higher positions in a group hierarchy that at the beginning was characterized by total equality.

More symmetric forms of learning may obtain better results with respect to understanding, i.e., high degrees of semantic correspondence, and they may also obtain decreasing degrees of dev, i.e., rising degrees of democratic structures. Yet in our experiments with groups of totally democratic structure the C-values also only seldom transcended the thresholds shown in figure 3. “Democratic” structure

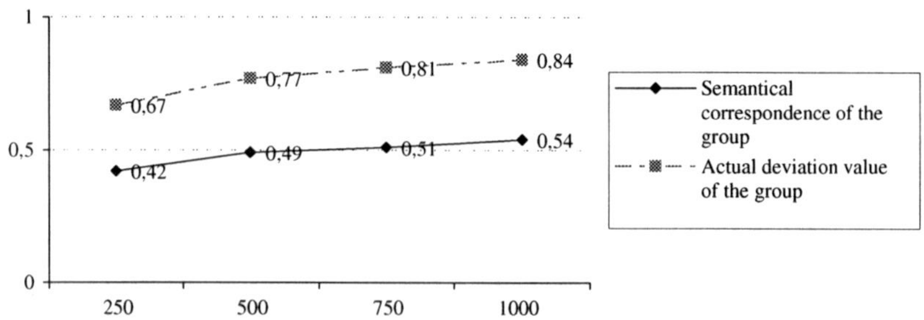

Figure 3. Initial values: C = 0.2, dev = 051 (a mixture of an egalitarian structure and hierarchical components). Further runs showed that C = 0.55 and dev = 0.85 is an attractor state

means in our model that the learning processes are symmetric, i.e., A learns from B and vice versa. Therefore, these limits of the degree of semantic correspondence must be explained.

If one takes a closer look at the communicative behavior of the artificial communicators one sees that in particular in long runs the communicators tend to always come back to the same topics, i.e., they will repeat certain messages after some time even if these messages have already been sent and/or received some time steps ago. The communicators do this despite the fact that they have other topics at their disposal and could, therefore, communicate about themes that have not been "discussed" before. Speaking in human metaphors it looks as if the artificial communicators have some favorite themes which they wish to repeat and that they avoid new topics although they have them at their disposal. This behavior certainly has striking similarities to human behavior: we all know from our everyday experience that such repetitions of always the same themes are a common characteristic of human social groups and that often attempts from one member to change the topics and go on to other subjects will be countered by the other members by coming back to the original themes.[6]

Such a behavior, of course, hinders the permanent increasing of semantic correspondence. Indeed, if the communicators only deal with a part of the possible topics then mutual learning will take place only with respect to these topics and will not raise the semantic correspondence in regard of the other ones. Hence, it is a logical consequence that the C-value of the group cannot transcend certain thresholds and will usually never reach a value of 1. That is why even a radical democratic structure with dev $= 0$ and accordingly only symmetric learning processes will not lead to very high degrees of mutual understanding.

This "human" behavior of our artificial communicators was not originally intended by us when we constructed the model and it may be looked at as an "emergent" phenomenon. We just implemented the rules that a) messages must consist of concepts that have rather strong connections and b) that when choosing a new theme the message must consist of concepts that are strongly connected. Because a random semantical network has only some clusters of concepts with strong connections, the rules a) and b) apparently are sufficient to generate such a strikingly human-like behavior. Yet we assume that these rules are empirically valid in the sense that human communicators also tend to speak about themes of which they have a large and strongly connected association field.

Despite the fact that this simplified model already exhibits types of behavior that we know from human groups, a more strict validation of the model is certainly desirable. That is why we undertook the comparison of this model with some social experiments.[7]

---

[6] When we gave lectures on this model at conferences or at university courses we more than once got the feed back from listeners that this behavior of our artificial communicators is by itself a strong indicator for the empirical validity of our model.

[7] These experiments were performed with our instruction by several of our students, in particular by Jochen Burkardt for his MA-thesis (Burkardt 2004) in communication science.

(B) Communication as Social Experiment

The main idea behind these experiments is to compare predictions of the "Communicator-Model" with the result of experiments performed with different groups of human communicators. The dimension of comparison is the respective degree of semantic correspondence in the human groups and the artificial group, i.e., the result of the runs with the same initial values as those of the human groups.

The social experimental groups always consisted of human experimental subjects. Mostly these subjects were students of the University Duisburg-Essen of Educational Science, Communication Science and Computer Science, but other groups, e.g. members of specific clubs, also took part in these experiments. At the beginning the experimental persons got three different themes, for example "eating", "Christmas", or "University". The first task for the participants then was to construct an associative network for each topic. To do this they had a specific form in which they should insert those concepts they associated within five minutes with respect to the particular subject. The form contained a structure, which can be called a "weighted semantic cluster" and which looks like this; the example consists of the theme "Paris":

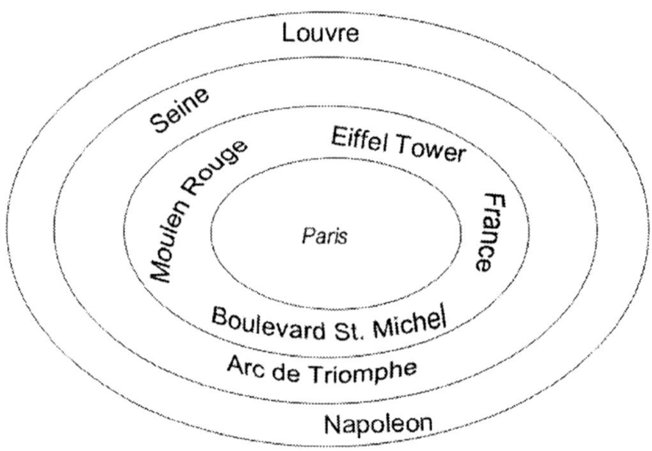

The particular theme was inserted in the center of the concentric circles. The experimental subjects should write the first three or four concepts they associated with the central concept – in this case "Paris" – in the first ring, counted from the central concept, the next three concepts into the second ring, the next three or four ones into the third circle and so on. Usually the participants only filled out the first three circles, i.e., they associated about nine to twelve concepts with the central one. The participants got as a guide how to use the form this example of "Paris";

we did not use the ambiguity of this concept to make things as simple as possible for the experimental subjects.[8]

After the filling out of the forms the participants should discuss each theme for about 15 minutes. To be sure, this is a rather short time for groups consisting of about 8 to 15 members. But because the participants were all volunteers, i.e., they did not get paid for their time we decided to keep the experiment as short as possible. After the discussions the participants again obtained three forms with the same central concepts. These forms should be again filled out. This task was given to them because the new forms should be compared with the initial ones.

We chose this method of weighted clusters because it is easy to understand and because the participants could structure their respective semantical networks by themselves. In this sense this method has more advantages than other methods of obtaining associative fields of experimental subjects. Remember that the definition of weighted connections in semantical networks we frequently used is that the strength of the connections determines the order in which different concepts are associated. Therefore, the filled out forms can be quite simply inserted into the semantic networks of the Communicator-program:

By again neglecting a connection between the central concept and itself we defined that the connection weight $cw(C, C_{next})$ of the central concept to the concepts in the next circle is $cw(C, C_{next}) = 1$; the connection weight from the central concept to the concepts in the second circle is $cw(C, C_{sec}) = 0.8$; the concepts in the third circle are connected with $cw(C, C_{third}) = 0.6$ and so on. For our example with "Paris" we obtain the list

cw(Paris, France) = 1;
cw(Paris, Eiffel Tower) = 1,
cw(Paris, Moulin Rouge) = 1;
cw(Paris, Boulevard St. Michel) = 1;
cw(Paris, Seine) = cw(Paris, Arc de Triomphe) = 0.8;
cw(Paris, Napoleon) = cw(Paris, Louvre) = 0.6.

As "Paris" is a central concept we assume that the connections from the other concepts to "Paris" are usually at least as strong as reversely. In other words, one more frequently associates "Paris" when thinking of "Louvre" than the other way around. Therefore, we defined

$$cw(X, \text{Paris}) = 1, \text{ if } cw(\text{Paris}, X) = 1,$$

$$cw(X, \text{Paris}) = 0.8, \text{ if } cw(\text{Paris}, X) < 1.$$

[8] The experiments were, of course, performed in German. One of the themes was "Eating", which in German is "Essen". This is the same word as the name of the city of Essen, where most of the participants live. It is interesting to note that frequently the participants did not realize the ambiguity of this concept and associated either only concepts concerning "food", "drinking", and the like, or only concepts concerning the town, e.g. "Ruhr" (the river at which Essen is situated) These participants were much surprised when the other experimental subjects brought in the respective other concepts.

With these definitions the filled out forms of the experimental subjects could be inserted as structured semantical networks, i.e. as weighted graphs, into the program.

When the participants after the three rounds of discussion filled out their final forms, the semantical correspondence of the experimental group was computed. The assumption is, of course, that the degree C of semantical correspondence would increase as a result of the discussion rounds. The exact computing of the semantical correspondence should not only take into account the number of common concepts for all participants but also the specific structure of the semantical networks of the experimental subjects before and after the discussions. Therefore, we defined:

By considering that for two communicators A and B the number of concepts at the disposal of the communicators is important we define the *quantitative* correspondence C_k as

(7.2.2) $C_k = 2*j/(n+m)$,

if j is the number of common concepts and n and m are the number of concepts of A and B respectively.

For the computing of the *qualitative* (or structural) semantical correspondence C_u we must consider the weight of the connections between the central concept and another certain concept. If for a concept X the weight in the semantic network of A is $cw_A(C, X) = r$ and in the network of B cw_B $(C, X) = s$, then for this concept the qualitative correspondence is

(7.2.3) $C_u = 1 - |r - s|$.

By combining the qualitative correspondence for all common concepts i we obtain a weighted average

(7.2.4) $C_{uw} = (\sum_I C_{ui})/q$,

if q is the number of common concepts.

The whole semantical correspondence C can then be defined as

(7.2.5) $C = C_k * C_{uw}$.

In other words, by this definition one not only takes into account the number of common concepts in relation to the number of concepts A and B have at their disposal but also the structural integration of these common concepts into the two networks of A and B.

For the semantical correspondence of a group of more than two communicators one has to compute C_{XY} for each pair of communicators X and Y, and subsequently again compute the average of these values. Thus we obtain for a group G

(7.2.6) $C_G = (\sum C_i)/t$,

for each pair i of communicators, if t is the number of pairs of communicators.[9]

Obviously $0 \leq C_G \leq 1$. $C_G = 0$ is, of course, a case where no semantical correspondence at all exists in the group; the members of the group literally cannot understand each other. $C_G = 1$ is a case where the semantical networks of all group members are identical, not only with respect to the concepts but also to the structure of the networks. We mentioned in the last chapter that this can be the case only with people who have known each other for a long time and have become accustomed to each other, e.g. a couple, which has been married for many years. The usual case will be that C_G is somewhere between these two extreme cases, as we also observed in our experimental groups.

The analysis of the increasing semantical correspondence in the experimental groups and the comparison with the prediction of the program was the main research question. To be sure, it can be interesting to analyze the changing of the individual networks of the participants and to compare it with according predictions of the program. In some individual cases we did it to demonstrate the learning effect of the discussions. A quite amusing example is this, shown in figure 4.

The student who took part at a discussion about the English Rock Star Ozzy Osbourne apparently did not know much about this musician. Yet obviously she got rather interested in the discussion and learned a lot of it.[10]

But in general it makes not much sense in the context of these experiments to prognosticate the individual changing of particular networks. The main reason for this is the simple fact that the participants had not much time to generate their respective networks for each theme, i.e., only five minutes. We explained the practical reasons for this restriction above; it can be assumed that the individual networks inserted in the form would have been much larger if the participants had more time at their disposal (with the exception perhaps of the student in the example of "Ozzy Osbourne"). Hence, we decided to concentrate not on individual changing processes but on the effect the discussion had on the whole group, i.e., on the increasing of semantical correspondence of the group. To be sure, as we demonstrated with the example of "Tom" in chapter 4., it is under other experimental and observational conditions quite possible to predict individual processes with suited models and programs as well as group processes.

Comparisons between the initial semantical correspondences for each theme and each group and the final ones showed that the C-value in each case indeed increased, yet not always to the same degree. In the average the higher the initial C-values had been the larger was its increase and vice versa. An explanation for this result may be that those groups whose members had much in common with respect to one

[9] These definitions were not exactly used in the computer experiments described above in paragraph (A) because in the random networks no central concepts were defined. The definition applied in these experiments used a more complicated equation for the structural correspondence, i.e., the difference between *any pairs* of concepts in the respective semantical networks.

[10] The three subjects of the group discussions were always selected by those students who organized the respective group sessions.

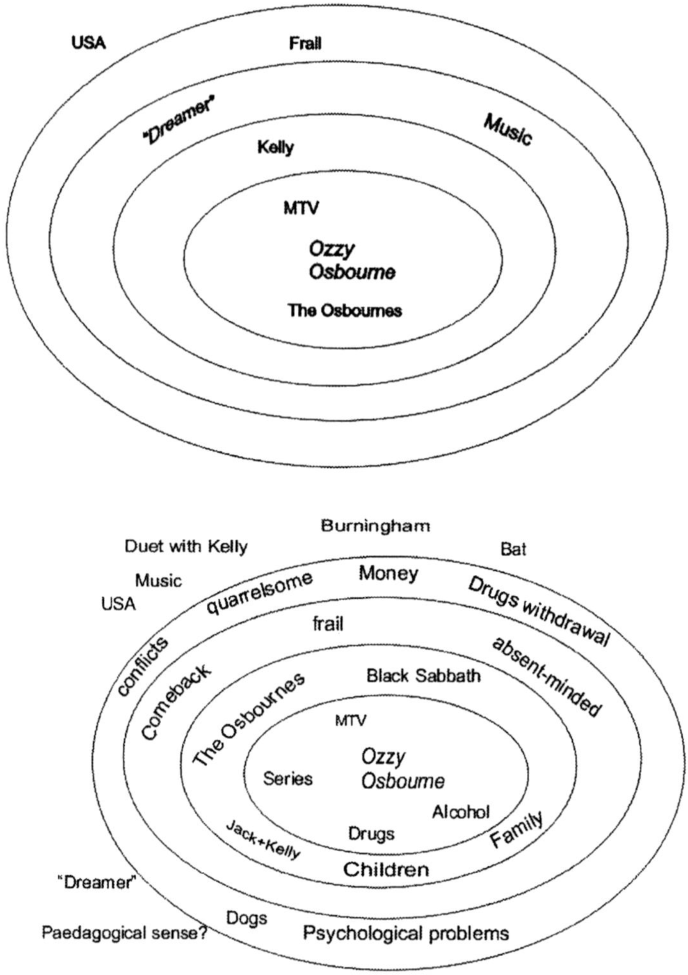

Figure 4. Two semantical networks of "Ozzy Osbourne" before and after the discussion about this interesting theme

subject had more discussions about the respective subjects, in which all members were interested. Conversely, if a group had only small initial C-values the members had not much in common about these topics and hence not much to say about it. Accordingly low were the final C-values.

For the simulation the dev-values were always inserted as zero, that is the social structures of the different groups were always assumed as "radical democratic" with according symmetric learning processes. The reason for this restriction is that we did not know anything about the social structure of these groups that did not exist before the experiments and completely consisted of *socially* equal members. To be sure, the group members differed in many aspects, in particular with respect to their knowledge about the different subjects and their rhetorical competence. Yet we assumed, not knowing the most of the group members either, that in the average these individual differences would not be of great importance. According to this restriction we also assumed that the learning processes would be mostly symmetric.

Factual human communicative processes depend not only on general rules and structural group characteristics but, as we frequently mentioned before, also on individual factors and sometimes on specific situational conditions, which cannot be captured in such general models as the "Communicator-Model". To take such individual and situational aspects into account the simulation runs were performed not once but fifty times. The results, i.e., the fifty respective final C-values, then were combined by the arithmetical mean; only this result was compared with the result of the human groups. The runs differed mainly with respect to the beginning of the simulation, i.e., which artificial communicator would start the communicative process, and accordingly which communicator would continue with which other. These succession were generated at random, but according to dev = 0 each communicator should approximately take part in the process as much as any other. Such a "distribution rule" is not always realistic, as we shall see in one example.

To be sure, the initial values of the program were just the initial semantical networks of the human communicators. Because each human communicator had to discuss three themes, each artificial communicator consisted of three independent interactive networks, each containing one semantical networks with the initial concepts and connections for the human communicator the artificial one represented.[11]

These experiments were performed with 10 different groups of human members, mostly, as we said, students from our university, but not always. The most important results are the following:

In six cases, i.e. six different groups, the prediction of the program differed only about 5–10 percent from the factual outcome of the respective human groups. The computing of these differences occurs, of course, by computing the difference between the factual outcome and the prediction of the program for each subject and by combining these three different values via the arithmetical mean. For some themes the difference was even lower, i.e., less than five percent. In three cases the difference was about 10–15% and only in one case the difference was more than twenty-five percent.

Speaking frankly, we did not expect such good results of most of the experiments because we knew how simplified the model still is. Yet the positive results hint at the probability that human communication is often rather simple and follow rules that are not much more complicated than the rules of our model. In other words, the themes that were all taken from common everyday knowledge of the

[11] This is again different to the experiments described in paragraph (A) where each artificial communicator consisted of just one interactive network with concepts and connections distributed at random.

group members apparently only needed simple social and cognitive rules in order to generate interesting discussions. Remember the human-like behavior of our artificial communicators that we described in paragraph (A). Indeed, when we questioned many participants after the experiments they mostly said that they found the discussions quite interesting and that they sometimes learned a lot (see the example of the semantical network containing Ozzy Osbourne).

In one case the program was much in error, i.e. its result significantly differed from the factual results. The initial C-values were rather low in this group and the program predicted a significant increase of them. But factually the final C-values were not much higher than the initial ones. Luckily we made video recordings of some of the groups in order to analyze the factual communicative behavior of the members and this group was one of them. By looking at the recording we found out that nearly all of the nine members practically said nothing at all during the experiment and only two of the participants tried – mostly in vain – to motivate the other members in joining the discussion. But they refused and kept silent.

We concluded that the silent members were not interested in the respective subjects and accordingly did not wish to learn anything about it. Therefore, the initial C-values did not rise in contrast to the prediction of the program. Because the program "assumed" that each participant would approximately speak as often as the others, and as this assumption was not correct in this case, the bad result of the program could be explained as a problem of a very special case of communication.[12] In this sense this group is an illustrative example of the impact of individual and situational factors on the dynamics and results of communicative processes: The frequency of actively participating in a communicative process obviously determines the learning results of the individual communicators. If not all communicators actively participate in the discussion then learning will not occur or only in a much restricted manner. Accordingly low is the increase of the C-value.

On a first sight the predicting validity of our Communicator Model seems rather astonishing, considering the relative simplicity of its rules and theoretical assumptions. Yet, as we mentioned, human communicative processes are frequently not very complex, i.e. difficult to understand, and of course we tried to define the model's rules as empirically adequate as possible. In addition, the social experiments only contained rather simple forms of human communication, namely the exchange of messages about common knowledge. It goes without saying that human communication is often much more complex than the communicative processes of our social experiments. Therefore, as satisfactorily the results of the comparisons of the simulation runs with the factual outcomes of the human groups are from a scientific point of view, we certainly do not want to overestimate them. Hence, we

[12] The explanation of the strange behavior of most of these group members was rather simple, as we learned afterwards: Nearly all of the members were students of us who would soon begin their final examinations and the writing of their final thesis under our supervision. Hence, they were afraid not to say something stupid because they of course knew that we would look at the recording – a classical case of Hawthorne effects.

developed some expanded versions of the basic Communicator-Model in order to capture some more complex aspects of human communication.

7.3. EXPANDED MODELS

In several respects the basic COMMUNICATOR is not sufficient with regard to our theoretical basis and to everyday knowledge about communicative processes. For example, each communicator may take up new concepts during his turn in the communication if he is not able to construct sentences with the concepts or related concepts of his predecessor in the communicative process. In addition, the order of communicative acts is usually chosen at random, but human communicators follow a certain order: they prefer to talk to somebody and avoid to talk to another and so on. Neither rule is very realistic: if one defines a "culture" as the knowledge of a group as we did in the preceding chapters, then this culture regulates the connections between different concepts. Accordingly, semantic networks are not totally different for two members of a social group with a common culture. In addition, a communicator is not simply allowed to talk about any subject he wishes to discuss. On the contrary, if a group has chosen a theme, then the communicators have to deal with it. Changing a theme is only allowed in certain cases; in particular, if the communicator has a rather high social position or if the group as a whole has agreed to change the theme. Other deficits of the COMMUNICATOR-model will be discussed below with respect to more advanced models, in particular the problem of "who talks with whom".

According to these deficits we enlarged the rules of COMMUNICATOR in three steps, i.e., by developing more and more complex models. These models will be described here in just a general way; readers who are able to read German may contact us for the detailed description of the models (cf. Toellner 2004; Kaczor 2004; Honke 2006).

(A) The combination of the COMMUNICATOR with the Moreno approach

This first extension of the original COMMUNICAOTR model is developed in order to represent a certain group culture on the one hand, and to define a socially determined order of the different communicative acts between two members of a group on the other. To do this we first had to define a certain ordering of the concepts.

The connections between the concepts that constitute the group culture are the same for each communicator, although the communicators still differ with respect to their initial concepts, i.e., the concepts they select to start a communication. Several concepts are "clustered"; i.e., they are connected by connections with cw-values $\neq 0$. Such clusters are defined as a "theme"; i.e., as the set of all concepts that are directly or indirectly connected with cw-values $\neq 0$. In other words, a theme consists of concepts that can be combined in a "sentence" with a probability $p > 0$. An artificial communicator now consists of a large network that contains sub networks representing different themes. Those themes may be connected by certain "bridge" concepts like "Paris" in our examples or they are separated. Note that the connections of the concepts of a theme can be very different. Two simple examples may illustrate this:

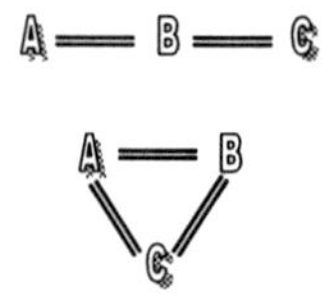

Figure 5. A theme consisting of three concepts, structured in two different ways

In the first case, A is connected with C only via B. In the second case, all concepts are directly connected. Accordingly, we defined the *semantic compactness* *sc* of a theme by the ratio of the factual direct connections and the possible direct connections (in the case of n concepts the number of possible connections is, of course, $(n^2 - n)/2$ if one counts only a connection from A to B and not the connection from B to A). This gives us a semantic parameter, sem, by defining the compactness of the whole culture as the (arithmetical) mean value of all themes of this culture:

$$(7.3.1) \quad sem = \sum \frac{sc_i}{k}$$

for k themes i.

In addition, we defined for each theme a *degree of rigidity ri*, which is the probability by which a communicator is allowed to change a theme (see above chapter 3.). The reason for this definition is the observation that different themes allow only in differing degrees their enlargement or change. Talking about politics may lead to themes of history, prejudices, gender, sex, and so on. Talking about mathematics usually forces the communicators to stay with that theme or to persuade the others if and how to change it. Speaking in the terms of chapter 6. we introduced a semiotic production rule as a particular h-function.

In this expanded model the communicators interact in the following way: The person of highest rank starts the communication by choosing a theme and generating a sentence, i.e., a triple of two to three concepts from this theme. The next communicator has to "answer"; i.e., he repeats the first concept (or another concept from the sentence if he does not have the first concept) and adds one or two new concepts from the same theme. If he is not able to answer with such a sentence, he either may choose a new theme, although only under rather restricted conditions, or remains silent and the communication passes to a third communicator.

In other words, we expanded the first model by introducing certain semiotic production rules and looked for the effects on the degree of understanding of the whole group. As a general trend we obtained that the semantic compactness of the group culture plays a decisive role insofar as high values of sem generate higher values of C.

Another shortcoming of the basic COMUNICATOR-models is the assumption that each communicator is able and willing to communicate with every other communicator. Real groups do not behave this way because, e.g., if communicator A does not like communicator B then A will try to avoid communications with B. Other factors of "who will communicate with whom" play according roles. This expanded version of the COMMUNICATOR takes this into account by substituting the simple rules of interaction of the basic model with rules based on a socio-matrix. In other words, we combined the logic of the COMMUNICATOR model with the approach for modeling differentiating processes of groups with the "Moreno approach" we described in chapter 4.:

The artificial communicators are placed as cells on the grid of a cellular automaton (CA), as was demonstrated in 4.1. Empty cells represent as before space to move in if the communicators so wish. The basic rule is again that a communicator tries to become a member of such a subgroup, which is represented on the CA-grid by the Moore neighborhood, where he feels better than in other subgroups. Accordingly each communicator looks for suited neighborhoods, and either stays in his initial one or moves into a "better" subgroup. The computing of the feelings of the communicators is done approximately the same way as in the simpler experiments of 4.1. One difference is that the socio-matrix contains not only values of 1, 0, and −1 but that the values are arranged on a scale from 0 to 10. The interpretation of these values is roughly the same, i.e., the lower the values of the matrix are the less the communicator likes the respective group member and vice versa.

Each communicator consists of several semantical networks that are ordered in the manner described above. The communicators have as in the basic communicator-model the ability to learn, to communicate, and as an additional capability the possibility to change the values of their socio- matrices. This is done the following way:

As in the simple CA-model of 4.1. the program starts with the evaluation of the respective subgroups and with the selecting of new neighborhoods if that is possible. If the program generates a point attractor this process stops, i.e., a first differentiation of the whole group into different subgroups has occurred. If the program does not reach a point attractor after 30 time steps then the program also stops. This rule, of course, takes into account the fact that no human group will endlessly search for a global optimum, i.e., a differentiation where all members are to a maximum satisfied. The members of the group will accept positions where they are satisfied only to a certain degree.

After the stop of the differentiating process communicative processes will begin like in the basic COMMUNICATOR model but each communicator only interacts with the group members of his own Moore neighborhood. The decisive point at this stage of development is that the individual communicator "evaluates" the answers he gets from the other members. If he receives answers in form of concepts he also has in his semantical network, and if the communicator perceives that the other member has a similar concept structure as he has, then his emotional value with respect to his communicative partner will rise. "Similar concept structure" means that the concepts of the answer are in the same order as the sender has these concepts in his network. If, for example, the first communicator has the concepts A, B, and C with direct connections in his network and if he receives an answer (A, B, C) then the first communicator perceives this as a similar structure. Accordingly, if the answers of his partner do not exhibit a similar ordering structure, then the emotional value with respect to his communicative partner in the socio-matrix of the first communicator will decrease. If not only the structure of the concepts of the partner is not similar but the concepts themselves are different from those of the first communicator, then the emotional values will decrease even more. Note that these variations of the socio-matrix only occurs with respect to the communicators of the Moore neighborhood.

It is important to note that the raising or decreasing of the values of the socio-matrix is only a result of the factual communication processes between the group members. As in "real" life the communicators are not able to perceive the semantical networks of their communicative partners in a direct way but they can only orientate their matrix values to the answers they get. In addition, we use in this model the same assumption as Schelling did in his quoted model (1971), namely that people prefer to be in the neighborhood of other people that are or at least seem to be comparatively similar to themselves and that they avoid being together with people who differ from them in certain aspects. Accordingly a communicator selects a new partner if his first partner is not able to communicate about the same theme. The values in the respective socio-matrices, therefore, are changed according to the experiences of similarity or dissimilarity. After 25 time steps the communicative processes stop, the communicators evaluate their situation, again with respect to the whole group, and change their neighborhood if the communicative processes have varied the socio-matrices so much that the selection of a new neighborhood is desirable. Subsequently new communicative processes start and so on. The whole simulation run stops if a point attractor for the whole group has been reached or if a certain number of time steps has been performed by the program.

The research question that lead to the construction of this extension of the basic model is if the semantic compactness of themes and their degree of rigidity have any influence on the communicative processes. That is indeed the case as a lot of simulation runs demonstrated: On the one hand high values of the semantical compactness sem generate, as we already mentioned, accordingly high degrees of semantic correspondence and vice versa. On the other hand the degree of rigidity acts as a control parameter: the higher the rigidity of the themes is the more different subgroups emerge, that is subgroups with different sub-cultures, consisting of different sets and structures of concepts. Consequently, the semantical correspondence *in* these subgroups becomes rather high and the semantical correspondence for the whole group decreases. This seems to be a quite realistic result: the more specialized different themes are the more special become the subcultures of those subgroups that define themselves with these themes. In this sense even an initial homogenous culture with a rather high degree of semantical correspondence becomes differentiated into specialized subgroups. In the end of such processes the members of the subgroups only communicate with members of the same subgroup and remain there. The original group literally becomes dismantled into isolated subcultures.

To be sure, in "real" societies these differentiating processes do not go on until the total decomposition of the society. There are always counter factors as, e.g., common laws and interests that form a common bond for the whole society. Yet our simulation experiments demonstrate that tendencies of radical differentiation, which we can observe in modern societies of the Western type, can easily happen if there are no common bonds or if such bonds have no real binding forces. A high rigidity degree of sub cultural themes can be enough to set such process of differentiation into motion. Only if the initial values of rigidity are not high ($ri \leq 0.5$) then admittedly differentiation into subcultures will nevertheless occur but the semantical correspondence of the whole group will remain quite high, i.e., the subcultures are not isolated islands.

The ri-degree was used in these experiments as an independent variable, i.e., its respective value was fixed for each simulation run. That is, of course, a simplification because the rigidity of certain themes is by itself a result of foregoing communicative and other social processes. Therefore, it would have been more realistic if the ri-degree is not constant. Yet the model is just complex enough that it allows to demonstrate how the characteristics of themes, that is of the semiotic dimension of communication, are under certain conditions sufficient to generate the emergence of new cultural and social structures.

(B) Second enlargement: the association of concepts with perceptions

Even the expanded model just described is still not sufficient in several additional respects. On the one hand the communicators are still just modeled by directed and weighted graphs that can be enlarged and changed during the communicative process. Yet these graphs are not such dynamical systems as "real", i.e. human communicators. Such dynamical models were described in chapter 7.1. On the other hand, and even more important, the concepts of the semantical networks the communicators consist of are only associated, i.e., connected with other concepts. In this sense the directly connected concepts represent the mediate meaning of certain concepts but the fact is omitted that concepts as symbols refer not only to other concepts but also to certain characteristics of perceived or just cognitively constructed objects. The quoted scholastic definition of a symbol as "*aliquid stat pro aliquo*" refers to that fact that of course semantical networks and their concepts always must have some reference to something "aliquo", i.e., to the *designatum* of the symbols. Communication via the use of certain symbols is not just an exchange of these symbols as in the preceding models but also an exchange of symbols *and* the *designata* of the symbols.

In order to model these relevant aspects of communication too we introduced a certain combination of different neural nets as the representation of an artificial communicator, namely by using so called hetero-associative feed-forward networks

(HN) and self-organized Kohonen maps (KM). To be more exact, each artificial communicator consists of two hetero-associative networks, of one Kohonen map and of one semantical network. The latter is the result of the foregoing operations of the HN and the KM.

The two HNs have the task to associate the characteristics of a certain concept with the concept itself and vice versa. The reason for this sub-model is, of course, that communication often consists in the naming of characteristics on the one hand and the adding of the respective concept on the other. If a child, e.g., says, "look, something small with four legs and it makes noises" and the answer is "this is a dog" then the child will associate these characteristics with the concept "dog". Conversely, if one hears the concept "dog" one associates characteristics like those the child has told. The HNs in our model perform just these tasks.

The KM whose basic logic we described in chapters 4. and 5. is able to generate a semantic net from the concepts and their respective characteristics in a self-organized manner.[13] Therefore, the artificial communicators in our expanded models do not need to get their semantic networks by the user of the program but they are able to construct their networks themselves. It is obvious that this model allows not only the study of the emergence of group understanding and in this way the emergence of a certain culture but also the study of individual learning processes in dependency of the communicative processes in the according group. Before we go into some technical details we give an overview of the operation of the model.

Imagine two artificial communicators A and B. A consists of the two hetero-associative nets HN_{A1} and HN_{A2}, the KM_A, and the semantical net SN_A, and accordingly, B consists of HN_{B1}, HN_B2, KM_B., and SN_B. If A sends, as usual in our models, a triple of concepts (X, Y, Z) then there are several possibilities for B:

a) B knows all concepts of the message, i.e., they are all contained in SN_B. In this case B associates via HN_{B1} the characteristics, i.e., the *designata* of the concepts via associating, e.g., the concept X with a vector $(x_1, \dots, x_n)$ consisting of the characteristics of X. If, for example X is "cat" then B associates "small", "purring", scratching" etc. Note that these associations may be wrong, at last from the point of view of A. Perhaps A's association with "X" is a vector $(x'_1, \dots, x'_n)$. Of course, when talking about cats the probability is very high that A and B have roughly the same associations, i.e., they associate vectors that are rather similar. But if a member of a Christian culture and a Moslem are talking about "marriage" then the associative vectors will differ in at least one component: The Christian will associate "marriage" with the imagination of one man and one woman, whereas the Moslem will probably think about the possibility that one man may marriage several women. Such different associations can happen even in science: if a physicist and a mathematician

---

[13] A Kohonen map is able to learn in an "unsupervised" manner. That means, generally speaking, that it is able to order the concepts it obtains by their own logic, i.e., by their relations. Because a "dog" is more related to "cat" than to "fish", a KM will place "dog" nearer to "cat" than to "fish". Remember the biological example we gave for the operation of a KM in chapter 4.

both talk about "field" then they are not necessarily aware that the first means a certain physical structure associated with, e.g. waves, and the second one talks about an algebraic structure, i.e., a set defined by two algebraic operations and a mapping to the space of real numbers.

b) B does not know one or several concepts of the message. In this case B "asks" for the "meaning" of these unknown concepts, i.e., B asks for the associative vectors of the concepts. When A answers with the vector(s) B inserts the vectors into his KM. The KM orders on the basis of the associative vectors the new concepts, i.e., it integrates the new concepts into the semantical network of B. This integration is in the first step a pure topological one, i.e., the KM decides which old concepts are most similar to the new ones. "Similarity" means the similarity of the respective associative vectors which is measured either by the Hamming-distance or the Euclidean distance. As a result the new concepts become placed in the neighborhood of the similar concepts.[14]
Subsequently the weight of the connections between the old concepts and the new ones is again determined by the Hamming distance: if the vectors of an old concept X and a new concept Y differ in only 10% then the connection weight is 0.9, if the vectors differ in 20% then $cw(X, Y) = cw(Y, X) = 0.8$ and so on. By using the Euclidean distance it is possible to determine the cw-values even more detailed but for experimental purposes the simple measure via the Hamming distance is sufficient.

If A does not send concepts but "talks" about perceived characteristics of some object, i.e., A sends one or more associative vectors, then B of course has to associate the sent characteristics with the concepts he knows already. This is the task of HN_{B2}, which obtains the sent vectors as input and associates the according concepts as output. B in this case "knows" what A is talking about. Note again that also this association may be wrong, i.e. that A has quite another concept in mind. If, for example, A sends a vector ("small", "ugly", "four legs", "smelling badly") then B may associate a little dirty pig. But A just saw the small dog of his neighbor, whom he dislikes as well as the dog. If B could by his HN associate the sent vector with one of his known concepts he answers with a message of his own.

If the HN_{B2} of B cannot associate a concept with the message then B has to ask for the concept A has used in his message. When B gets it the KM of B again has to decide about the insertion of the new concept X′ into the semantical network. This procedure is basically the same as in the previous case when concepts were sent, i.e., the KM computes the topological places and weight connections for the new concepts.

Technically a HN is a multi-layered feed-forward network that learns by a variant of the mentioned back-propagation rule. The number of units, and of the different layers are not determined before but they are constructed during the training process

[14] The Hamming distance H simply measures the number of components in which two vectors differ. For example, a vector (1, 1) and a vector (1, 0) differ in one component, hence the Hamming distance is $H = 1$. The Euclidean distance E of two vectors (x_i) and (y_i) is given by $E = (\Sigma(x_i - y_i))^{12}$.

by the so called Flex-Net algorithm. The final size of the HN depends of course on the number of concepts and associative vectors, including their dimensions, which the artificial communicators have at their disposal. If, e.g., in several of our experiments 100 concepts are at the disposal of the communicators, if there are 10 communicators, if the dimension of the vectors of characteristics is 6, and if there are 10 "starting concepts", i.e., concepts, which each communicator has at the beginning of each simulation run at his disposal, then the resulting HN contains about 50–60 units and it is differentiated in 7 different layers, i.e., input layer, output layer, and five hidden layers.

We performed several experiments with this model, which apparently concentrates on the cognitive dimension of communication. No social factors are taken into account for the simple reason that the (cognitive) complexity of the model should be studied without the influence of other factors. One experiment shall be described in some detail, which measured the influence of wrong associations on the communicative process.

The messages in this experiments consist again of triples of concepts (X, Y, Z). In contrast to the experiments described so far we introduced a certain "noise" into the communication, i.e., a distortion of the messages. If a communicator B asks for the associative vector of a new concept then the answer of A becomes distorted by a certain percentage; accordingly B receives an associative vector for the new concept that differs from that of A in several components. For the sake of simplicity we used only vectors with a bi-polar coding, i.e., the components either had the value 1 or -1. Hence it is sufficient to use the Hamming distance for the measure of the difference between two vectors and the distortion is simply the changing of 1 to -1 and vice versa.

Now we defined a "measure of confusion" Co for a group of communicators. For two communicators this measure is computed by

$$(7.3.2)\quad Co = \sum_i H_i,$$

if H_i is the Hamming distance for an associative vector i in both networks of A and B, that is a vector that is associated in both hetero- associative networks with the same concept. As $H_i = 0$ for identical vectors obviously this definition only takes into account the vectors that differ in at least one component.

In the case of three or more communicators, Co is computed by adding all Co-values for each communicator with respect to all other communicators and dividing the result by the number of communicators. Accordingly we obtain for the measure of confusion Co_G of a whole group of n communicators

$$(7.3.3)\quad Co_G = (\sum_i Co_i)/n,$$

if Co_i is the confusion measure of one communicator i with respect to all other communicators.

In the experiment whose results are shown below we increased the rate of distortion after each communicative step, i.e., after each communicator has sent and received a message from one other communicator. The first communicative step was distorted with a factor of 10% , the next step by 20% and so forth until a distortion rate of 90% was reached. In another experiment the distortion rate was increased only after three communicative steps but the outcome of this experiment was approximately the same as of the first one.

The influence of the distortion rate on the confusion measure is shown in figure 6:

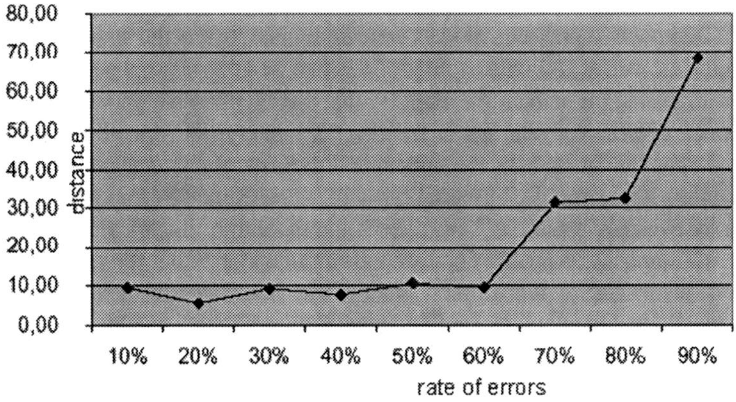

Figure 6. the x-axis is the distortion rate, the y-axis the measure of confusion

Although the increase of the distortion rate is linear the resulting increase of the measure of confusion exhibits quite another course. Apparently the whole system is able to "compensate" the increase of the distortion rate for some time, i.e., it increases its measure of confusion just in certain phases and that only after a significant rise of the distortion rate. The distortion rate had to reach an apparently critical value of about 70% in order to increase the measure of confusion also in a linear fashion. This on a first sight rather counter-intuitive result may have its counterpart in human communicator groups too: Even if human communicative processes become more and more distorted the individual errors in taking over new concepts with wrong associative vectors may compensate each other for some time: If one communicator A learns a wrong vector from B, then A will send it in the wrong version to C who receives it again in a distorted fashion. In several cases this second distortion may "correct" the wrong vector A has received, which will reduce the distance of that vector of C to the according vector of B. Apparently, as our results show, such compensating processes and even more occur at least if the distortion rate will not transcend first a threshold of 60% and then finally a threshold of 70% . Such compensating distortion processes and probably even still others might explain why it is possible for human communicators to talk with each other in such a distorted fashion, and nevertheless have the partially correct impression that they understand each other quite well. It will be worthwhile to examine the details of this model more thoroughly in this aspect.

By the way, it is quite easy to imagine human discourses where the participants exchange messages, containing of commonly known concepts, without checking the according characteristics, i.e., without asking about the *designata* of the conceptual symbols. Frequently discourses in the humanities may only be understood by assuming that the communicators do not care if they mutually agree on the *designata* of the symbols they use. In such cases high measures of confusion do not matter in a practical sense.

(C) The integration of models (A) and (B)

In a final step the two previous models were combined, that is the communicators on the CA-grid of model (A) consist now of the two hetero- associative networks, the Kohonen map, and the semantical map. By that combination we obtain a model with the complex cognitive dynamics of model (B), namely the capability to associate perceived characteristics with the conceptual symbol of the *designatum*, together with the interactive structure of model (A) that is determined by the changing values of the respective socio-matrix. The rules of interaction in this integrated model are roughly the same as in model (A): each communicator looks for those others he likes best, according to the initial values of the socio-matrix, selects his Moore neighborhood, communicates with the communicators in this Moore neighborhood, i.e., his initial subgroup, changes his socio-matrix according to the result of the communication, selects if possible and desirable a new subgroup and so on. To be sure, these processes of perceiving others as similar or not now is more complicated than in model (A): In this model the criterion of similarity is only defined by the number and the order of common concepts. In the combined model (C) the similarity of associative vectors must also be taken into account.

To guarantee this the formula for computing degrees of similarity had to be extended *but only for the cases* where the communicators know the respective associative vector of the other communicator. This is simply done in the way that the respective degree of similarity of two vectors with the same associated concept is multiplied with the percentage of similarity of the vectors. If, for example, two semantical networks have a correspondence degree of 0.5 and if the 10-dimensional vectors of two concepts whose vectors are known have an average value of their Hamming distance of 4, then the factor 0.4 is multiplied with the degree of similarity which obtains in this example a total value of 0.2. In other words, the respective degree of similarity can be much lower by this more complex computation if the associative vectors are taken into account too.

Another important aspect must be mentioned: In the integrated model the communicators can forget, that is under certain conditions some concepts get removed from the semantical networks of the communicators. The general rule for forgetting in this model is that concepts will be removed if the communicators did not use them in communicative interactions with other communicators for a certain time, i.e., a certain number of time steps. The justification for this rule is not only the famous assumption of Hebb (loc. cit.) that certain synaptic connections in the brain weaken or even vanish if these parts are not used for a longer time, but also everyday knowledge about forgetting facts when they are not necessary for some time. In human brains such forgetting often occurs by transferring the forgotten facts from short-term memory to long-term memory; because in this model there is no distinction between these two forms of memory the concepts are removed until they will be learned again.

The main experiments with this model consisted, as is the case with model (A) in the analysis of the emergence of isolated sub-groups or subcultures respectively. In addition to the experiments described in section (A) we concentrated on the measurement of confusion on the one hand and the so called rate of forgetting on the other. "Rate of forgetting" means that the number of time steps or of communicative acts respectively, after which one of the not used concepts is removed, can be defined as a control parameter for the emerging and the characteristics of different sub-groups. Communicative processes in these experiments consisted only of concept messages, i.e., messages containing vectors of characteristics were neither sent nor received with the exception of questions about new concepts. Because in such cases and in general in the case of communication consisting of vectors of characteristics the vectors became identical only the "conceptual" form of communication was used.

The measurement of confusion apparently has no influence on the emerging of sub-groups. This is mainly due to the fact that in most cases the computing of the degree of correspondence had only to take into account the different concepts because the according vectors of characteristics were not known to the communicators. Indeed, such vectors are only known after the receiver asks for it and then – see above – no confusion can arise.

Quite another effect have the different rates of forgetting. The result of five experiments with different rates of forgetting is shown in figure 7; the rates of forgetting were

Experiment 1: no forgetting;
Experiment 2: forgetting after 2 time steps;
Experiment 3: forgetting after 5 time steps;
Experiment 4: forgetting after 8 time steps;
Experiment 5: forgetting after 12 time steps.

One sees that the degree of correspondence is dependent on the forgetting rate. In these experiments the whole group of 10 members rather quickly differentiates into two sub-groups that have no contact with another after an average of 15 time steps. The degree of correspondence varies in dependency of the forgetting rate: the higher this degree of the whole group is the more different are the subcultures of the two subgroups and vice versa. High rates of forgetting obviously favor the emergence of radically isolated sub-groups whose members only interact with one another and whose subcultures have not much in common. Accordingly high are the values of the socio-matrix within a subgroup and significantly lower are the values with respect to the whole group. At the end of section (A) we already discussed the sociological relevance of such results. In addition we may say that the human

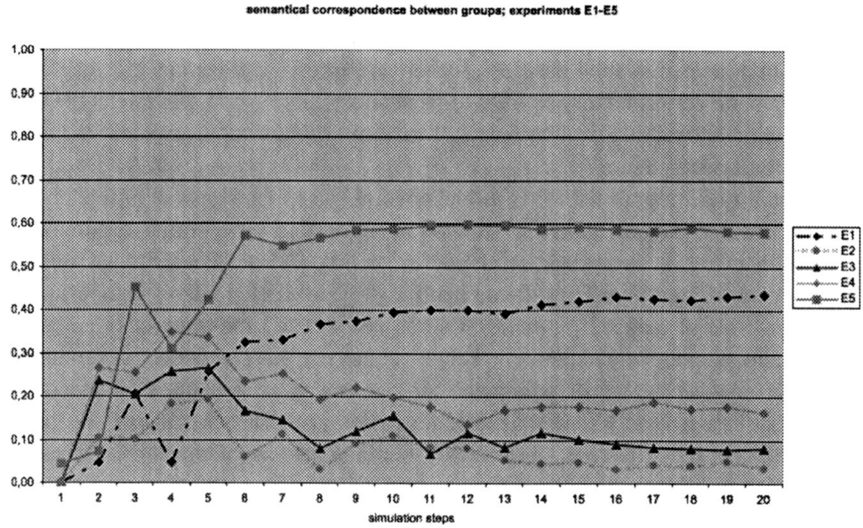

Figure 7. 5 experiments

tendency to be influenced by a certain social milieu in the way that humans forget the facts and concepts that are outside of the own subculture, even accelerates such differentiating processes.

The main goal of this chapter was the demonstration that and how it is possible to transform the general theoretical insights and terms into specific computer programs. In other words, the general theoretical frame developed in particular in chapter 6. can be operationalized by the construction of according computer programs. We have demonstrated in 7.2. that in simple cases it is rather easily possible to empirically validate such programs. Other and more complicated social experiments will be performed in order to validate the more complex programs too. Yet even before an exact empirical validation of these programs one can see how much more can be understood about regularities of human communication by experimenting with programs such as these. They are the methodical and operational basis for any mathematical theory of communication.

CHAPTER 8

EPILOGUE: THE MATHEMATICAL CONDITIONS OF HUMAN COGNITION AND COMMUNICATION

Some years ago the British magazine "Punch" published a little picture that showed a kingfisher sitting on a branch and observing a fish in the water below. The kingfisher busily calculated the refraction angle in order to catch the fish by using the well known equations of refraction. (Figure 1)[1]

The humor of this charming little picture is, of course, that the idea of a bird using some complicated equations if trying to catch a fish is quite absurd. Equally absurd would be the idea that a human fisherman would use these equations if he tried to get the same fish with a spear. Although physicists are without doubt correct in assuming that refraction angles of light into water must be computed via these equations, no living organism that has to deal with these problems in a practical way would apply such equations, even if it should know them. Indeed, even a physicist who is well acquainted with such mathematical formulas would not apply them but would rather rely upon his practical knowledge in such matters.

Hence, the lesson one could learn from this picture is that mathematics on the one hand, and solving practical problems of cognition and action on the other hand are two very different matters that should not be combined. In quite another context the psychologist Gardner (1985) reports a similar observation: when people were asked which proposition is more probable a) "Jane is a successful manager" and b) "Jane is a successful manager and a feminist" most people answered that they think b) to be the more probable of the two. In some sense this in contrast to the laws of propositional calculus because b) is only true if both parts of the sentence are true; for the truth of a) it is sufficient that only this sentence is true. Hence, proposition a) is the more probable. Therefore, as Gardner concluded, people do not think according to the laws of mathematical logic when confronted with problems of everyday life.[2]

Yet as always here things are not so easy as it would seem on the first sight. What does the kingfisher really do when he prepares for the dive into the water?

In remembrance of our models of cognitive processes in the preceding chapters the answer is principally quite easy: Presumably by the phylogenic evolution of

[1] This is not the original from "Punch" although the equations are the same, i.e. the correct ones. We owe this drawing to Jörn Schmidt who also told us the correct form of the equations, which we had forgotten.

[2] These little experiments were performed in the early eighties when feminism was at its peak. It may well be that the same question would be answered today in a different fashion because the number of engaged feminists among professionally successful women has decreased (our subjective impression).

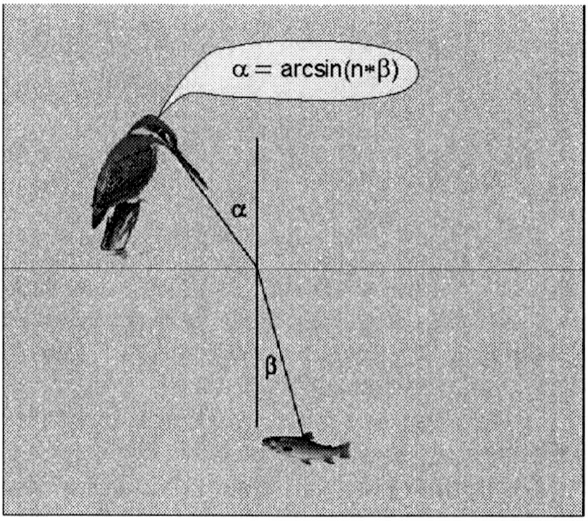

Figure 1. A kingfisher using the equations of refraction (drawn by Jörn Schmidt)

its species the kingfisher has acquired certain neural networks in his brain that get activated when it sees a fish. The according attractor of these nets activate other parts of the brain that react on the first attractor with some signals to legs and the rest of the body to take a certain posture and to activate the muscles of the legs in a certain manner. As a result of these operations of the brain and of the respective body actions the bird jumps and catches the fish, if the fish has not moved in the meantime. Principally the same is the case with a human fisherman with the difference that the respective topology of his brain is not acquired by phylogenetic evolution but by individual learning processes, i.e., by ontogenetic development. Therefore, in both cases the brain operates according to a certain topology and a particular flow of activation that result in the generation of according attractors and the successful actions.

In their classical study "The Computational Brain" Churchland and Sejnowski define the general meaning of "computational systems": "...a physical system is a computational system just in case there is an appropriate (revealing) mapping between the system's physical states and the elements of the function computed". (Churchland and Sejnowski, 1992, 62). In other words, a (dynamical) physical system is a computational system if the states and in particular the succession of states can be interpreted as the physical representation of a suited formal system that allows the computation of the succession of states, i.e., the dynamics of the system, and if necessary the changes in the succession of recursively generated states by the changing of the rules or functions of interactions. We defined these concepts in chapter 2. If the "mapping" of Churchland and Sejnowski is a bijective one then we may in addition speak of a complete representation of the formal system by the physical one and vice versa.

Our representation of cognitive processes by the use of artificial neural nets and additionally the representation of social processes by the use of neural nets and cellular automata we have apparently fulfilled the conditions of this definition of computational systems. In this sense we may safely call the kingfisher's brain a computational system and also that of the human fisherman. Hence, the kingfisher, of course, does not apply some complicated equations and neither does the fisherman. Yet in another sense both brains operate in a fashion that can be mathematically described and understood: both brains "compute" when they prepare the body for the catch by applying their cognitive topology and their function of activation. To be sure, neither of them does that in a conscious way. But as far as most of the brain's operations are done in an unconscious manner the computation of the right angle for the body of the kingfisher or the arm of the fisherman are computations although unconsciously performed, as well as the resulting dive or throw of the spear.

The same argument, by the way, must be applied to the observation of Gardner with respect to mathematical logic: people are usually not aware that there are laws of mathematical logic and they certainly do not apply them in a conscious way. Even professional logicians will not do this in everyday life. Instead of that the probands of Gardner were via the rise of feminism used to the fact that rather often female professional success was combined with a feministic attitude of women. Accordingly the probands had adjusted their respective neural topologies and generated an attractor of the sort "female success and female feministic attitudes mostly go together". This was done according to the learning stimuli from the environment and had, of course, not much to do with a conscious application of mathematical logic. Yet it is computation and the more so because the processes of biological neural nets certainly obey the laws of mathematical logic, although not in the way experimental and theoretical psychologists some times seem to believe.

The considerations and in particular the models we presented in the preceding chapters all demonstrated that it is possible and even necessary to understand cognitive and communicative systems according to the definition of Churchland and Sejnowski as computational systems. In this sense we may say that there are mathematical conditions for cognition and communication likewise. To be sure, the term "mathematical condition" does not mean that communicators act in a conscious mathematical way by applying some equations like, e.g., those of chapter 6. This is not more the case as in those of the kingfisher and the fisherman. Yet the dynamics and outcomes of cognitive, social interactional and communicative processes can be characterized in a mathematical way by understanding these processes as computational systems. The cognitive and social processes that together constitute communicative ones are regulated by a certain logic that can be expressed in mathematical or computational formalisms in a similar manner than physical or chemical processes. To be sure, the mathematics that must be applied in our case is very different from the mathematical methods of physics or chemistry. Yet they also belong to the wide domain of mathematical tools that are not to be reduced to those of the mathematical natural sciences. It is no objection that human communicators are not conscious of these regularities that can be mathematically expressed. Neither are physical elementary particles or chemical molecules. Yet no physicist or chemist doubt the validity of their respective laws.

These final considerations allow a last reflection of the term of "understanding". We defined this difficult term as the common sharing of semantical sub - networks, including concepts and connections. In remembrance to the model (B) and (C) of chapter 7.3. we have to add the common sharing of the *designata* of the different concepts. Yet, of course, these semantical structures can never be directly observed in other people and frequently wrong assumptions about the other's semantical structure lead to serious processes of misunderstanding.

The interpretation of cognitive and communicative processes as computational systems gives us an additional possibility of "understanding" other communicators. Remember the social experiments with human communicators described in chapter 7.2. In most cases, as we reported, the COMMUNICATOR-program predicted the outcome of their discussions with a high degree of exactness. Therefore, we may say that we "understood" the communicative processes within the discussion groups and to a certain sense also the cognitive processes of the individual communicators by representing them in our network model and by analyzing the specific rules of these networks. The two "Ozzy Osbourne" networks of the one participant we showed, for example, are understandable in their changing, i.e., the first as the initial and the other as the final one, if and when we assume that this changing was performed via the rules of the model. The understanding of the learning processes of this student was made possible by the formal reconstruction of the networks and the rules of the changing processes. The simulation program did exactly that, i.e., it assumed that such learning processes would occur and that they would lead to the correctly predicted rise of semantical correspondence.

By generalizing this example we obtain the following definition of understanding:

The exact understanding of other communicators is only possible by formally reconstructing the underlying cognitive processes and the communicative processes as well, that is by mapping these processes into a suited formal system (cf. Churchland and Sejnowski loc. cit.). *Understanding, hence, means that we are able to reconstruct the logic of these processes in a formal, i.e., mathematical way.*[3]

The analysis of understanding usually is the domain of hermeneutics and that means the field of philosophy and the humanities. If "understanding" is additionally meant in the manner just defined we may obtain something like a "mathematical hermeneutics", namely the understanding by the application of mathematical methods. Yet our extension of the methods of understanding must not necessarily be seen as a contradiction to the classical methods of hermeneutics. We all are used in everyday life that understanding of other people often is tried with the attempt to find oneself in the other. In cognitive science one frequently uses the

---

[3] One of our students, Bianca Kirschstein, is analyzing documented real discourses this way in her MA-thesis in Communication Science.

term “mental representation” in this context. The definition of understanding we have just proposed is nothing else than the construction of mental images of the others by the application of certain mathematical methods. In this sense we wish that this book may be understood not as a contradiction to everyday understanding of communication or a contradiction to more classical approaches to our subject but as an extension and an enlargement of their methodical tools.

The history of the natural sciences is full of examples that scientific progress is always the extension of well - known fields to new ones *but by preserving the already reached results and insights*. The most famous example of such extensions is the often quoted extension of Newtonian mechanics by relativistic mechanics. We understand our own considerations just this way, namely as an extension of those fields of communication science that are well confirmed and will be preserved.

BIBLIOGRAPHY

Anderson JA (1996) Communication theory. Epistemological foundations. The Guildford Press, New York London

Axelrod R (1987) The evolution of strategies in the iterated prisoner's Dilemma. In: Davis L (ed) Genetic algorithms and simulated annealing. Morgan Kauffman, Los Altos

Bandura A (1986) Social foundations of thought and action. A social cognitive theory. Prentice Hall, Englewoods Cliff

Barwise J, Perry J (1987) Situations and attitudes. MIT-Bradford, Cambridge (MA)

Bateson G (1970) Mind and nature. A necessary unity. Chandler, London

Bateson G (1972) Steps to an ecology o mind. Chandler, London

Berger P, Luckmann T (1966) The social construction of reality. Doubleday, New York

Bertalanffy Lv (1956) General systems theory. In: General systems. Yearbook of the society for the advancement of general systems theory, vol 1. University of Michigan Press, Ann Arbor

Burkart J (2004) Bedeutung und Information. MA-Thesis in communication Science. University of Duisburg-Essen

Chomsky N (1966) Aspects of the theory of syntax. MIT Press, Cambridge (Mass.)

Chomsky N (1959) A Review of B. F. Skinner's *Verbal Behavior*. Language 35(1):26–58

Churchland P, Churchland, P (1990) *Could a Machine Think*? In: Scientific American, vol 262, pp 32–37, Jan 1990

Churchland P, Sejnowski T (1992) The computational brain. MIT Press, Cambride (Mass.)

Dehaene S (1997) The number sense – How the mind creates mathematics. Oxford University Press, Oxford

Devlin K (1991) Logik and information. Cambridge University Press, Cambridge (MA)

Elman JL (1995) Language as a dynamical system. In: Port RF, van Gelder T (eds) Mind as motion: Explorations in the dynamics of cognition. MIT Press, Cambridge (MA)

Edelman GM (1992) Bight air, Brilliant fire – On the matter of the mind. Basic Books, New York

Eder K (1976) Die Entstehung staatlich organisierter Gesellschaften. Suhrkamp, Frankfurt (M)

Falk R, Jablonka E (1997) Inheritance. Transmission and development. In: Weingart P, Mitchell SD, Richerson P, Maasen S (eds) Human by nature. Between biology and the social sciences. Lawrence Erlbaum, Madwah London

Fararo TJ (2000) Social action systems. Foundations and synthesis in sociological theory. Praeger, Westport (CO)

Favre-Bulle B (2001) Information und Zusammenhang. Informationsfluß in Prozessen der Wahrnehmung, des Denkens und der Kommunikation. Springer, Wien New York

Forrester JW (1973) World dynamics. MIT Press, Cambridge (Mass.)

Freeman W (1990) On the problem of anomalous dispersion in chaoto-chaotic transition of neural masses, and its significance for the management of perceptual information in brains. In: Haken H, Stadler M (eds) Synergetics of cognition. Springer, Berlin

Gardner H (1985) The mind's new science. A history of the cognitive revolution. Basic books, New York

Garfinkel H (1967) Studies in Ethnomethodology. Prentice Hall, Englewood Cliffs

Geertz C (1973) The interpretation of cultures. Basic Books, New York

Gehlen A (1956) Urmensch und Spätkultur. Frobenius, Bonn

Gell-Mann M (1994) The Quark and the Jaguar. Freeman, New York

Giddens A (1984) The constitution of society. Outlines of the theory of structuration. Polity Press, Cambridge (UK)

Greene B (2000) The elegant Universe. Superstrings, hidden dimensions, and the quest for the ultimate theory. Norton, New York

Grush R (1997) Yet another design for a brain? Review of Port and van Gelder (eds) Mind as Motion. Philosophical Psychology 10:233–242

Habermas J (1968) Naturwissenschaft und Technik als "Ideologie". Suhrkamp, Frankfurt (M)

Habermas J (1981) Theorie des kommunikativen Handelns. Suhrkamp, Frankfurt (M)

Hannemann RA (1988) Computer-Assisted Theory Building. Modeling Dynamic social Systems. Sage, Newbury Park

Hartley RVL (1928) Transmission of information. In: The bell system technical journal 7:535–563

Hebb DO (1949) The organization of behavior. Wiley, New York

Hill J (1974) Hominid Proto-Linguistic Capacities. Commentary 3, In: Language origins, Norton, New York, pp 185–196

Holland J (1975) Adaptation in natural and artificial systems. University of Michigan Press, Ann Arbor

Holland J (1998) Emergence. From Chaos to Order. Addison Wesley, Reading (Mass.)

Homans GC (1950) The human group. Harcourt Brace Jovanovich, New York

Homans GC (1974) Social behavior: Its elementary forms. Harcourt Brace Jovanovitch, New York

Hondrich KO (1987) Die andere Seite sozialer Differenzierung. In: Haferkamp H, Schmid M (eds) Sinn, Kommunikation und soziale Differenzierung. Suhrkamp, Frankfurt (M)

Honke J (2006) Kommunizierende und lernende Agenten in strukturierten Multiagentensystemen. MA-Thesis in domputer Science. University of Duisburg-Essen

Hopfield JJ (1982) Neural networks and physical systems with emergent collective computational abilities. In: Proceedings of the National Academy of Science, vol 79

Kaczor G (2004) Evolution neuronaler Netze im sozialen Kontext. MA-thesis in Computer Science. University of Duisburg-Essen

Kauffman S (1993) The origins of order. Oxford University Press, Oxford

Kauffman S (1995) At home in the Universe. Oxford University Press, New York

Klüver J (2000) The dynamics and evolution of social systems. Kluwer Academic Publishers, Dordrecht (NL)

Klüver J (2002) An essay concerning socio-cultural evolution. Theoretical principles and mathematical models. Kluwer Academic Publishers, Dordrecht (NL)

Klüver J (2004) Considerations on the logical structure of evolutionary theories. In: Klüver J (ed) Sociocultural evolution. Special Issue of Computational and Mathematical Organization Theory 9(3)

Klüver J, Schmidt J (1999a) A: Social Differentiation as the Unfolding of Dimensions of Social Systems. Journal of Mathematical Sociology 23(4):309–325

Klüver J, Schmidt J (1999b) Control parameters in cellular automata and Boolean networks revisited. From a logical and sociological point of view. In: Complexity 5(1):45–52

Klüver J, Sierhuis M, Stoica C (2004) The emergence of social order in a robotic society. In: Lindemann G, Denzinger J, Timm IJ, Unland R (eds) Multiagent system technologies. Proceedings of the second German conference MATES. Springer. Lecture Notes in Artificial Intelligence, Berlin Heidelberg New York

Klüver J, Stoica C (2004) Detektive aus Bits und Bytes. In: Gehirn und Geist

Klüver J, Stoica C, Schmidt J (2003) Formal models, social theory and computer simulations. Some methodological remarks. Journal of Artificial Societies and Social Simulation 6, no 2, http//jasss.soc.surrey.ac,UK/6/2/8.html

Klüver J, Stoica C, Schmidt J (2005) The emergence of social order by processes of typifying: A computational model. In: Klüver J, Stoica C (eds). Emergence of social order. Special Issue of the Journal of Mathematical Sociology 25:3

Klüver J, Hildebrandt F, Schmidt J (forthcoming) Recent results on ordering parameters in cellular automata and Boolean networks. To be published in Complex Systems

Krallmann D, Ziemann A (2001) Grundkurs Kommunikationswissenschaft. Wilhelm Fink Verlag, München

Lakoff G (1987) Women, fire and dangerous things. What categories reveal about the Mind. The University of Chicago Press, Chicago

Lakoff G, Núñez RE (2000) Where mathematics comes from. How the embodied mind brings mathematics into being. Basic Books, New York

Langton CG (1988) Preface. In: Langton CG (ed) Artificial life. Cambridge University Press, Cambridge (Mass.)

Langton CG (1992) Life at the edge of chaos. In: Langton CG, Taylor C, Farmer JD, Rasmussen S (eds) Artificial Life II. Addison Wesley, Reading (Mass.)

Libet B (2004) Mind time: The temporal factor in consciousness. Harvard University Press, Cambridge (MA)

Luhmann N (1984) Soziale Systeme. Suhrkamp, Frankfurt (M)

Mainzer K (1997) Thinking in complexity. The complex dynamics of matter, mind, and mankind. Springer, Berlin

Marquardt B (1984) Die Sprache des Menschen und ihre biologischen Voraussetzungen. Narr, Tübingen

Maturana H (1982) Erkennen: Die Organisation und Verkörperung von Wirklichkeit. Vieweg, Braunschweig/Wiesbaden

McLeod P, Plunkett K, Rolls ET (1998) Introduction to connectionist modelling of cognitive processes. Oxford University Press, Oxford

Mead GH (1934) Mind – Self – Society (ed by CW Morris). Chicago University Press, Chicago

Michalewicz Z (1994) Genetic Algorithms + Data Structures = Evolution Programs. Springer, Berlin

Milgram S (1967) The small world problem. Psychology Today 1:61–67

Moreno JL (1934) Who shall survive. Nervous and Mental Disease Monograph 58, Washington DC

Morris C (1970) Foundation of the theory of signs. Chicago University Press, Chicago

Nowak A, Lewenstein M (1996) Modeling social change with cellular automata. In: Hegselmann R, Mueller U, Troitzsch KG (eds) Modeling and simulation in the social sciences from the philosophy of science point of view. Kluwer Acadmic Publishers, Dordrecht (NL)

Parsons T (1968) The structure of social action. Basic Books, New York

Peirce CS (1878) How to make our ideas clear. Popular Science Monthly 12

Pimm SL (1991) Balance of nature? Ecological issues in the conservation of species and communities. University of Chicago Press, Chicago

Pinker S (1994) The language instinct. Morrow, New York

Polk TA, Seifert CM (eds) (2002) Cognitive modeling. MIT Press, Cambridge (Mass.)

Pollack JB (1995) The induction of dynamical recognizers. Jordan B Pollack in Port und van Gelder, (eds)

Popper KR (1969) Die Logik der Forschung. Tübingen: Mohr (English translation: The Logic of Scientific Discovery)

Port RF, van Gelder T (eds) (1995) Mind as motion: Explorations in the dynamics of cognition. MIT Press, Cambridge (MA)

Rasmussen S, Knudsen G, Feldberg R (1992) Dynamics of programmable matter. In: Langton CG, Taylor C, Farmer JD, Rasmussen S (eds) Artificial life II. Addison Wesley, Reading (Mass.)

Ritter H, Kohonen T (1989) Self-organizing semantic maps. Biological Cybernetics 61

Rosch E (1973) Natural categories. Cognitive Psychology 4

Roth G (1997) Das Gehirn und seine Wirklichkeit. Suhrkamp, Frankfurt (M)

Schelling TC (1971) Dynamical models of segregation. Journal of Mathematical Sociology 1

Shannon CE, Weaver W (1949) The mathematical theory of communication. University of Illinois Press, Urbana

Searle J (1990) Is the brain's mind a computer program? In: Scientific American 262:26–31

Sestito S, Dillon TS (1994) Automated knowledge acquisition. Prentice Hall, New York Sydney

Singer W (2000) Ein neurobiologischer Erklärungsversuch zur Evolution von Bewußtsein und Selbstbewußtsein. In: Newen A. und Vogeley K. (Hrsg.): Selbst und Gehirn. Paderborn: Mentis

Stadler M, Kruse P (1992) Zur Emergenz psychischer Qualitäten. Das psycho- physische Problem im Lichte der Selbstorganisationstheorie. In: Krohn W, Küppers G (eds) Emergenz. Die Entstehung von Ordnung, Organisation und Bedeutung. Suhrkamp, Frankfurt (M.)

Stoica-Klüver C, Klüver J, Schmidt J (2006) Soft computing. Die Modellierung von Komplexität durch natur-analoge Modelle.Verlag w3l, Herdecke-Bochum

Thagard P (1996) Mind. Introduction to cognitive science, 2nd edn. MIT Press, Cambridge (MA)
Toellner T (2005) Von der Gruppe zur Subkultur. Simulation von gruppendynamischen und kommunikativen Prozessen. MA-Thesis in Communication Science. University of Duisburg-Essen
Vanberg VJ (1994) Rules and choice in Economics. Routledge, London
Watts DJ (1999) Small worlds: The dynamics of networks between order and randomness. Princeton Studies in Complexity. Princeton University Press, Princeton
Watzlawick P, Beavin JH, Jackson DD (1967) Pragmatics of human communication. A study of interactional patterns, pathologies, and paradoxes. Norton, New York
Weisberger JL (1962) Die sprachliche Gestaltung der Welt. Schwann, Düsseldorf
Wuensche A (1994) The ghost in the machine: Basins of attraction in random Boolean networks. In: Langton CG (ed) Artificial life III. Addison Wesley, Reading (Mass.)
Wuensche A, Lesser M (1992) The global dynamics of cellular automata. Attraction fields of one-dimensional cellular automata. Addison Wesley, Reading (Mass.)
Wolfram S (2001) A new kind of science. Wolfram Media, Champaign (Il.)
Zoozmann HW (1917) Über die Experimente des Herrn Dr. Pawlow. In: Sitzungsberichte der Preußischen Akademie der Wissenschaften, Berlin

INDEX

THEORY AND DECISION LIBRARY

SERIES A: PHILOSOPHY AND METHODOLOGY
OF THE SOCIAL SCIENCES

Editors: W. Leinfellner (*Vienna*) and G. Eberlein (*Munich*)

1. G. Zecha and P. Weingartner (eds.): *Conscience: An Interdisciplinary View*, Salzburg Colloquium on Ethics in the Sciences and Humanities (1984). 1987 ISBN 90-277-2452-0
2. R.W. Scholz: *Cognitive Strategies in Stochastic Thinking*. 1987 ISBN 90-277-2454-7
3. H. Nurmi: *Comparing Voting Systems*. 1987 ISBN 90-277-2600-0
4. M. Schmid and F.M. Wuketits (eds.): *Evolutionary Theory in Social Science*. 1987 ISBN 90-277-2612-4
5. C.L. Sheng: *A New Approach to Utilitarianism*. A Unified Utilitarian Theory and Its Application to Distributive Justice. 1991 ISBN 0-7923-1301-1
6. F. Forman: *The Metaphysics of Liberty*. 1989 ISBN 0-7923-0080-7
7. G. Bernard: *Principia Economica*. 1989 ISBN 0-7923-0186-2
8. J.W. Sutherland: *Towards a Strategic Management and Decision Technology*. Modern Approaches to Organizational Planning and Positioning. 1989 ISBN 0-7923-0245-1
9. C. Vlek and G. Cvetkovich (eds.): *Social Decision Methodology for Technological Projects*. 1989 ISBN 0-7923-0371-7
10. P. Hoyningen-Huene and F.M. Wuketits (eds.): *Reductionism and Systems Theory in the Life Sciences*. Some Problems and Perspectives. 1989 ISBN 0-7923-0375-X
11. K.G. Grunert and F. Ölander (eds.): *Understanding Economic Behaviour*. 1989 ISBN 0-7923-0482-9
12. G. Antonides: *The Lifetime of a Durable Good*. An Economic Psychological Approach. 1990 ISBN 0-7923-0574-4
13. G.M. von Furstenberg (ed.): *Acting under Uncertainty*. Multidisciplinary Conceptions. 1990 ISBN 0-7923-9063-6
14. R.L. Dukes: *Worlds Apart*. Collective Action in Simulated Agrarian and Industrial Societies. 1990 ISBN 0-7923-0620-1
15. S.O. Funtowicz and J.R. Ravetz: *Uncertainty and Quality in Science for Policy*. 1990 ISBN 0-7923-0799-2
16. J. Götschl (ed.): *Erwin Schrödinger's World View*. The Dynamics of Knowledge and Reality. 1992 ISBN 0-7923-1694-0
17. R. von Schomberg (ed.): *Science, Politics and Morality*. Scientific Uncertainty and Decision Making. 1993 ISBN 0-7923-1997-4
18. J. Baron: *Morality and Rational Choice*. 1993 ISBN 0-7923-2276-2
19. M. Allais and O. Hagen (eds.): *Cardinalism*. A Fundamental Approach. 1994 ISBN 0-7923-2398-X
20. E. Carlson: *Consequentialism Reconsidered*. 1995 ISBN 0-7923-3547-3
21. J. Götschl (ed.): *Revolutionary Changes in Understanding Man and Society*. 1995 ISBN 0-7923-3627-5
22. A. Camacho: *Division of Labor, Variability, Coordination, and the Theory of Firms and Markets*. 1996 ISBN 0-7923-3832-4
23. R. Hegselmann, U. Mueller and K.G. Troitzsch (eds.): *Modelling and Simulation in the Social Sciences from the Philosophy of Science Point of View*. 1996 ISBN 0-7923-4125-2

THEORY AND DECISION LIBRARY: SERIES A

24. J. Nida-Rümelin: *Economic Rationality and Practical Reason*. 1997
ISBN 0-7923-4493-6
25. G. Barbiroli: *The Dynamics of Technology*. A Methodological Framework for Techno-Economic Analyses. 1997 ISBN 0-7923-4756-0
26. O. Weinberger: *Alternative Action Theory*. Simultaneously a Critique of Georg Henrik von Wright's Practical Philosophy. 1998 ISBN 0-7923-5184-3
27. A. Carsetti (ed.): *Functional Models of Cognition*. Self-Organizing Dynamics and Semantic Structures in Cognitive Systems. 2000 ISBN 0-7923-6072-9
28. J. Nida-Rümelin and W. Spohn (eds.): *Rationality, Rules, and Structure*. 2000
ISBN 0-7923-6326-4
29. J. Klüver: *The Dynamics and Evolution of Social Systems*. New Foundations of a Mathematical Sociology. 2000 ISBN 0-7923-6443-0
30. V.A. Lefebvre: *Algebra of Conscience*. Revised Edition with a Second Part with a new Foreword by Anatol Rapoport. 2001 ISBN 0-7923-7121-6
31. J. Götschl (ed.): *Evolution and Progress in Democracies*. Towards New Foundations of a Knowledge Society. 2001 ISBN 1-4020-0063-4
32. N.J. Saam and B. Schmidt (eds.): *Cooperative Agents*. Applications in the Social Sciences. 2001 ISBN 1-4020-0190-8
33. B. Verbeek: *Instrumental Rationality and Moral Philosophy*. An Essay on the Virtues of Cooperation. 2002 ISBN 1-4020-0639-X
34. J. Klüver: *An Essay Concerning Sociacultural Evolution*. Theoretical Principles and Mathematical Models. 2002 ISBN 1-4020-0750-7
35. T.J. Fararo and K. Kosaka: *Generating Images of Stratification*. A Formal Theory. 2003
ISBN 1-4020-1500-3
36. O. Dahlbäck: *Analyzing Rational Crime – Models and Methods*. 2003
ISBN 1-4020-1657-3
37. E. Oeser: *Evolution and Constitution*. The Evolutionary Selfconstruction of Law. 2003
ISBN 1-4020-1784-7
38. A. Carsetti (ed.): *Seeing, Thinking and Knowing. Meaning and Self-Organisation in Visual Cognition a Thought*. 2004 ISBN 1-4020-2080-5
39. N. Gontier, J.P.v. Bendegem, D. Aerts (eds.): *Evolutionary Epistemology, Language and Culture. A Non-Adaptationist, Systems Theoretical Approach*. 2006
ISBN 1-4020-3394-X
40. J. Klüver, C. Klüver: *On Communication. An Interdisciplinary and Mathematical Approach*. 2007 ISBN 1-4020-5463-7

Printed in the United States
83759LV00002B/175/A

9 781402 054631